# IN DEEP

# IN DEEP

## HOW I SURVIVED GANGS, HEROIN, AND PRISON
## TO BECOME A CHICAGO VIOLENCE INTERRUPTER

# ANGALIA BIANCA
### WITH LINDA BECKSTROM

CHICAGO
REVIEW
PRESS

Published by Chicago Review Press Incorporated
814 North Franklin Street
Chicago, Illinois 60610
ISBN 978-1-64160-041-5


**Library of Congress Cataloging-in-Publication Data**
Names: Bianca, Angalia, 1958– author. | Beckstrom, Linda, 1954– author.
Title: In deep : how I survived gangs, heroin, and prison to become a
    Chicago violence interrupter / Angalia Bianca, with Linda Beckstrom.
Description: Chicago, Illinois : Chicago Review Press, [2019]
Identifiers: LCCN 2018027635 (print) | LCCN 2018029207 (ebook) | ISBN
    9781641600422 (PDF edition) | ISBN 9781641600446 (EPUB edition) | ISBN
    9781641600439 (Kindle edition) | ISBN 9781641600415 (cloth edition)
Subjects: LCSH: Bianca, Angalia, 1958– | Female
    offenders—Rehabilitation—Illinois—Chicago—Biography. | Female gang
    members—Rehabilitation—Illinois—Chicago—Biography. | Community
    leaders—Illinois—Chicago—Biography.
Classification: LCC HV6248.B496 (ebook) | LCC HV6248.B496 A3 2019
    (print) | DDC 364.106/6092 [B] —dc23
LC record available at https://lccn.loc.gov/2018027635

*Unless otherwise indicated, all images are from the author's collection*

Typesetter: Nord Compo

Printed in the United States of America
5 4 3 2 1

**Angalia Bianca**
To my grandma, whose prayers kept me alive,
Aunt Louise, who never gave up on me,
My son Sean, who never stopped loving me,
And to every addict who is still suffering.

**Linda Beckstrom**
To Blake, for keeping my feet on the ground.
To Lane, for making my heart soar.

The first revolution is when you change your mind.

—Gil Scott-Heron

# Contents

# Foreword

WE WERE INTRODUCED TO BIANCA through a brother when we found ourselves in a difficult situation with the Illinois Department of Corrections. Kevin had been released from prison but still wasn't being allowed to travel for work in order to provide for our family and furnish employment to those who depend on us. Bianca worked relentlessly and tirelessly, contacting anyone and everyone she knew who could possibly help. She went to bat for us, and we knew from our first follow-up phone call that she was either going to fix the situation or come pretty close to fixing it! Unfortunately, Kevin wasn't granted travel for work, but we would soon find out why Allah (God) had placed us in each other's lives.

After many conversations with Bianca, we learned a little bit about her past and the work she does with Cure Violence. It was absolutely mind blowing to hear about her commitment to helping at-risk youth change their lives. We know from our own experience through our foundation that it takes a special person to get through to the youth, and Bianca is definitely one of them. She told us countless stories of her fearless encounters with at-risk youth, many of which are described in this book—stories about how she *literally* saved lives. From that point on, we knew our purpose in meeting her, and we soon joined forces to continue our mission to save the youth.

*In Deep* is a book that you will *not* be able to put down. I opened the first page of the book and was still reading at 3:00 AM when Kevin walked into the house. I was sitting at the table, then looked up like a deer in headlights, and he asked, "Dreka, what's wrong?" I had spent the past few hours reading 197 pages of the book, and had he not walked in, I probably would have finished the entire book in that one sitting! I was in absolute disbelief and shock over her story.

This book needs to be read by *everyone*! It doesn't matter what type of background you come from. It is a real eye opener to see the many different aspects of addiction and/or unexpectedly ending up in a life of crime and violence. Those who are lost and need to be "scared straight" will see that it's only so long before your chances run out. But Bianca's story will also show you the persistence and endurance that it takes to come out of these situations. You'll learn that the world is yours and that anything is possible. Your past does not have to dictate your future!

Much love to Bianca for sharing her story with us and the *world!* She has become a lifelong friend and sister to us. She deserves all of the success in the world!

Love,
KEVIN GATES AND DREKA GATES

# Part I

# Go Ask Alice

# 1

# Sister Morphine

I WAKE UP TO MY PHONE ringing at seven in the morning on a Sunday. Although it is an unknown number, I answer anyway. Something could be happening on the street that I need to know about, and if I can help, I will. The young woman's voice on the other end has a touch of urgency mixed with the special brand of resignation that comes with finding oneself in unwanted but familiar territory.

"Hey, is this Bianca?" she asks.

"Yeah. Who's this?"

"I'm Lil D's girlfriend. He told me to call you. He's in Cook County again."

"Oh, shit," I sigh. "What for?"

"They got him on possession of a gun last night. But he's on the visiting list for today from nine to three. He needs to see you so you can help him get his shit straight with this. Can you come?"

I hesitate for just a second. It is a typical January morning in Chicago, a brutally cold thirteen degrees, with a subzero windchill. I am exhausted, having spent the entire night before out on the streets working with my Cure Violence team,* moving from one potential shooting to another, talking kids out of killing one another, trying to change their

---

* Cure Violence was formerly known as CeaseFire Chicago, but I'll generally use the current name for clarity.

minds about violence. Today is my day off and I was planning to spend most of it staying warm and cozy under the covers.

I pause for the briefest of moments, but I can't say no. "OK, baby. I got you. I'll be there. I'll see what's going on." Of course I go. I always go. "Give me his full last name and his ID number, no nicknames."

She gives me the information, and then says, "Can you put some money on your phone account at the jail so he can call you himself?"

"No, honey, I'm sorry. I can't do that. If I did that for everybody who asked me, I couldn't pay my rent, you feel me? I don't have that kind of money. But I will come and see him today. When you talk to him, tell him I'll be there for sure."

I force myself out of bed, shower, bundle up, and am in my car by eight o'clock, heading from the far north side of Chicago to Cook County Jail on the Southwest Side, about a thirty-minute drive on this deserted Sunday morning. I try to find parking on the street as close as I can get to the entrance for the division where Lil D is being held. It is crowded as usual, and I end up three blocks away, an excruciating distance in the biting wind. I'm no stranger to Cook County Jail, but it has been a while since the last time I visited. Lately, I have been seeing my guys in the penitentiary, where I can stay for several hours and have a real conversation across a table. It is a longer drive, but the visits are always more meaningful. No matter how well you get to know the ropes at Cook County, the jail is notorious for changing the rules almost weekly when it comes to who gets in, when and how you have to enter, and what is allowed inside. I know I have to leave my phone, my keys and large key chain in the car, but I tuck my rubber Cure Violence–branded key chain with my car key on it into my pocket, leaving my purse in the car, too. When I get inside, I'm told I can't bring the key chain in, so I walk those three grueling blocks back to my car, slip the key off, and head back to the jail entrance. I can't help smiling to myself thinking about how many times I tried so hard to get out of Cook County, and here I am working my ass off to get back in.

After passing that initial security check, I'm inside the compound, a collection of buildings as gray as the winter sky, separated by open-air courtyards. I walk across to the next entrance. The buildings offer no shelter from the wind, so I walk as fast as I can. Once inside, I have to check in to make sure that my guy is on the visiting list and show the officer my driver's license. I am told to take a seat and given a token for a locker, so I can put away my coat, hat, gloves, and scarf if I want. The only completely forbidden article of clothing inside Cook County is a hoodie, so if you dare to show up wearing one, you have no choice but to leave and come back without it. The seating area is so crowded, as it always is, and I am so bundled up that I start to sweat. I find a locker, peel off my layers, and stuff them inside. I put my locker key, car key, and my driver's license in my jeans pocket. Now the waiting begins.

I find a seat sandwiched in between a young woman and an older man. The atmosphere in this room is unlike that of any other kind of waiting area I've experienced. There is impatience, a touch of excitement, the tension of trying to keep young children calm and entertained, and an underlying sense of drudgery. Many of the people here have been waiting for weeks to get thirty minutes with a husband, father, boyfriend, best friend, son, or grandson. If it's a busy day, the time is cut to twenty minutes. Some have traveled for hours on public transportation, shivering on the El platform in the cruel morning air, hoping against the odds to get good news about release or trial dates, some fretting over having to deliver updates on a bad situation at home to someone who is helpless to do anything about it. This room is one of the saddest places I know. Like a recurring dream, the scene plays out over and over again every Sunday, in the stifling heat of August or the bone-chilling cold of January, and the pain, while familiar, seems to cut deeper each time. I have been on both sides, the visitor and the visited. I know the emptiness of that day when there is no one to answer when your name is called.

I sit there for two hours, an average wait. Many of those around me would be there for much longer. Just before eleven, I hear Lil D's real name called. I get up and get in line to go through yet another metal detector. Once cleared, some of us are directed to the left and some to the right, some carrying babies or very small children. This leads me into the actual visiting area, a long narrow room set up with a tall, thick, bulletproof glass partition that runs the length of the room, with nine metal stools on the visitors' side. The stools on the inmate side are empty. We're told to take a seat. One by one, the inmates walk through a door on the other side of the glass to take the seat in front of their visitors. From their side, it is hard, at first, to see who is visiting and most don't know exactly who has come, so they bend down and look up through the glass to see who it is before they sit down. Because the glass is so thick, it is difficult for people to hear one another. A round porthole in the center of the glass has enough small holes in it to let the sound of a voice in if you lean right up to it when you speak, making it physically impossible to look at the person as you talk. It has been decades since Cook County had phones for visitors and inmates to use; that's a Hollywood image long gone in the interest of tightened security, since anything an inmate can hold in his hand can become a weapon.

All around me I watch fathers hold their hands up to the glass as their baby mamas take the small hand of a toddler and place it up against the glass on the other side. Girlfriends and mothers bend toward the porthole to speak. Many inmates at Cook County have not seen a family member for months. They are held in cells on tiers of about one hundred prisoners each, and only around twenty get to be part of any given visitor's day. The powers that be will allow four or five people to squeeze together and visit an inmate all at once, but it is a very tight space and almost impossible for everyone to get a chance to talk. Often an inmate has nobody. Some people don't have the money to get there, some don't care, and some, as my family eventually did, have simply given up on the person inside. Lil D was lucky to get on the list so quickly and to have a girlfriend advocating for him. He knew I was coming.

He takes the seat on the other side of the glass. Visitors can't see the guard from their seats, but I know from having been on that side so many times that he is standing at the inmates' entrance. The guards watch every movement on both sides of the glass to halt impulsive acts like a girlfriend flashing a body part or any other inappropriate behavior. It happens. Trying to have a conversation under these conditions is a test of patience. People are screaming into the porthole, and every conversation in the room is echoing throughout. Almost every sentence is punctuated with "Wait, what did you say?" or "I can't hear you, say again."

Lil D and I have our thirty minutes. I know he's going to the penitentiary since this is his fourth gun charge, and there is no way he can beat it. I'm not a lawyer, but I've been in and out of the system so many times that I can predict most outcomes. My role is one of support. I want him to be hopeful, so I'm reluctant to tell Lil D that he is going to Stateville from here, and that eventually he'll be assigned to a more permanent prison. He will find out soon enough.

"Let's wait and see what happens," I say, knowing that trying to maintain your sanity and remain calm in Cook County Jail takes a herculean effort of self-restraint. He has been here before, which will help him but will also work against him in many ways. He knows how bad the conditions are, and he knows how long his case might linger.

"I gotta get outta this hole, Bianca."

I recognize the desperation in his voice and know all too well what he's going through. "I know, baby. Just keep fighting it. Let me know if you need anything. Do you need any money?"

"No, my girlfriend's got me covered. Thanks."

"Awright, let me know what's going on," I tell him as we get the three-minute warning from the guard. "I love you, baby. Don't give up. Be positive and don't get in trouble in here. I'll be back." This was my standard pitch, but I know that Lil D, like so many others, will cling to those words as perhaps the only positive thoughts in his head, and I know from experience just how much it can help.

I leave the waiting area, get my stuff from the locker, bundle up, and head out. No one stops you when you're leaving. Back in my car, shivering and waiting for the engine to warm up, I hit my CD player and blast the Rolling Stones, hoping to shake the sadness and worry I shouldered for Lil D. I counsel many young men in similar situations; for them, packing a gun is like carrying a wallet. Violence infects their neighborhoods like a disease, along with poverty and the hopelessness that comes from seeing no future and having few choices. I know from my training that it is possible to change their behavior, but it takes dedication and persistence. Every day I vow not to leave them, not to forget them. I tell myself that saving one life is worth every effort. I really believe that my job, my calling if there's such a thing, is to do whatever I can to help, for as long as I'm able.

Driving up California Avenue toward home, I'm dreaming of my nice warm bed and catching up on my sleep, trying not to let the desperate look in Lil D's eyes haunt me. I stop at a red light on Harrison Street. There is a car stopped in front of me, and to my left I notice a group of young men standing on the corner in front of a convenience store. Suddenly and for no reason that I can see, the car in front of me starts backing up and is about to hit my car. I look up and see another car in front of that one. I turn my CD player off and that's when I hear the gunshots. Three gunmen are leaning out the car windows and shooting directly into the crowd of kids on the corner. Even though I have to back up to keep the guy from ramming my car, I see the shooting go down right in front of me and watch as a teenage boy hits the ground. I know he's been hit, and I know I have to help him.

The car in front of me takes off, but all my instincts and violence training kick in. I have to get to that kid. People are running away, and even after he falls to the sidewalk the shooters keep firing randomly as they abandon their car and flee in several directions. I go into survival mode as I listen to the gunshots, but I keep my eyes on the wounded kid. I pull onto the wrong side of the street, drive a few yards toward where he has fallen, slam my car into park and turn it off. I open the door, wait until the last few shots are fired, and I see that all the shooters have scattered and are out of sight. I run to the boy who is now just a few feet away from me. As I get closer to him, my worst fears are confirmed.

He looks to be about fourteen or fifteen years old and is lying there, alone in the street. The blood streams from his body, forming an expanding dark pool around him. I drop to my knees and can see that he is in shock and terrified, desperately trying to get up.

"Look at me, look at me, baby!" I scream. "Stay still. Don't move. Don't move! Somebody call 911. I need an ambulance!"

Kneeling there, I try to find the source of his bleeding. My hands are covered in blood and my light-colored blue jeans are soaked up to my thighs. I can't tell how many times he's been shot, but I can see that a lot of blood is coming from his groin, and I know I have to do something immediately or he is going to die. I put my hands inside his pants and can feel the bullet hole.

"Look at me! Look at me! This is gonna hurt, baby, I'm sorry, it's gonna hurt," I tell him as I use my hand to put pressure on the wound. I press as hard as I can. "I'm sorry, baby, I have to do it. Just keep looking at me. You're gonna be OK."

I bear down and stay like that, not moving my hands or even acknowledging anyone else at the scene until the ambulance arrives and the paramedics can take over. The police get there almost immediately, since the precinct is only blocks away, but the ambulance is taking forever. Word has spread around the neighborhood, and the boy's mother appears, kneeling beside me, calm and ready to take over.

"OK, thank you, we got it from here, honey. That's my baby, I got him," she says, not entirely grasping just how badly he's hurt.

"I'm not letting go until the ambulance gets here!" I yell at her, going into shock myself at that point. She backs away, and a young woman who was standing nearby starts crying and says, "Oh my God, that's my cousin!"

Finally, the ambulance pulls up. The paramedics have to physically move my hands and inch me away from him. They put the boy on a stretcher and carry him to the ambulance, leaving me standing there, completely covered in blood, shaking and crying. I look around to get my bearings and process what has just happened. I am a mess. I can see that my car is now inside the crime scene tape. A policeman comes up to me, asks a few questions about what I saw, and tells me I can't leave until the detectives come and finish marking the scene, since my car is part of it. Now the adrenaline is wearing off, and I am freezing, so the officer says I can wait in my car to get out of the cold.

As I sit in the car, shaking and praying for another young life to please, please make it, I know that this war, this senseless plague, will not end anytime soon, and my heart is broken once again. Then I get angry. I look at my hands and realize I have an opportunity to make a statement. I want people to see the effects of violence; I want the scores of young men who follow me on social media to see what it looks like.

I take a picture of my bloody hand and post it on Facebook with the caption "Come on Chicago the killing gotta STOP the shooting has to STOP." I take a deep breath, trying to calm myself down as I wait, looking out at a scene that is all too familiar.

I am no stranger to street violence, but it never gets any easier to witness. I light a cigarette and notice that my hands are still shaking. I glance around to remind myself of where I am, which corner I'm on, and my mind starts to wander. So many corners in this city have my footprints on them. I realize that I'm close to an alley that had once been my home, in a time when I could barely remember who I was or had ever been.

It was the late 1990s, and I was drug addicted and homeless, stealing jewelry or perfume from Chicago's finest stores to sell for drugs. I had not seen my five children, or anybody in my family, in more than sixteen years. After decades of trying to help me, they had finally opted to protect their broken hearts and had left me to my own hell. When I was a child, I was surrounded by boisterous, unbounded love, the kind of love that is demonstrated, not just pronounced. I smile to myself whenever I remember those voices, loud and laughing and always there for me . . . until they were gone.

I remember a long-ago Christmas Eve when I wandered this same alley, abandoned and alone. At that point I still had my three-month old daughter Alia, the youngest of my five children, and we were living on the streets. That night was like this one, deathly cold. I had bundled my baby up as best I could, carrying her in a baby sling across my chest. It was a slushy, icy day. I strayed for hours, trying to find someone who would let Alia and me sleep in their house, but it was a holiday and no one wanted us. Cold set in as it got later and darker. My shoes were soaking wet, and my feet were freezing. I found a half-boarded-up abandoned apartment with rotting furniture in it. All I had was a bit of powdered baby formula, a bottle, and one diaper. I climbed in the window. The apartment wasn't much better than outside. There was no heat and no electricity. The minute I got inside I could hear the rats scurrying across the floor, and I prayed that I was the only junkie who had crawled into this hole. In the faint glow from the streetlights, I found a bed, held up my butane lighter to check for roaches, picked up an old dirty blanket from the floor, climbed in with Alia, and wrapped the blanket around us. I remember her crying. She must have been so cold and hungry. I felt guilty and sick, but I held her as close to my chest as I could for warmth. I was scared, but I tried to be strong for Alia.

I woke on Christmas morning from whatever sleep I had managed and shivered as I glanced at the filthy walls and cracked ceiling. I forced myself to get up and out of there. It almost felt warmer outside. I walked three blocks to the University of Illinois Hospital and took Alia into the ladies' room in the lobby, a place I knew would be open. I held my sweet little baby under the hand drier to warm her up. I laid her on the changing table and made a bottle of formula. I used paper towels to give her a bath, put on the only clean diaper I had, and washed her little outfit in the sink, holding the wet clothes under the hand drier. Through all this I fought off waves of dope sickness, trying not to vomit, and falling deeper into heroin withdrawal. Being dope sick was one of the worst feelings I had ever experienced, worse than the pain of childbirth. At least childbirth ends. Being dope sick happens every time you fall asleep and wake up, a clawing need that never gets off your back. But I knew I couldn't give in to it. I had to make sure Alia was warm, clean, and fed before I carted her off with me to look for a bag of dope. I loved her as much as any mother could, but I knew deep in my heart that I couldn't take care of her while living on the streets. I'll never forget that Christmas Eve, the night I knew I would have to give up my youngest child. Soon I was alone on the streets again, unencumbered, with only my habit to feed. Once again, dope would win.

I blink back to the present. A few hours have passed since the shooting, the scene has been examined and processed by the police, the blue lights on their squad cars flashing like strobe lights, the yellow crime scene tape strung like so much crepe paper around another deadly dance, evidence markers placed like tiny tents on the sidewalk, cops standing all around, squawking into their shoulder radios, all of it playing out like a vicious dream that would not end. I can still see the pool of blood where the boy had lain.

One of the detectives comes over to my car window and motions for me to open it.

"Are you Bianca?"

"Yes, I am."

"It's cold out. Do you mind if I sit in your car?"

I say sure, pop the lock, and he slides into the front seat. He hands me his card, and I can see that he's of Italian descent, just like me, so we joke and share some small talk about that, a moment of normalcy in this horrific day.

Then he says, "I just want to ask you a few questions. What exactly did you see?"

"I really didn't see anything. I know there were three shooters, but while they were shooting, I was looking at the boy. I never got a clear look at any of them."

He writes his report and I give him my Cure Violence business card. He knows about the organization, and I tell him I work in Chicago, nationally, and internationally.

"OK, just wait a few more minutes while we do a final sweep for casings and you can go. And I want to thank you for what you did today, for helping that kid."

"I just hope that he lives," I say.

"Yeah, let's hope he makes it." He sounds sincere. There isn't the usual touch of sarcasm in his voice, a symptom of seeing too many young men getting hurt and returning to the same behavior over and over again. He opens the car door and leaves. A few minutes later, one of the officers waves for me to go, and I also leave. I have stopped shaking just enough to drive.

I make my way home and can feel the exhaustion spread over my entire body. I peel off my blood-caked clothes and throw them in the garbage. I take a long hot shower, trying to wash it all away. There is even blood in my hair. I finally crawl under the covers, but I know I won't be able to sleep right away. And then my phone rings. I answer. It's the detective.

"Hi, Bianca," he says, "I'm just calling to let you know you did good work today. You saved that boy's life. Nice job."

"Thank you," I murmur, fighting back another round of tears. "How is he, what do you know?"

"All I know is that he came out of surgery OK. He's still got a long way to go. I don't know his condition or the medical report, but I do know that he's going to make it. That was pretty heroic what you did."

"Well, thanks, but I don't really think of it that way. I am not a hero. I just want him to live and thank God he will," I say, "and thank you for letting me know."

I hang up and realize that my cellphone has been vibrating with notifications. In the five or so hours since I'd posted it, the picture of my hand had gone viral. In a few days, the boy's family would find me. I would meet them and visit him in the hospital and eventually become his mentor. But at that moment, I'm just grateful that I was there to help him.

This is my life's work now. This is what I do to make the full weight of my own journey count for something positive. It's how I live. I know the streets, have experienced the violence, and understand the toll that drugs and bullets exact. Addiction and violence take away everything that feels human, until they eventually take away lives. Every kid with a gun thinks he will win. Every addict believes he or she is above being consumed by drugs and can stay ahead of the wolves. I learned the hard way that neither is possible, but it took almost thirty-six years of my life. At the start of it all, I was a spoiled kid who thought she was invincible and the coolest thing ever to hit the street. I never believed the street would hit back and take everything from me.

# 2

# Another Brick in the Wall

In 1963 I was five years old. I was lying in bed when I heard a noise, so I got up and saw my mother standing inside our back door. It is an image that remains seared into my mind like an unfading photograph. A beautiful woman who loved to dress well, she was wearing a stylish tweed coat with a fur collar and, as always, high heels. Her Chanel No. 5 lingered, a scent that, to me, meant she was near, yet there she stood with suitcases at her side.

"Mommy, where are you going?" I whispered.

Quietly, she said, "Out to buy milk for your breakfast, honey. Go back to bed, baby."

I knew she wasn't coming back. I grabbed the bottom of her coat and pleaded with her, "Mommy, please don't go. Let me come with you."

She pried my tiny hand from her coat and replied, "I promise I'll be back. I'm just going to buy milk, honey. Go back to sleep."

With that, she walked out the door. I stood there for a while feeling afraid to cry. I thought of myself as a big girl, and big girls didn't cry, so I held back the tears. I climbed back into bed. The cold that had settled over the city left the sky clear, and from my bed I could look out the window and see the full moon hanging there, peeking in between the other buildings around our apartment. When I gazed up at the sky I could see a few bright stars and they comforted me for a while, but I couldn't hold back the tears for long.

I fell asleep, but my baby sister, Christine, crying from her crib in the other room, woke me up. She was barely a year old and we called her Crickie. The two of us were alone in the apartment. My father lived with us, but he worked nights and went out after work, a routine that usually didn't get him home before sunrise, and this day was no different. As soon as I walked into Crickie's room, she stopped crying and smiled at me. I struggled to get her out of the crib—a challenge for a five-year-old, but I managed. She was hungry, and her diaper was so wet that it was falling off. I had watched my mother and grandmother change her diaper many times, so I figured I could do it, but every time I tried to hold her down to get the clean diaper around her, she wiggled and squirmed and tried to run off. I gave up and let her go.

We were both hungry, so I decided to try my hand at making eggs while Crickie ran around the house naked and played with her dolls. I took the carton of eggs out of the refrigerator and pulled a chair over to the kitchen sink. I loved watching my mom make breakfast, cracking eggs over the sink with a deft hand, and I figured if I did the same, the result would be scrambled eggs. I watched the sink quickly swallow up each egg I cracked until I emptied the carton. By then, Crickie was standing next to me, crying again. In the middle of all this, my father walked in the kitchen door.

"What the hell is going on?" he hollered. "Where is your mother?"

I could not stop the tears this time. "Daddy, Mommy left last night to buy milk and never came back."

He helped me down from the chair and took Crickie into his arms. He must have called his mother immediately because the next thing I remember Grandma rushed into our house. She picked Crickie up and wrapped her in a blanket, took my hand, and led us to the taxi that was waiting outside. We took the long drive from the west suburb of Elmwood Park to her home on Polk Street in Chicago's Little Italy, where she lived with my grandpa and my father's brother and sister. Crickie and I stayed there most of the time after my mother left.

I sat at Grandma's front window for hours every day, peering up and down the street. Seeing how sad I was, Grandma would say, "Ang, go play with your dolls."

"No, Grandma, I'm waiting for my mommy to come back."

My mother did come back years later, when I was about nine, but my father would not let us see her. Grandma intervened and started sneaking us out, but it would be a long time before my father gave us permission to visit her, when Grandma finally convinced him that girls need their mother. Later in my life, lost in a haze of drugs, I would inflict the same pain on my own son, leaving him behind to be the one waiting at the window for a mother who was never going to come back.

Both my parents were young and unmarried when I was born in 1958. They got married when I was about a year old. When my mother found out she was pregnant she left and went to live with friends in Nashville, but after I was born, she must have realized the true burden of her new responsibility, so she bundled me up, came back to Chicago, and stood on the doorstep of my grandma's house. Grandma was overjoyed to see her son's baby girl. There had not been a baby born in the family since the 1940s, when everyone was dirt-poor thanks to the Great Depression. Grandma grabbed me, held me tight, and I realize now that she never let me go. I don't know why my mother gave me such a difficult first name, but Angalia must have sounded beautiful to her. I immediately became Angela or Ang to my family, and after years of creating aliases later in life, I simply went by Bianca and continue to use that name today. Grandma moved my mother and me into her home where my father still lived, but made my mother sleep in a different bedroom since they weren't married. It was 1959, and she wasn't going to put up with an unmarried couple sleeping together under her roof. Grandma was a sly old Sicilian, and she knew that would be the push my parents needed to tie the knot. By the time Crickie came along, they were married and had a place of their own.

But my parents were young and attractive and used to being free. They weren't ready to settle down. I don't know if they even knew how to settle down. My father was a real player, and there was no way he was going to let a wife and kids stop him. He had other women, so my mother played, too. She went out at night while he was working, leaving Crickie and me with a string of babysitters, whoever she could get to watch us. If my grandma called our house and, God forbid, a babysitter answered the phone, she would jump right into a taxi, pay the babysitter, put us in the cab, and off we'd go back to her house. Morning would come and, with it, our mother, yelling at Grandma.

"Those are my babies," she'd shout at the top of her voice.

Grandma's standard reply was to call her a whore and swear at her in Italian, "*Buttana!*" Back and forth they went as my mother scooped us up and took us back to our house. This happened about every other day. I was too young to know exactly what was going on, so it seemed completely normal to me, and my sister was just a baby.

When I was four, something happened that I doubt my mother ever thought was possible. Even though I was young, it was so traumatic I would never forget it. My mother wanted to go out with her girlfriend but didn't have a babysitter. Her friend had a son in his teens who said he would watch us, so out they went, leaving Crickie asleep in her crib and me alone with this boy. When the adults left, the boy pulled me into my bedroom, turned off the light, and pulled out his penis. He told me he wanted me to suck on it. I said I didn't know what he meant. I was scared. He was a big, tall, mean teenager, and I knew he could hurt me. I had no idea what I was supposed to do. I wiggled away from him and went to sit in the window to look out at the stars, something that I would do many times in my life, as if the star-filled sky was a safe zone for my psyche, a place to escape whatever was happening to me, even later, when I was living on the street and sleeping in alleys.

He went into the kitchen and got a jar of peanut butter, spread it on his dick, and pulled me back on top of him. He told me to lick off the peanut butter, and when I hesitated he shoved my head down and stuck it into my mouth, making me gag. He kept trying to shove it down my throat, and I was so sure I was going to throw up I started sobbing and gasping for air. He finally left me alone, made me swear not to tell anyone, and I went back to the stars, trembling with fear and anger. I knew what he had just made me do was bad. As soon as my mother and her friend came back, I ran into the kitchen and told them everything. My mother and his mother pushed him up against the wall and screamed at him. I never talked about it after that, not to anyone. Years later, when I was about thirteen, I told my stepmother, Pat, the whole story. When she shared it with my father, he said he knew all about it and that I should never think about it again because he took care of that kid a long time ago. I had no idea exactly what that meant, nor would my father ever tell me, but I could guess and I'm sure it wasn't pretty.

That day, I started building a wall around my heart to keep the fear and sadness out. As I grew up, my solution to being afraid was to become a real badass. Every con I pulled, every drug deal, every crazy, dangerous move I made added another brick in the wall. I have many regrets when I look back on my life, but I truly loved that badass feeling because I never felt vulnerable. I used my wits and my unrelenting drive to win, to survive, and, in my immoral universe, to thrive. But I learned the hardest way possible that there is no winning when your moral compass is upside down.

Throughout those years, before I turned five and my mother finally left, she and my father were both cheating on each other. He became determined to catch her in the act, so my father's uncle Eugene hired a private detective to follow my mother. One evening while my father was at work he got a call from the detective. "Your wife is sitting at the bar making out with her boyfriend."

My father's hair-trigger Sicilian temper kicked in, and he quickly got his gun, ready to go to the club and kill both my mother and her boyfriend. He would have done just that had it not been for my uncle, who took the gun away from my father and went to the club himself, making my father promise to stay behind. When Uncle Eugene arrived, he walked in and saw my mother, close and friendly with the strange man.

"You're a whore!" my uncle yelled at my mother, who was shocked to see Eugene standing in front of her. "Go home, pack your things, and get the fuck out," he told her.

"I will, I'll take my kids and leave," she cried.

"No, you're not taking those kids anywhere." And that was final. My mother knew she had to get away as soon as possible and must have decided to make her move in the middle of the night, before my father got home, leaving him to guess where she went and when, if ever, she would come back. That was how they played one another; she left him before he could throw her out.

I was spoiled and out of control from the moment my mother walked out on us. Even at the tender age of five, I realized almost immediately that I now had an angle to work. The adults in my family started to overcompensate to make up for my mother leaving, and I saw an opening. My older Italian relatives were always telling my grandma, "Oh, those poor little girls." To me, that meant I could get anything I wanted with just a cute, slightly sad smile. I perfected that lost look and milked it for all it was worth, again and again.

I had an easy target in Grandma. She would cover things up and help hide them from my father to avoid his wrath, and I could wrap her around my little finger whenever I needed an ally. She and my father tried to get me under control by sending me to Catholic schools, but at the same time they bent to my every whim. I threw tantrums and screamed horrible things at them until they gave me what I wanted because they just didn't know what else to do. I even forced them to give me my own room, which meant that Crickie had to sleep on the couch. She slept on the couch for many years, the entire time we all lived together. I was easily bored, a thrill seeker and a tomboy from an early age. I never learned the value of a dollar, never put much stock in telling the truth, and learned to bulldoze the grown-ups to get my way. I could wear my father down to the point of submission even when my demands were crazy. I would find ways to beat him at his own game, conning him like a little pro. I remember feeling victorious every time I won. I had to smile to myself, proud I had learned how to game my father and win, and sometimes I would catch him smiling to himself because he knew I was not only just like him but maybe even better at the game than he was.

My father started dating Pat soon after my mother left, and my sister and I grew very close to her. She was a good mom to us. At first, Pat and my father lived in another apartment while we lived with Grandma. When the city began to build all around Little Italy, dismantling the old neighborhood, our apartment building was sold under eminent domain and my father moved all of us out to Oak Park, the first suburb west of Chicago. Daddy visited every Wednesday to bring Grandma money, so every Monday and Tuesday we heard, "Your father is coming over so you better behave." "Who cares?" I would say, but on that Wednesday I became the perfect kid. I would run to the door to ask, "Did you bring hot dogs, Daddy?" He always brought us hot dogs from the family business, a lucrative restaurant that was famous in Chicago and the suburbs.

I was about nine years old the first time I got drunk. A neighborhood friend about the same age stood with me outside the National Grocery Store in Oak Park until we got a man to buy us some Boone's Farm wine. But we didn't stop there. Another little friend, Keith, and I made a discovery. His father was dying of cancer, and we started stealing his pain medicine and taking it like candy. We didn't know what it was, but we knew we liked the way it made us feel. Giggling uncontrollably over nothing, stumbling across Keith's perfect lawn, and staring up at the clouds, I loved the numb, fuzzy buzz in my head. Only years later did I realize it was morphine. Keith's mother caught us once and chased us out of the house, hollering at us, "Come back right this minute!" but we got away and got high, really high. I wanted to do it over and over again.

Many of my firsts came at a young age. I was like a child of Babylon, left to wander a world filled with fascinating and dangerous distractions not so much out of neglect but because Grandma, my father, and the rest of my family all failed to tame me. I soaked it all up, wanted to try everything, and became impossible for them to discipline or control. Guilt remained over my mother leaving, coloring their judgment, and I never let them forget it. I wanted to consume, experience, touch, and eventually conquer the whole world, whatever that meant. And almost from the day I was born, I would do anything to get what I wanted.

Pat spent a lot of time with me and could see what a hyper child I was. As an outsider, Pat was less accepting of behavior that our family deemed normal and could see that the way I was being raised, with so much freedom and zero sense of responsibility, was creating a monster. But my father, while he loved me unconditionally, had no idea how to be a father. His primary role model, his own father, was a straight-and-narrow guy with no shady affiliations, but he was a raging alcoholic, which left my grandma alone with only her own wits to raise her kids. Pat could see that I needed something more, but it was not an easy sell.

The old Sicilian ways ran deep in my grandma and my father, so when Pat suggested I see a psychiatrist they were appalled. "She's fine! She'll grow out of it," they would argue. But Pat persevered and eventually got my father to agree.

As usual, my father insisted on the best for his daughter, but this shrink's fee was a hundred dollars an hour, a hefty bill back in 1968, and I knew it. I was only ten years old, but I was so mad at my father for giving this guy that much money instead of spending it on me that I was determined to get back at him by making sure he got his money's worth. I lied about everything, telling the psychiatrist that Grandma beat me and my father never gave me anything or took care of us and concocting any other atrocities that my ten-year-old hyperactive brain could dream up. The doctor prescribed Mellaril (thioridazine), a form of phenothiazine commonly indicated for psychotic disorders like schizophrenia with side effects that include dizziness and drowsiness. It left me lethargic. I would sit in my bedroom in the dark and stare at my low-lit aquarium for hours, just watching the fish swimming around in the ethereal light. It was such abnormal behavior for me that Grandma had a fit.

"Petey!" she hollered at my father, "She's not right. She can't stop looking at those damn fish. Go see that doctor!"

After a few weeks and several appointments, my father insisted on a consultation. When he heard what I was telling the unsuspecting psychiatrist about how I was beaten and neglected at home, my father just shook his head and acknowledged that I had him. I think part of him was secretly proud that I was such a good con, but that was the end of the psychiatrist for me. Once again, I won.

But Pat didn't give up as easily as my father. She got me to see a counselor in school, a young woman that I really connected with. At the time I was in fifth grade and even though I was always getting into trouble for acting out in class or smoking on the playground, I was put into the academically accelerated program because I had a high IQ, and when I did participate, it showed. But most of my friends were not in the advanced classes, so I failed my tests on purpose in the hopes of getting moved in with them. My teacher knew exactly what was going on and supported my visits to the counselor. But the outcome was just too weird for my family. During a visit to the principal's office for yet another infraction, my grandma and I sat outside waiting to be called in. I was facing suspension yet again.

"What the fuck did you do now, you *somm-an-a-bitch*?" Grandma did not censor herself at all and added a little slap upside my head for good measure.

"I didn't fuckin' do anything, Grandma! What the fuck is your problem?"

Understandably misinterpreting this loving exchange, the principal and counselor were appalled. After a few sessions with her, the counselor gave us a mandate. She wanted Grandma and me to speak softly and kindly to one another at all times, and she wanted my father to monitor our progress. Otherwise, suspension loomed.

We tried. In the most stilted manner imaginable, Grandma and I tried to speak in civil tones and words. But it was so hard and so unnatural that we were both miserable.

"Ang, dear, what would you like for breakfast?"

"I would like toast with jam, please, Grandma."

"OK, I'll get that for you now."

It was ridiculous and made me so unhappy. One day, I lost it and stormed into the counselor's office in tears. "I miss my grandma," I sobbed. "I want things back the way they were right now. I don't care if I get suspended!"

Over the years, Pat would continue to help me, always concerned for my safety and well-being until I was too far gone for anyone to make a difference. I spun further out of control, and as I got older the trouble I got into became more serious and much harder to fix.

Daddy married Pat when I was in the ninth grade. A few years after they were married, Daddy and Pat moved into our Oak Park home. I don't think my father wanted to get married again, but Oak Park River Forest High School would not let me in unless my father lived in the district and Grandma would not let my father and Pat live in the same house without being married, so there he was with another wife. Grandma was still the boss, Crickie still slept on the couch, and for the most part we all got along fine. Daddy and Pat had a son named Michael who was born when I was a teenager. We were a close Sicilian family. Daddy would play Frank Sinatra records, crank up the volume, and sing along with every word. We all loved Sinatra and because of their "connections," my family knew him. Whenever Frank came to Chicago, my father and his uncles partied with him, and my grandma would bake Sicilian cookies just for him. Sinatra would say that he had not had such great cookies since the last time he was in Italy.

Aunt Louise and Uncle Joey, my dad's sister and brother, lived nearby. Aunt Louise was very precise and refined in everything she did. It fascinated me. Her outfits were color coordinated, she had the perfect salon hairstyle, and her nails were always done. She had two sons, my cousins, Mark and Anthony. Aunt Louise was like a second mom to me next to Grandma. She would tell Grandma, "Ma, you're too soft on Ang." Grandma would reply, "I know I am, but I can't help myself. I just love her."

I was my grandma's whole life and she was mine, and I knew I was the favorite kid out of the whole bunch, cousins included. That was how I got away with everything. Grandma saw a lot of herself in me. We both knew how to get what we wanted, one way or another, and my grandma could charm anyone. She knew how to work a room and was always in charge. Her kitchen was off-limits to everyone. I never learned how to cook, wash a dish, or even use a mop until I got to prison and was assigned to kitchen duty. The inmate in charge had to show me how to do everything and was constantly in awe of my ineptitude at the most basic tasks.

Uncle Joey was a completely different personality. He was a legitimate businessman in every sense of the word. I always looked up to him. We were very close, but I hated how he would try to discipline me in my father's absence. I would say, "You're not my father!" I am sure it hurt him, but at the time I didn't care. He had friends who would catch me hanging out in bars and local taverns before I was of age, acting loose, wearing makeup, and flirting with older guys. I think he thought my wild behavior was a phase and hoped I would grow out of it. Uncle Joey was honest and hardworking and, unlike my father, paid for everything on the up-and-up. I thought he was such a classy guy. He threw fancy dinner parties at his home, traveled to Mexico, and had wonderful taste. He knew a lot of high-society folks, inside and outside Chicago. He took good care of Grandma and hated that I was so spoiled and disrespectful toward her. But he had a bad Sicilian temper, too, and could get mean. I remember him chasing me and screaming at me: "You spoiled little bitch." I would always get away. I never doubted that Uncle Joey loved me and only wanted the best for me. He used to say how smart and pretty I was. "You got the world by the balls, sister," was one of his favorite comments. But nothing could hold me down.

When I was about thirteen I started to get in trouble with the law for petty crimes like stealing makeup and clothes. Each time Grandma would do whatever it took to get me off, and then hide it from my father. She was always yelling in broken English, "Your father is going to bust!" as she bit the tip of her thumb, an Italian gesture that basically translates to "fuck you." Grandma was old school and never meant any harm when she yelled at us. I knew that, but it didn't stop me from playing her when I had to. She was an easy mark, even though she knew all the tricks, because she couldn't say no to me.

Without even realizing it, Grandma had taught me a few things. I was about six years old when we were on a routine shopping trip with my aunt Camille. We always went to Bill's, a corner grocery store about two blocks from our apartment, even though Grandma complained about how high Bill's prices were. She had her own method of cutting costs.

"Go flirt with Bill and keep him busy, Camille," Grandma said, once we got inside the store.

I watched while Aunt Camille started a conversation with Bill. Then, Grandma took a dozen eggs and gently stuffed them into her girdle. I can still see her calmly looking around and reaching up under her dress to stash the eggs. She moved down the dairy case and took a pound of butter and stuffed that into her bra. She took my little hand, and we calmly walked out while Aunt Camille said good-bye to Bill, who never caught on. Not only did I observe the art of distraction and get a chance to study the calm execution of a successful heist, to this day

I still stash things in my bra, just as a place to hold them. I don't give it a second thought.

Traditional Italians, my family rolled out the red carpet whenever there was a holiday or special occasion. I was the first generation in an Italian immigrant family to enjoy the extravagant effects of their New World prosperity. Along with running the hot dog stand, my father had a range of other "projects" in the works. He was always bringing home a new appliance or some fancy jewelry that "fell off a truck." He would tilt his head to one side, give a little shrug, and say, "I know a guy." There was a high-profile jewelry heist in Chicago in the early 1970s, when I was around fourteen. It was on the front page of all the papers. I don't know how my father was connected to it, but one day I came home and our long dining room table was covered in opened velvet jewelry rolls full of glittering gold chains, silver cuff links, and diamond bracelets. My eyes grew big as I walked around the table trying to take it all in. My father invited me and Crickie to take whatever we wanted. I never heard anything else about it.

My father worked hard, but he liked to play hard, too, and he was a real ladies' man. He loved my sister and me to no end, but he never knew how to be a father. Grandma would say, "Petey, you better spend some time with these girls!" He tried to do the best he could in the family department, but he always had too many balls in the air. I remember a little field trip he took us on when we were very young, to a fancy Lake Shore Drive penthouse where we could swim in the pool. He watched us in the water as he sat by the pool making time with yet another pretty woman. I thought my dad was the coolest guy in town. He knew everyone, and everyone knew him. I would hear him talk about being at the club with this guy or that guy, and all the names I heard were famous Chicago crime figures. When I asked Grandma about them, she'd say, "Keep your mouth shut." I'd shrug my shoulders and say, "OK." Back in those days, it seemed like everybody around us knew someone or had a relative who was involved with "connected guys." That's just the way it was. When I was a teenager, I had my own princess phone with a private number. Once I got a threatening phone call on my line that was intended for my father. The guy's voice was menacing, and that made me really angry, so I let my father have it, "Now you've got these people threatening *me*! I'm afraid to go to school! Am I going to get kidnapped because of something you did?" He promised to take care of it, and that was my perfect excuse to stay home from school. I wasn't scared, but I never wasted a good angle.

Weddings were big occasions and one of the few times all the connected guys would show up in public together. The whole family went to my father's cousin's wedding, a big extravagant affair with close to a thousand people. Some of the "guests" at the hotel where the reception was held were undercover FBI agents there to take photos and watch the men, like a scene out of *The Godfather*. My father brought a date with him, and they began to argue. I have no idea what it was about, but my father had a hot temper. He and his date walked to the lobby. It was getting very loud, so a man walked up to them to try to calm the situation. My father was so crazed that he punched the man right in the face and knocked him out, not knowing that the man was an FBI agent. My father was quickly arrested and hauled off to the nearest Chicago police precinct. As expected, my father's uncle left his own daughter's wedding immediately to bail my dad out of jail before Grandma even knew he was gone. This was normal for my family. I never thought twice about any of it.

Eventually, my father got deeper into the drug game. I always knew he smoked pot; Crickie had been stealing weed from his bedroom drawer for years. He must have known, but he never said anything. It was the early 1970s, a time when a younger generation of connected guys, many the children of impoverished immigrants, started to look at other activities beyond the basic rackets (like car-theft rings and robbing merchandise from trucks) that their elders were into. My dad started to realize that there was a lot of money to be made in the drug trade. His uncles were against it, so they stayed away and my father never told them. But he moved with the times and started using and dealing cocaine. I learned from my father how to taste the coke, how much is in a kilo, and how to cut up a kilo. In fact, he gave me my first triple-beam scale.

This all came about by accident when Crickie found out from a friend that my father was dealing. One afternoon I was at her apartment, and she and her husband wanted some coke. We were in our twenties.

Crickie said, "Daddy does everything for you, Ang. Call him and ask him for some, he'll give it to you."

"Sure," I said without hesitation, but as I started to think about what might be in it for me, I knew I needed an angle. Once I got him on the phone, I said, "Daddy, I've got a proposition for you. I know I ask you for a lot of money and maybe you don't really want to give it to me, so I thought if you gave me a couple ounces of coke and told me exactly how to break that down and how to sell it, I could do that. I'll make money, you'll make money, it's a win-win."

He simply said OK. He told me he was on his way out, but the coke would be hidden under the fruit bowl in the kitchen and to come and get it. So I started dealing coke, just like that, and it kept me rolling in money.

After my mother left, my father had a lot of girlfriends, but he always took care of our material well-being. Daddy regularly delivered wads of money to Grandma for Crickie and me. A child of the Great Depression, she never believed we were wealthy, and refused to put her money into any bank. Instead, Grandma kept it in her mattress and a few other hiding places, but I always knew where it was. I would peel off twenties without her knowing. My sister and I enjoyed the nicest things money could buy. We wore new clothes, rode around in my father's Cadillac, and dined at fancy restaurants. I developed a taste for the best of everything, and the pursuit of the nicest, most expensive, and coolest things became an obsession. I never thought I had too much money: there was always more to be made and more to buy. It was an attitude that drove my criminal career—a long résumé of one con job after another, stealing only high-end merchandise, embezzling as much as I could from any one source before getting caught, and eventually supporting my expensive, unrelenting heroin addiction.

Despite my father's dangerous influences, he also gave me a love of music. We had a baby grand piano in our apartment, and my uncle played classical music all the time. My father bought me a portable phonograph when I was about ten and the Beatles' *White Album*. He sat on the floor with me, opened the record player, and put the album on. We listened together, and I fell in love. Like so many kids of my generation, I spent all my money on albums. I knew everything about my favorite bands, and whenever a new album came out, I had to have it, no matter how I got the money. Music became another lifelong obsession that would help me get through some of my worst days, until one day—when I was in my lowest place, dope sick, homeless, and penniless again—I realized that, like everything else that mattered to me, I had no music in my life.

Not long after he bought me the *White Album*, my father introduced me to California and the glitter of Hollywood. I spent many summers as a kid outside Los Angeles, where my family owned a few houses. My aunt Philly lived in one of them. My father must have thought it was a good idea to send us away for a while and give Grandma some relief, so we stayed with Aunt Philly and I drove *her* crazy. My aunt tried to make sure we were amused. I remember many car trips to Palm Springs, the Calico Ghost Town, and Disneyland.

But Hollywood beckoned. There was so much trouble to get into, and I didn't waste a second. The rock music scene, with its sexy stars, and the allure of the Sunset Strip were on my radar from the time I got that turntable from my father. I went to my first concert in 1969 with my California friend, Francine, at the Forum in Los Angeles. I was only eleven, but most parents didn't know what happened inside a rock concert back then, and Aunt Philly certainly didn't have a clue. Francine's father got us tickets and told us where to go to get to our seats, how to act, and where to meet him afterward. It was Three Dog Night, not the coolest band in the rock 'n' roll galaxy, I would later decide, but when her father dropped us off and we walked into that arena, I entered a world I wanted to be part of, mesmerized by the musicians and the audience. I saw people dressed the way I wanted to look, doing things I wanted to do—like smoking pot. I knew I had to get my hands on some of that.

Music and weed were connected in my mind. I was in fifth grade, and now my summer in Los Angeles meant sneaking away to Hollywood to buy weed. Francine, the local girl, knew all about Hollywood and together we decided we had to go to the strip. We figured out how to take the bus all the way from Aunt Philly's house, right to the Whiskey a Go Go. We couldn't go in, but we managed to cop some weed just standing there. We went to a head shop and bought a mini hookah pipe, loaded it up, and smoked right on the street. Like Jodie Foster in *Taxi Driver*, we were eleven-year-old girls wearing platform shoes and halter tops, strutting along and getting high on the strip. I saw pimps and hookers and drug addicts. I realized that Hollywood and Vine was a spot for movie stars only in myth. In fact, there weren't any movie stars there at all, only street people hustling and getting high. My family eventually figured out what I was up to and tried to stop me, but like so many times to come, it didn't stick.

Aunt Philly was much stricter than Grandma, but even her methods didn't work. She and my uncle took Crickie and me on car trips all over California. When we went to Palm Springs, Bel Air, and Beverly Hills, I had to endure the tedious driving tour of famous Italian celebrities' homes, Frank Sinatra's house, Dean Martin's house, something they were so proud of but that drove me into fits of boredom. One place I really did want to see was Sea World in San Diego, and Aunt Philly knew it. She decided I had to be punished for running off to Hollywood, so she made me stay behind while Crickie went with them to Sea World. Of course, I did not stay home as instructed. Francine and I got high and went back to the strip as soon as the family car drove away. My family was learning that there just wasn't a cage, physical or emotional, that was strong enough to hold me.

High school was one place that I simply could not endure. Oak Park in the early 1970s, during the end of the hippie days, was full of wealthy kids partying and spending their parents' money on drugs and whatever else they wanted. The age of free love was giving way to unbridled consumerism. Designer everything became the new craze, and none of us cared about anything beyond ourselves. I would go to huge parties at friends' mansions when their parents were away. We were getting high all day, every day, taking LSD, smoking weed, and popping reds, quaaludes, yellow jackets (nembutol), and the Cadillac of barbiturates, Christmas Trees (Tuinol). I dropped out of Oak Park River Forest High School at sixteen. I figured I knew all I needed to know and I didn't have time to study. I started partying when I was very young and didn't see any reason to ever stop.

I was bored and restless, and there was too much trouble waiting for me outside of high school. I found many ways to escape. One of my great escapes was in 1974 when I took off on a cross-country road trip with my boyfriend and two other guys. They were all seniors, and I was fifteen. I had always been more like one of the guys than a girlie girl, but they were skeptical of a girl tagging along. I convinced them that I could and would do whatever they would do. I wasn't afraid of anything, and I could talk my way into or out of any situation. They drank more than I did, but I could match them one for one with any drugs. In fact, I probably got high and popped pills more than they did, so I was in. The plan was to hit the road in a car the guys bought, an old station wagon, stop on the way to see a couple of national parks, like Glacier and Mount Rushmore, and eventually get to Expo '74 in Spokane, Washington. I was so excited. But we had to have enough cash and decided that we needed four hundred dollars each before we could leave.

I had to figure out how to get the money from my father. I didn't ask his permission to go. I *told* him I was going and demanded the money. He said, "Absolutely not, you are not going anywhere, go back to school and stop wasting space!"

But, in my unrelenting way, I wore him down. I made him a proposition. We could split it. If I could raise half, he would pony up the other half. Deal, he agreed, thinking he had me because there was no way I could ever raise two hundred dollars. And, admittedly, I had no idea how I was going to raise it, either. My father thought he was slick, but I knew I was slicker. He told Grandma not to give me a dime, so that was out. He knew that I was smart. I knew that he was proud of that, and it made me happy. He might have worried a little about what I would do, but he probably thought a kid couldn't get into that much trouble. He didn't fully understand yet that I would do anything to get what I wanted. I needed a plan.

I will never know how this came into my head, but it was my first con outside my family members, and I was a natural. I had been milking my uncles and Grandma for petty cash for as long as I could remember, but now I was taking it to the street—literally. I was a cute little girl at age fifteen, and I could make myself look older or younger, depending on what the situation demanded. I decided to put on my frilly pink-and-blue one-piece bathing suit and my flip-flops, hold my swim cap in my hand, drape a beach towel over my arm, and stand on the corner of State and Lake in downtown Chicago. To anyone who would stop and listen, I made a pitch in my most innocent, little-girl-lost voice.

"Um, excuse me, I lost my money at the beach, and I can't get home to Oak Park, so could you just give me a couple of dollars for the bus? I really need to get home. My grandma is going to be so worried." A man stopped and gave me a five-dollar bill, and I felt such a thrill. It was hard to keep up the destitute act and not laugh out loud.

I panhandled for a full day on that spot and, while some people gave me bus tokens, I actually collected $150 cash! I was not going to leave that corner until I made as much as I could before the crowds thinned, and it started getting dark. It was easy money, and I loved it. A hustler was born. But I didn't stop there. I was determined to raise all the money and still take the two hundred from my father. So I went to one of my favorite antique stores in Oak Park. It was run by two friendly unsuspecting little old ladies and I went in often to look at the fancy estate jewelry and beautiful old things, so they knew me and seemed to like me. The nice lady took some of the jewelry out of the case to let me see it and while my cute little self charmed her, one of my hands grabbed a very expensive emerald ring and stuck it in my pocket. I hitchhiked to a pawnshop on North and Ridgeland Avenues and got one hundred dollars for it. Now I had $250, but I didn't want to stop there. The next week in school I did what a lot of my friends did and stole money from other kids' lockers. Even though I was only a freshman, it didn't take me long to catch on. Many of the kids at my high school were from wealthy Oak Park families and carried all kinds of cash and even checkbooks. In the gym room I broke into a girl's locker and stole her wallet and checkbook. I started writing checks and cashing them at the Certified Foods in Oak Park. It was so easy! I ended up with more than $400.

I often wonder how different things might have been if I had been caught and punished a few more times when I was young. But I kept getting away with everything, and that only fueled my sense of being invincible, something that would drive me to go all the way with so many illegal activities. The game always fascinated me more than the possible consequences, whether it was my father's wrath or serious jail time. Nothing scared me.

I went back to my father with most of the money safely tucked in my bra, just like Grandma taught me, and only showed my father $200. He was shocked. But being an old Sicilian, he was a man of his word, and I knew it. He could not go back on his promise. I was an adorable and crazy fifteen-year-old and he had every reason to be worried, but he knew he couldn't stop me now. After a lot of shouting and cursing, he handed over his half of the cash, made me promise to be careful and stay in touch the whole time. Off I went with the older guys. We stayed away for a couple of months. We camped and hiked, took drugs and drank, and had a blast. My boyfriend and I had our own tent, so we could have sex every night. We were free spirits, went wherever we wanted, whenever we wanted, and did whatever we felt like. We were high all the time on one thing or another, but barbiturates were my favorite, and I popped them like candy.

The trip was a psychedelic, drug-fueled tour of the West: the mountains outside Butte, Montana, Glaciers National Park, and many other magnificent stops along the way. Peanut butter sandwiches with granola on top became our standard fare. We tried to cross the Canadian border, but looking like the complete hippies that we were trying to be, in our beat-up station wagon, with towels and other laundry hanging out of the windows, when we pulled into Canadian customs of course we were stopped and searched. The agents found some pot seeds, but after harassing us, taking us into custody, grilling us, and tearing the car apart, they sent us back through US customs, denying us entry to Canada. My father was screaming at me to come home every time I called, but I told him there was no way, and we just kept moving. We made it to Spokane and the Expo and then moved on to the coast, went to see the redwoods, and toured the California highways. It really was the trip of a lifetime for me, something my family never would have done. I was flying high. It was one adventure after another, until we hit a major snag.

Outside Big Sur the brakes on the car gave out on one of those long downhill patches. We slammed into another car with two older women inside. We had to be cut out of the car, but nobody was badly hurt. We were all high on quaaludes, loose and feeling no pain. Now we were without wheels, and two of the guys decided to hitchhike home. But I refused. I was on my way to L.A., and that's where I was going. Somehow I convinced my father over the phone to buy my boyfriend and me plane tickets and wire me money. We got a hotel room near the strip, did lots of coke, and eventually went home. I was so passed out on the plane from a couple of drinks and a handful of barbiturates that the flight attendants had to shake me to get me out of my seat when we landed at O'Hare International Airport in Chicago. My father picked us up and that was the end of that adventure. But it was the beginning of my drug-fueled wanderlust.

A few weeks after I got back home, my friend Rainey* and I decided to hitchhike to the Ozark Music Festival, one of the biggest rock festivals in history. Dressed in the shortest shorts and low-cut halter tops, me in my laced-up leather knee-high moccasins, we used our female charms to get all the drugs we wanted and hung out with guys in their twenties. Eventually, as I always did, I became one of the most enthusiastic participants, and after seeing so many naked hippies I took off my top and joined the crowd. We saw Aerosmith, the Eagles, Lynyrd Skynyrd, and many others, and got home in August, in time to start school in September.

But I could not stay put. I was developing the soul of a nomad and I just had to move. I hitchhiked across the country ten or fifteen times. It was free and easy for a fearless girl like me. Rainey called me one day that August and said she was near Key West and I just had to come down there. I left almost immediately and stayed for five months. It was a beautiful place called Stock Island, and she was living in a little hippie outpost, swimming in the ocean every day, fishing off a boat for dinner, sleeping in a tent on the beach, and, of course, doing drugs all the time.

---

* For the sake of privacy, her name has been changed.

The moment I got off the phone with Rainey, I called my father, told him I needed airplane tickets to Miami and cash for the trip. He said no at first, but I wore him down. He booked the flight, Rainey and the older guys she was hanging with picked me up, and soon I was living on Stock Island, a sun-drenched, free love, drug-hazed paradise.

Every morning I walked out of my tent and the ocean was at my feet. I would stop by the campground office every single day because, to assuage her worries as much as anything else, Grandma mailed me twenty dollars a day in an envelope. Soon my father started doing the same, unaware of Grandma's contributions, so I got forty dollars every day, which in 1974 was not a bad deal. But my mind always looked for a scam to get more and somehow I managed to get on public aid in Florida at age fifteen. I have no idea how I did that. I was a minor, had no home or children to support, but along with my forty dollars a day in the mail, I was also collecting forty-eight dollars a month in food stamps. Rainey and I would go to Piggly Wiggly, stand out in front and offer to pay for a shopper's food with our food stamps in exchange for their cash, and it worked. But we would hold back a few food stamps, then hitchhike to Key West and go to a deli we really liked, where we could use food stamps to pay for conch chowder, our favorite. We'd often spend the day in Key West or hitchhike there at night to watch the sunset with all the hippies in Mallory Square. It was a lifestyle that I reveled in. I learned how to fish and scuba dive. I was living a dream.

I stayed on Stock Island much longer than I had expected. By the time I decided to come home, it was December and I had missed the first half of the tenth grade. While I was gone, the school called every day. Grandma was livid, but I told her there was no way I could ever go back inside that school now. I had tasted freedom. And it seemed that the world was yielding to my desire to buck all semblance of a normal life. My high school had adopted a modern education model that included something called the XP, an experimental program. This was an attempt to keep kids engaged by letting them use real-life experiences to get high school credits. You were supposed to have exceptional grades and test scores. Somehow my father got me into the program. I don't know how he did it.

I managed to fake my way through enough credits to make up for my time on Stock Island with the XP curriculum. According to the teachers, it qualified as a life learning experience. My imagination went to work and I wrote about the island, scuba diving, and the different types of fish I encountered, about Key West and Ernest Hemingway, crafting yet another successful scam. Living in a hippie commune, sleeping with a twentysomething guy, smoking weed, popping pills and acid every day, all at age fifteen, was a learning experience, for sure. But what I was learning was that high school was a joke and I could do or be or have anything I could imagine.

I did well in school when I wanted to because I was a bright kid. Grandma liked to say I was too smart for my own good. I thought I knew everything because I never studied and still got good grades. In today's world of childhood testing, I might have been diagnosed with ADD, but there was no understanding of that yet. I was a thrill seeker and a tomboy from an early age. I scored above average on the tests I managed to take, but never did any schoolwork, so I had no grades at the end of each term. My main activities in high school were sitting on the school mall, selling drugs—weed, pills, acid—doing those drugs, and smoking cigarettes, while the regular students passed by on their way to class. But the XP program kept me enrolled. You were considered in attendance as long as you were completing an assignment anywhere in the Chicago metropolitan area. I would skip school all day, get high, and compose essays about my pretend trips to places like the Art Institute, write poems and stories, and get credit for all of it. I managed to make it through the tenth grade.

When I was sixteen I lied and said I was eighteen to get a summer job at the Chicago Board Options Exchange. It wasn't difficult. The most common careers in Oak Park were lawyer, doctor, stockbroker, funeral director, or in the mob. Many of my friends' parents were brokers, so a couple of us went down to the board of trade to see if we could get jobs. We managed to get passes to the trading floor and went from booth to booth asking if they needed summer help. I got to EF Hutton and the guy there asked me if I wanted to be a runner. I had no idea what that was but said yes and started almost immediately. My only problem with the job was that EF Hutton had the ugliest gold-colored jackets and I did not like wearing one, so I spent my first three weeks on the floor schmoozing other companies with cooler jackets. Front Street Securities hired me. I got a better-looking jacket, and that summer I learned a lot. I was good at retaining information. In many ways, the fast-paced, erratic world of the stock exchange was a perfect match for my hyper personality. Summer ended and I tried but could not go back to school. I skipped all the time and took a few more hitchhiking trips out west to get away. Whenever I felt the urge to wander, I stuck out my thumb and back to California I went, exploring San Francisco and the Haight-Ashbury scene, another drug-drenched trip. Back home again, the truant officers were at our door, threatening Grandma with jail or me with the juvie home.

I would sleep until noon, get up, and watch television. Grandma would yell at me and say, "You somm-an-a-bitch, you gotta go to school!"

I had a perfect position in front of the TV in my room, placed just so by my father on a shelf that made it exactly right for me to watch from the plumped-up pillows on my bed, tuned to *The Bozo Show*. She would venture in with my coffee and cinnamon-sugar toast, and I would yell at her, "That's not my problem, Grandma. You're the guardian, you figure out what to tell them. I gotta watch *All My Children* later! I can't miss Erica Kane!"

Grandma would curse in Italian and leave the room.

At night, I hung out in downtown Chicago, around the popular club scene on Rush Street. From that first time as a kid standing on the corner of Lake Street in my bathing suit, conning passersby out of petty change, I learned the art of manipulation. I was always thrilled by how easy it was, and I always went all in. Even when men tried to take advantage of me, I managed to turn it on them and get as much as I could out of it. A destination for throngs of wealthy tourists, Rush Street was also where the city's elite went to party, from local celebrities to politicians, to sports stars and gossip column regulars. They mingled with the pimps, strippers, and dealers who also hung out every night. It was prime pickings for high-end hookers, hustlers, and skilled thieves.

One night on Rush Street, when I was sixteen, I was hanging out with a bunch of friends, just walking along, dressed in a short skirt, low-cut top, teased hair, and far too much makeup, when a black limo pulled up. The window slid down to reveal an older man sitting in the backseat. He gestured toward me and said, "Come 'ere for a minute." I didn't think much of him—he seemed a little creepy—but the hustler in me figured the limo was something that I had to get near.

"Get in the limo," the older guy said.

"For what?" I asked.

"I'm going to make you a proposition."

"For money?" I immediately wanted to know.

"Yes," he said, "a good amount of money."

I asked him how much money, he said a thousand dollars, and I said, "Open the door."

I got into the car and noticed another guy sitting in the backseat, Creepy Guy's security guard. Creepy Guy, it turned out, was a high-ranking city official.

"I want to have sex with you, and I'll pay you a thousand dollars," he said. In 1975 dollars, that was a huge amount of money. I wasn't a hooker, but I was ready to hustle. There I was, in a limo with a thousand dollars dangling in my painted-up sixteen-year-old face, so I decided to go with it. He took me to the Ambassador East hotel, one of Chicago's finest, home of the famous Pump Room restaurant—"playground to the stars," as it said in the brochure, and, I would soon learn, the place where high-ranking city officials took young girls like me for fun and not-so-cheap thrills.

We got out of the limo in front of the hotel, and Creepy Guy already had a room, so up we went. I found myself in an opulent suite, with two bedrooms, one connected to a huge, marble-lined bathroom. He told me to run a bath for him. But before I would go any farther than the threshold of the suite, I made a demand.

"You said a thousand dollars. I need it first," I said without a second's hesitation. I wasn't thinking that this was what a hooker should do; I just knew that nobody was going to scam me. He tried to convince me to take half first, and the rest later, but I said no, I needed the whole thing first or we don't have a deal. He gave me ten hundred-dollar bills right then and there. I tucked the money into my purse and went into the bathroom, never letting my purse out of my sight, somehow channeling the instinct that hustlers call "ugly game" even at that age, and ran the bath. When I came back to get him, he was already naked. He was a sight I would like to forget: a short fat man with a forest of thick black hair on his chest and back. Never in my life had I seen such a hairy back. I was grossed out and for a brief moment calculated my chances of running out of the suite with the money, leaving this asshole right where he was sitting. But the security guy, who had followed us, was in the front room. So instead of running, I went along with Creepy Guy, closed my eyes, and washed his back, trying not to gag. When he decided I was done, he got out of the tub and told me to take off my clothes and lie on the bed, and in a very short time he got his thousand dollars' worth. The brevity of it all convinced me that I had made a good choice. He may have been on top of me, but I had definitely come out ahead in this deal. Hairy back aside, I made a thousand bucks in five minutes. All I had to do was block out the sound of his old-man grunts by mentally counting the thousand dollars. I got dressed, left the room, walked back to Rush Street with the money, and got my hair done and a manicure in one of the most expensive salons in the city. Then I bought myself a cute outfit in one of the pricey boutiques nearby.

Over the next few months, I saw him again. When he pulled up to me, I recognized the limo and got right in. During our time together, I was told to be quiet and not tell anybody about any of this because of who he was. His position was highly visible, so he could get into a lot of trouble, he told me. I didn't care about any of that. All I cared about was the thousand dollars, and as long as I got it up front, we were good. I gave him my phone number at Grandma's house, and he would call me to meet up, sometimes with one of my girlfriends. He took us to the Pump Room and other exclusive restaurants near Rush Street and State Street and apparently didn't care who saw him doing that. We were young girls, so maybe he figured he could say we were his nieces. I do know that I consumed a lot of lobster and filet mignon. He ordered us champagne with strawberries in it and even bought me a sexy white strapless dress with a slit all the way up to my thigh and a pair of black heels to wear. This went on for many months and really only ended when I went to Tucson about a year later.

I gave up on high school for good and went back to the board of trade to become a full-time runner. No one ever asked me for identification, and it was before the days of brokers being vetted and bonded. I was quick to learn and especially good with numbers, so I managed to work my way up to phone clerk and then assistant broker, the one responsible for holding the deck, keeping all the orders straight, who's selling, who's buying, standing in the pit with the broker. I ran an arbitrage line, a hotline straight to the New York Stock Exchange. I did all this without a high school diploma, lying about my age the entire time.

The charged atmosphere of the trading floor never intimidated me. I was aggressive, unafraid of the risks, and I loved the action, the shouting in the pit, the rapid-fire rise and fall of fortunes. The bosses and the brokers loved me. I was making good money, but I lived as if I had a lot more, and whenever I was short I would hit up my father. He would comply, so I never thought about money. Ever the chameleon, I fell into a fast lifestyle that was the height of glamour to me, and I went as far as I could go with it. No more frolicking hippie living on the beach—now I was a city babe who wanted a piece of everything money could buy. My drug intake was rising all the time. Coke, pills, and weed were already staples of the stockbroker culture, and a lot of guys regularly snorted coke on the trading floor, so there I was, in what seemed like my perfect job. I was seventeen, looking twenty-one, attractive and sexy, partying with rich older men. One of the brokers at my firm let me live in a furnished, but unoccupied, condo he owned on the eightieth floor of the John Hancock building, giving me a swanky Magnificent Mile address, on top of the world. I loved spying on this new world and gazing at the stars from the high-powered telescope that came with the condo. I bought or stole designer everything, rode in limos, took expensive cab rides just for fun, went to the priciest restaurants and hottest clubs in town, and hung out with influential, powerful men who thought they were taking advantage of me. But I always came out on top.

I started to think I was better than my family because I was hanging out with such high-society friends, people from old money and positions of power in Chicago. I told my father, "I'm a white-collar worker, Daddy, and you're just a blue-collar guy. I looked it up in the dictionary!" He was such a hard worker, and whenever he had a lucky streak gambling he would give my sister and me wads of cash, a few hundred dollars, but I was a mean spoiled brat, no matter what the poor guy did.

I would be in and out of the board of trade just like high school. As much as I loved the job and the lifestyle, I still had to get away whenever I felt like it, so when my friend Carrie suggested we take a two-week vacation to Key West, I was in. When I returned to the trading floor I found out that the company I had worked for had folded while I was gone. I was given a few weeks' severance pay, a glowing recommendation, and told to see a guy at another firm for a job. He was ready to hire me but the job required a drug test and a lie detector test, two things I knew I could not pass, so I figured that was the end of my career at the Options Exchange. I was cool with not working, and my father would give me whatever I wanted, so I went home to Oak Park and kept partying, hitting the clubs downtown every night, out until morning, snorting coke, smoking weed, and popping pills like everybody else. But I had made a reputation for myself at the board of trade as a hard worker and an aggressive one, so soon I got a call from another brokerage firm, and they hired me.

Now I decided I needed a car to match my white-collar job and started working on my father to buy it for me. It took a couple of weeks to wear him down. I would step away from the trading floor and use the pay phone to call him.

"Daddy, what are we doing about the car? I need it now!"

After two weeks of this, he finally caved. "Go inside my suit jacket in the closet, there's $5,000 in cash. Use that for the down payment."

"Thank you, Daddy!"

He told my stepmother to let me know that I should not come home with a foreign car, to find something practical and safe that would run well. I had no idea what any of that meant, I just knew a car should look cool and have a good stereo system. I went to the Ford dealer with my boyfriend. After a few minutes I decided, "Fuck this," and we wandered over to the Porsche-Audi dealership. We walked around looking at all the gorgeous cars until I saw exactly what I wanted, a beautiful midnight-blue Porsche. I took it for a test drive, and the stereo was great. It was a five-speed stick shift. I had been driving since I was twelve when my friends and I started stealing cars in Oak Park and taking them for joy rides, so I could drive anything. Since my family was well known in Oak Park, I told the dealer who I was and he immediately said OK and let me sign for the car, just like that. I gave the dealer the $5,000 and made sure all the paperwork was ready to go, but I couldn't drive it off the showroom floor until my father signed for the rest of the cost. I wasn't ready to face my father, so first I told Pat, my stepmother, who knew it was going to be bad when she heard it was a Porsche.

"Your father's going to kill you!" she hollered.

"I already signed and put the money down, so I have to get it," I said.

When he heard the news, my father said, "Absolutely not, no way." He said he was going to call the dealer and get the money back. Every day for the next week, two or three times a day, I called my father and cried over the phone.

"You don't love me, Daddy! I don't even have a mother. We can afford this! How can you say no?"

My poor father could only take this for so long. He finally relented, "OK, go get the fuckin' car!"

I loved that car more than anyone should ever love a car. I drove it everywhere, hanging out on Rush Street, or flying down the highway to see how fast it could go, sometimes being chased by the police. Once a cop asked me if I knew how fast I was going. I gave him a song and dance about how this was a Porsche, and you have to open it up to keep it running right. He threatened to write me a ticket and take my license away, so I told him who my family was and promised that he would be back walking the beat tomorrow because he had no idea how connected I was. This cop could not believe the nerve of this little smart-ass teenager and wrote me a ticket. I crumpled it up and threw it on the car seat. My father took care of the ticket, as I knew he would, but he schooled me on how to handle these things in the future.

"Never tell the cop who you are. Just take the ticket and let me handle it from there. This cop was so pissed at you, he didn't want to let it go. It took a long time to get him to change his mind." Lesson learned on my part, but I didn't really care about anything except getting my way.

I never got the hang of parking on the streets of Chicago, and many times I just left the car wherever I wanted to, near a club or restaurant or wherever I was going. I was too high to drive around looking for a parking space. If I got towed, I called my father, and he fixed it. I was getting as many as ten parking tickets every day. I lost count at a certain point and would just toss them into the glove compartment and bring a pile into the house when it overflowed. My father eventually asked me how many I had and I told him to look at the pile. I genuinely didn't understand why this was such a big deal. My father went crazy when he saw how many there were, and had to pay thousands of dollars to get them all fixed.

I was seventeen, behind the wheel of a Porsche, always high, and totally in control of my destiny, or so I thought. I spent another eight months back on the trading floor and again, I outran and outworked my peers. It was time for promotions, and I knew I deserved one that included a hefty pay raise and a fabulous office with a view. Instead, a runner with a bachelor's degree, a guy, got it. The company promised me a raise, the same money he was getting, but nothing else. I wanted that office more than the money. I told them just where they could shove their raise and walked off the floor in the middle of that day's rally, the worst possible time to leave. I never looked back. I decided to go to Tucson with my friend Jo to stay with her sister, MJ. I parked the Porsche at O'Hare, wrote a bad check for the airplane tickets, and stayed away for five weeks.

I loved Tucson. Jo and I partied with MJ's friends, hookers, bikers, and dope dealers. I thought they were all fascinating. Some of the dope dealers were members of the Mexican mafia and did regular smuggling trips over the border. I didn't know it at the time, but they kept MJ and her friends well supplied in heroin and coke. These characters were scary and attractive, tough and funny, and I wanted to find out more about how they lived. I was never satisfied with hearing stories or reading books about how other people lived. I had to know firsthand. If I discovered a group of people or a scene that captured my imagination, I had to be part of it. I loved the climate in Arizona, the hot, dry days and cool, crisp nights. And there were so many stars in the desert sky; I knew I would keep coming back.

After a few weeks, I finally called my father to ask him to wire me money. I told him where I was and he asked me where I had left the car. I said it was in the parking garage at O'Hare. He went ballistic, telling me the car would be stripped for sure. He really thought he had me this time. He decided that I should handle getting the car out myself, thinking there was no way I would have enough to bail out the Porsche. "You figure it out for once," he said. "You're a big girl." Once again, he underestimated me. I flew home and found the Porsche in one piece.

I pulled up to the checkout booth for the garage and turned on my innocent-little-girl persona for the guy, "Um, can you please help me? I don't know what to do, I lost my parking stub and I am so sorry!" I made my voice crack and even managed some fake tears.

He just asked me for the day fee, less than forty dollars, and waved me through. I went home, parked the car out front, and walked into the house. My father asked me if I had taken a cab home. When he looked out the window and saw the car, he was speechless, except to say for the umpteenth time, "You are too smart for your own good."

I drove that car into the ground and let the gunky oil wear down the engine. I parked it at home one day, told my father he could have it, and left home again. To this day I have no idea what he did with what was left of the Porsche.

When I got back from that first trip to Tucson, another brokerage firm offered me a job, and I found myself back at the board of trade. Once again, I was riding high and doing a great job. After work, I started hanging with more people in the music scene in Chicago, getting backstage passes, meeting the musicians, sleeping with the musicians, and again, discovering a lifestyle that fascinated me. The chameleon in me found another subculture that I had to try on for size.

The Who came to Chicago that year and I managed to meet them and even hang out at their hotel. I was backstage during sound check for their second Chicago show, and one of the roadies asked me to go onstage and talk into one of the mics for him, so I did. The house lights were still up and people were starting to filter in to their seats. It was an awe-inspiring view of a rock star's world from his vantage point, and I was dazzled beyond belief. Keith Moon asked me to go with him on the tour, and I didn't hesitate. But first, after the show that night, I had to go back home to Oak Park and pick up some things, so we drove there in Keith's limo. I can only imagine the neighbors peeking out of their windows when the big black car pulled up in front of my grandma's building. Keith came inside and said hello to Grandma, but it was clear they would not become friends. She was yelling at me not to leave, cursing in Italian, and even made a few remarks about his weird accent and haircut, so I made sure we got the hell out of there as fast as possible. We drove to the airport, and I boarded the Who's plane, high on pills and weed, and feeling like my whole life was some kind of groovy hallucination.

But a rude wake-up call was not far off. After many shows, insane hotel parties, more drugs than I could comprehend, and lots of crazy sex with Keith, he moved on to another cute starstruck girl, and I was out in the cold. I hung with the tour, now downgraded to riding on the bus, sleeping with roadies, assigned to an unglamorous bunk, and asked to help sell T-shirts and other Who merchandise at their shows. I had to actually work, packing and unpacking the merch, and carrying heavy boxes to and from the truck. This was definitely not my thing, so I walked away one day and hitched back to Chicago.

I naively assumed that I could waltz back to my job at the board of trade and nonchalantly showed up for work one morning, as if I had never left. It was after Christmas. My boss greeted me with the company gift, a nice cigarette lighter that everybody got, told me to go to the office for my severance pay, and to have a nice life. He told me that everybody knew I was on tour with the Who, not on sick leave as

I claimed. Since half the board of trade went to every big rock concert in Chicago, most of my coworkers had seen me walk onstage and speak into the mic during that sound check. I was busted, and no amount of sweet talk was going to get my job back.

Unfazed, I walked away, stuck out my thumb, and went back to San Francisco to hang with my hippie friends again. In what seems to me now a stunning example of how many second chances I got and promptly blew, I actually had a chance to go back to work when another brokerage firm called, but I turned it down. Instead, after San Francisco, I went back to Tucson, a move that would start the long downward spiral in my life.

# 3

# The High Life

It was the spring of 1976, and the electricity was turned off in the Tucson apartment where Jo's sister, MJ, lived. Rent had not been paid on the tiny one-bedroom in months. It was in one of the worst parts of the city, downtown, near the bus station. MJ was about eight years older than me; she was a real hippie and a heroin addict. Most of her neighbors were either addicts or dealers, or both. We sat on the floor one morning and in the candlelight I watched as she "cooked" heroin in a spoon. I was seventeen and about to shoot up for the first time.

Once I found out that MJ was using heroin, I was so intrigued that I begged her to let me try it. I knew she was doing something cool when our neighbor down the block, a Mexican guy named Dickie who was her dealer, came over to our apartment and they disappeared into the bathroom for a very long time. I just had to know what they were doing—I had a feeling it was something I wanted in on. Some days MJ would be in there by herself for a very long time. When she came out, she was in another place, a high that I could tell was different from any I knew. I had to find out what drug she was doing that got her so wasted, and how it felt. I wanted that feeling. She was always secretive about it because she didn't want her little sister or me to do it, and she didn't want us to see how badly strung out she was. Other girls, hookers who knew MJ, would come by in their little sports cars, disappear with her into the bathroom, and then stick around to party with us, drinking, doing pills, and smoking weed. I learned later that everybody knew MJ was the go-to for heroin.

We hung out in a local biker bar, played pool with the bikers who were regulars, and had a great time doing peyote, LSD, or mescaline with them. One day, I just asked MJ outright, "What the hell is going on in the bathroom all the time? You're doing dope, aren't you?"

"Yeah, I am, and it's horrible," she finally admitted.

"I knew it! I want to try," I begged her.

"No way!" she yelled. "You already love barbiturates way too much. If I let you try heroin, you're gonna end up an addict and a hooker on Cicero Avenue back in Chicago."

She was so right it was prophetic, but I couldn't see any of that coming. I just wanted to know what it was like to get high on heroin. And, as usual, I thought I was beyond invincible. Now that I knew, I dogged her from morning to night, trying to get her to let me have a taste. She said no over and over again, even saying she would tell her people not to sell it to me if I tried to get it on my own. She saw an addict in the making and she knew firsthand the hell of addiction. I even got to see a glimpse of that hell.

She woke me up one morning in really bad shape. "Do me a favor," she whispered, not wanting to wake up her sister. "I don't want to leave the apartment right now, and I don't want Jo to know. Take this money and go down by Dickie, knock on the door, tell him I sent you. Give him the money and he's going to hand you something and then bring it to me in the bathroom."

I thought, *Finally! I get to see what the hell is going on in the bathroom.*

I did what she said. Dickie was an intimidating character, and I found out later that he was one of the guys in the Mexican mafia— that's why he had the best dope. But he was always glad to see one of us and handed me a package wrapped in a dirty blue bandanna. I came back to the apartment and knocked on the bathroom door. MJ stuck out her hand, took the package, and forced the door closed. After a really long time, too long, she didn't come out, and I couldn't hear anything through the door. I started to worry about her, so I jimmied the bathroom lock open. There she was, sunken down in the bathtub water, turning blue. She had OD'd. I pulled her out of the bathtub, screaming, threw her on the floor, and started pounding on her chest while Jo called for an ambulance. I tried to give her mouth-to-mouth, but I didn't really know how. Her lips were ice cold and her face was wet and clammy. She looked like a corpse, and she was so still it was easy to believe she was dead. But she came to when the paramedics took over, loading her onto a stretcher and into the ambulance. When she got out of the hospital and walked into the apartment the next day, she was so angry with me, I couldn't believe it. I thought I had saved her life. The hospital had given her the antioverdose drug naloxone that blocks heroin in the system so the person can begin to breathe again. MJ woke up in the hospital sicker than ever, and when she got home had to get a bag right away.

"Don't ever do that again," she screamed at Jo and me for calling the ambulance, sending both of us into tears. "I would have come to."

"No you wouldn't have," I cried. "You were turning blue and sinking down in the water. You were going to drown!"

"No," she insisted. "It happens all the time. Now I'm really sick."

Even after seeing this, I wanted to know what could feel so good that she would go through all that and still want more. I asked her every day, wearing her down the same way I would work my father when I wanted something. By this time, my father was no longer mailing me money; instead, he and Grandma were wiring it to me. Every day I went to Western Union and got forty dollars, so I had plenty of cash. On that dark morning when I first shot up, MJ was in deep heroin withdrawal again, sick and desperate, and this time she had no money to buy dope. The rent was past due, the lights were turned off, and I knew I had her right where I wanted her.

"MJ, I will buy you a bag if you give me a little to try," I proposed.

I had a feeling she would get worse that day, and the misery of withdrawal would get so bad that she would have to give in to me, so I kept badgering her. Finally, she collapsed under my special brand of pressure and sent me down the block to buy *my* first bag of heroin. I know she never wanted to introduce me to this powerful drug, a demon she lived with every day. Heroin withdrawal is the worst hell to experience, taking people to places they never thought possible while forcing them to do anything just to get one more bag. This was in my future. Right now, I just had to know how it felt to get that high.

MJ tied my arm off with a belt, took the bag out of a bloodstained bandanna, cooked the dope in a dirty spoon, filled a dull used needle, and tried to find my vein. It was an ugly scene my first time. MJ kept sticking me in different places, as my whole arm started turning blue. Blood was dripping down my arm from each new hole she made. It hurt like hell, but my determination was stronger than the pain. I tried to wipe it up, so my hands were full of blood, too. "I can't see without any light, I can't find a vein," she said in frustration. Finally, she sent me down the block to see Dickie. He found my vein immediately and emptied the needle into my arm. I felt a warm sensation down my back, tingles rushed up my arms, my eyes grew heavy, and I was in a dream, only still awake. It was the strongest sensual feeling I had ever known, complete pleasure all over my body. No other drug or combination of drugs had ever put me there. I floated back to the apartment, and suddenly the feeling turned to nausea. I ran to the bathroom in the dark, felt my way to the toilet, and wretched uncontrollably, from deep inside, holding on tight to the cold porcelain. I must have thrown up for twenty minutes straight, but afterward that dreamy feeling came back, and I fell in love. I would be addicted within a month.

That first time I did only a very small amount. MJ said it was three cents' worth from what was called "a paper," ten dollars' worth of heroin. I realized after I became more familiar with the lingo that it was even less than that, what's called "a wet cotton," meaning what was left over on the cotton used in the spoon when you fill the needle. I know now that MJ was giving me as little as possible, and I'm grateful because if she had actually given me three cents' worth, I probably would have OD'd and died right then and there. But it was enough to give me a taste that led to an appetite that led to a killer habit.

I began doing heroin every day, soon several times a day. Jo started to catch on because I was going down to Dickie's all the time, and now I was the one hanging out in the bathroom for what seemed like hours.

My only problem was I couldn't do it to myself. I could never find a vein, and my veins were shallow, not easy to penetrate. I had no idea that sharing needles was a bad idea, a good way to transfer diseases. I just needed help shooting dope, so I took it from whoever was willing.

Every day for a couple of weeks it was a chore to find somebody to shoot me up. One time, MJ's boyfriend had a needle that was used and had a burr on it. He used a match to burn it, make it hot, and scrape it clean. I have a sulfur scar on my arm to this day from the shot he gave me with that needle, missing my vein and giving me a nasty wound, but I didn't care as long as he finally managed to get it right. I was getting high at least once a day, sometimes as often as four times. MJ was still trying to discourage me and would say no when I asked her to get us more, so I started going to dope houses on my own. I knew where she went and the junkies there had seen me with her, so they knew I was cool. Many of them were Mexicans, getting uncut heroin directly from across the border, so it was really potent. I started sleeping at different trap houses, too high to bother going home to MJ's apartment. I was perfectly happy to crash in one of the barely lit abandoned apartments or houses strewn with stained mattresses here and there, roaches racing across the dirty floor, a cloud of cigarette and marijuana smoke barely masking the smell of the junkies who crashed there, oblivious to the unrelenting Arizona heat. With senses dulled from dope, none of that mattered.

One day MJ came over to the place where I was crashing, woke me up, and asked me if I had been getting high over the last three weeks, since she first helped me. When I told her yes, she was livid.

"You've got a habit now," she said, and I could see the guilt on her face.

"No," I said, "of course I don't."

"Have you been doing it every day?"

"Yeah, three or four times a day, actually," I'm sure I smirked. I was so convinced that I knew what I was doing.

"You have a habit, just like I said you would." MJ was more sad than angry now. "If you try to go a day without it now, you will get really sick."

"No way!" I laughed. I really did not believe her.

The next day, I wanted to get high and was so impatient that I decided I would try to shoot up myself. I kept poking away at my arm but could not find a vein. Instead, the needle was filling with blood. I could see the little clots inside it. I got so frustrated I chucked the needle, throwing it into a potted plant in the house. I bought another small bag and got somebody else to shoot me up. But it wasn't enough. The next morning I woke up to a new feeling. I was sick. I had never felt this bad before and could not understand what was happening to me. In my world, you caught a cold or maybe had a stomachache. That was getting sick. This was something completely different. It seemed like my entire body was fighting against me. I had pain everywhere. I was shaking from the chills and sweating at the same time. I was throwing up while fighting off diarrhea. I was paralyzed and jumpy all at once. It was the first time I was dope sick, and it was pure misery. I had no money to buy another bag because I hadn't been to the Western Union that day to get Grandma's money. I remembered the needle I had tossed in the plant. I took it back and dumped the contents into a spoon, mushing up the dried blood clots to try to turn them back into liquid, adding drops of water, assuming there had to be some amount of dope still lingering in those clots. In the middle of all this, MJ walked in.

"What the fuck are you doing? Look at those clots, you don't want to shoot that!"

"I don't feel good. I'm really sick, and I just need to do this."

She tried to argue, but I found a vein and there was just enough dope left to make me feel better. Then MJ and I went to get my money and buy a bag. That was the day I realized I was a junkie and most of my friends were junkies, too. I don't remember being upset, just acknowledging the obvious. Now I had an expensive habit because my tolerance had risen and I needed more dope each time. The money my father and Grandma were wiring me wasn't even close to what I needed to feed this beast, so I had to find a way to make more. My new friend, Louise, whom we called "Sleazy Louizy," had the answer.

Louise was so glamorous to me. She came to MJ's to cop and get high after work, so I partied with her, and we became fast friends. She was from a wealthy family that lived in a mansion in the foothills of Tucson. Both her parents were psychiatrists, and Louise was the black sheep, something we had in common. Alcoholism and drugs took her life far too soon, but when I knew her, I wanted to be her. She drove a Triumph TR3 convertible sports car, with a stick shift, she wore the hippest clothes, and she was a prostitute. When I drove around in that car with her, I was in heaven. It didn't hurt that I was high and Louise was an addict who always had enough money to get whatever she needed, and then some. She said she could get me a job where she worked, a funky "massage parlor" called the Rendezvous way out in the desert outside Tucson in Pima County. It was well known and had plenty of customers, so the madam, BeBe, always needed new girls, especially young ones like me. The Rendezvous was owned by a short, stocky cocaine dealer. When Louise told me what the job was and how much money she made in one night, I was in.

It took at least an hour for Louise to drive us out there. We flew across the wide-open highway, curving through the painted desert hills, the hot wind in our faces. We pulled up to the only building we had seen for miles and miles. A flashing red neon light spelled out "The Rendezvous," pulsing like a perverted welcoming beacon. Clusters of tumbleweed drifted by on the road leading up to the house, just like an old cowboy movie. Posted at the front door was a guy I will never forget, Doberman Dave, a real biker in full menacing gear, black leather from head to toe, chains hanging from his belt, tattoos that signaled his membership in a gang. He earned his nickname from the dogs he bred. Although he scared me a little, he was so handsome underneath all that biker regalia, I was intrigued before we even walked in. Once we got past Doberman Dave, we walked into the house, and I got a glimpse of the front room. It was like a movie set, decorated like an iconic early whorehouse. Everything was red. Gaudy, red velvet couches lined the walls, the curtains were red paisley, even the lampshades were red. Women sat around the room in floor-length sheer negligees with nothing under them, or short tight lingerie. It was a scene that totally captured my heroin-tinged imagination and I wanted to be a part of it. I never hesitated.

Once we got inside, Louise introduced me to BeBe, who ran the place and kept the women in line. She was the classic aging prostitute who still had some of her charms, even though it was clear she was fading around the edges. I was seventeen, so to me she looked pretty old, but I couldn't guess her age—she could have been forty or even fifty. I thought she was the picture of elegance, with long, shiny black hair, porcelain skin, her sheer, lacy negligee brushing the floor when she walked, decorated with an abundance of flashy jewelry. She took me into the kitchen for a job interview that started with a cup of coffee made from General Foods' instant International Coffees, the Café Vienna flavor, which came in a little red can, something I had never seen before. This was so exotic to me. My grandma made espresso, that was it. BeBe had me with the coffee. She asked me how old I was, and I started to tell her the truth when Louise, who was nineteen, cut me off and said I was eighteen.

After a few more questions, BeBe looked me up and down, taking in my young, innocent look, and said, "Boy, she would make a lot of money!"

I was naive and dazzled by the atmosphere. In the front room I saw two women sitting on the couch and whispered to Louise, "Are they really hookers?"

BeBe heard me and called to them, "Darla, Sugar, come here and meet Angalia. I want you to take her in back, give her a tour of the rooms, and show her the ropes. And help her pick a name."

I was confused by the name part, so Sugar told me that all the girls had fake names, "You should choose one you like," she said, "It can be anything you want."

I decided to call myself Jacqueline, after Jackie O, because she was so elegant and mysterious and now I was, too.

So I got my job training. They took me in the back and showed me hard tables that had mats on them. It looked almost clinical, not at all what I thought rooms in a brothel would look like. If you didn't know better, you might believe that the Rendezvous actually was a massage parlor. That would be legal, but it didn't seem to matter, because it was outside the city of Tucson. The cops from the city had no jurisdiction, and the Pima County sheriffs didn't do anything to stop business because they got in-kind favors to keep them happy. We accommodated all the sheriffs, just like in the movie *Best Little Whorehouse in Texas*. That first night, I learned about all this and how to do the job, including what to charge, and what to offer and not to offer. The menu included a hand job for twenty bucks, forty for a blow job, sixty for what we called a "straight fuck," no touching, and a hundred for a "half and half," a blow job and a straight fuck combo. In a 60-40 split between the women and the house, we got 60 percent.

I was completely taken with all of it: the women, the men, the sexy atmosphere, and especially what I considered easy money. Because I was the youngest girl there and all the men wanted to try me, I found myself making more than $500 a day. Darla, Sugar, and Louise taught me how to do everything to keep the men from ripping me off and to keep my mind busy while I was working. "Think about how you're going to spend the money," they would tell me. So I thought about what color I was going to paint my nails and how much dope I was going to buy. I never had any trouble keeping the men under control; in fact, I was the meanest girl in the house. While most of the women had repeat customers who asked for them specifically, I never did because I was as cold as ice. I timed each trick and after four minutes, I told him to come now or pull out. I was never with a trick for more than five minutes, and if the guy didn't come, I didn't care. I had his money. I would let a man forgo using a condom only if he paid me more. If he touched my breast, I would holler, "Do NOT fuckin' touch me there." If he tried to kiss me, I would holler no. I stuck to the rules about no "romance," as the men called it. "If you want romance, go buy a fuckin' novel," I would say. They all called me the hooker from hell, but I still had plenty of business because there were always new men coming around who had no idea what they were in for; they just saw a young girl that they wanted to try. And of course, I was always high, above it all inside my perennial heroin bubble.

My time at the Rendezvous was job training I would fall back on often over the next few decades. I don't remember feeling bad or unhappy about any of it, just amazed at the money we made, the drugs we did, and the cool people we met. My fascination with different people and how they lived seemed to have no boundaries. I had to *live* it—I didn't want to just read about a lifestyle, I wanted to *be* the lifestyle, and I always went in deep. But I knew if or when I got bored or felt bad, I could just leave.

While in Tucson, I only strayed once from the protective haven of the Rendezvous. I had left work early one morning after an unusually bad night; I hadn't made any money. So I decided to try a little free-lancing. I went to a bar in a nice hotel downtown and ordered a drink. I might have been eighteen by then, but I had no trouble getting served. I sat there for a few minutes, nursing my drink. I was wearing a long black sleeveless dress with a glittery star on the front and my platform shoes. A man sitting nearby slid a matchbook down the bar to me. I looked at him, and he gestured with his head for me to look inside the matchbook. I flipped it open and found a tightly folded hundred-dollar bill and his room number written on the inside cover of the matchbook. *Oh, so this is how it works*, I thought. I closed the matchbook, tucked it inside my bra, and finished my drink. He nodded toward me again, and I followed him to the elevator and up to his room. Soon, we were in bed, completely naked, and he was getting his money's worth. Next thing I knew, his wife came walking in the door, laden with shopping bags. She started screaming, "What the fuck is going on here?" I slipped my panties on, threw on my dress, grabbed my bra and shoes, made sure I had the hundred dollars, and walked out into the hallway. I kept walking as the screaming faded in the background. I bought a bag, got high, and went back to work at the Rendezvous that night.

Even though the Rendezvous had the protection of the sheriff's department, we were raided by the Arizona state police occasionally, and I got arrested for prostitution a few times. The first time was traumatic, but I learned how to navigate the system. That night things were hopping as they usually were, especially on a Saturday. A group of new guys came in, and as most did, paid their cover charge to Doberman Dave and then walked into the front room where we were all on display like meat in a deli case, lounging on the couches, draped in sheer fabric and languishing in a dope-induced haze that made everything all right.

One of these new guys looked around and chose me. We took one of the few empty rooms in the back and once we were alone I asked, as I often did, if he was a cop. He said no. I would learn later that he was a veteran undercover agent, and I really had no chance up against him. As slick as I thought I was, I fell right into his trap. I was naive enough to think that it was illegal for a cop to show me his dick or to have sex with me. But when he asked me what I charged and I told him, he went to reach for his wallet and pulled out a pair of handcuffs to arrest me.

I screamed, "You showed me your dick. This is entrapment!"

He laughed and said, "Honey, for future reference, we're consenting adults here. Showing you my private parts when you ask is not against the law, unless you're a minor, then we could shut the place down." Thankfully, I was eighteen by then.

This kind of a bust happened about once every three or four months, probably as a result of people in the nearest town, like the suspicious wives of our customers, complaining that something had to be done. But the place was never shut down, and it was a minor harassment for Mike, the owner. The cops grabbed my purse, a designer bag that I really loved and had actually paid for at Marshall Field's on State Street in Chicago with my Options Exchange money.

In my purse they found the gun my boyfriend at the time had given me, a .32 Beretta, loaded and with one in the chamber. I was fascinated with guns, even though I didn't want to shoot anyone or any animals or birds or even threaten violence of any sort. I just loved guns. The law in Arizona at the time made it legal to carry a firearm if you were eighteen, but it had to be out in the open, like in the Wild West. (You couldn't buy a gun until you were twenty-one.) I was charged with carrying a concealed weapon and unauthorized use of a weapon because it was loaded and there was a bullet in the chamber. I was pretty scared because I didn't know what was happening or how to get out of it. I knew I couldn't call my father for this one. He had the cops in his pocket back home, but this was my first arrest out of state. I was taken to the Tucson police station and thrown in a cell. I was there for a few hours when a cop came in and said my bond was here. Mike, the owner of the Rendezvous, had a standing arrangement with the police. He paid the full bond of $1,000, and I was out. They gave me back all my belongings, but not the gun. I asked where it was, and they said I could not have it back. Mike hired me a lawyer, and I pleaded no contest and just had to pay a minor fine, but I really wanted that gun.

"Your Honor," I said when I finally had my day in court, "that gun was a gift from my boyfriend, legally purchased. I want it back."

He ruled in my favor since by this point I was nineteen, and gave me the paperwork to get the gun back. The cops knew that I was affiliated with a biker gang and made me carry the gun out in pieces, with the bullets in one baggie, the clip in another, and the gun in full display as I walked out. When I got back to my car, I put it back together, but from that day on I left it in full view on the car seat.

I made enough money working at the Rendezvous to cover my living expenses and my habit, which was getting more and more expensive. Most of the women there were junkies, but Mike did not like it, even though he was a cocaine addict. Sometimes we took so long shooting up in the bathroom that the men waiting would leave. Most of the time we didn't care. We already had his money, and we had to get high, but Mike would get really angry because the men wouldn't come back. To keep it on the down-low and to keep Mike happy, every day we'd choose someone to go on a dope run for all of us. As soon as we made some money, one of us would say, "Hey, who's gonna go? I'll cover for you. Hurry, because I feel like shit." We would take orders like we were going to the Jack in the Box for lunch.

One day when it was my turn, I borrowed a car and went to a dope house. I was already sick when I got there, so I decided to shoot up right there. After the dealer handed me all the bags for my order, I asked him if he had a needle. I knew nothing about catching diseases from used needles, and neither did anyone else back then. He handed me a shoebox full of used needles, some still with blood in them. I shuffled through and found one that looked sharp, and he gave me the common spoon with the cotton and residue still in it. I shot up, got fucked up, and went back to work with the orders for the other girls.

This was my new life. I had gone from hippie wannabe, to beach bum, to downtown babe in a Porsche, to a hooker with a very serious heroin habit. I spent my days getting high with other junkies, working at the Rendezvous, partying at Choo Choo's with my girlfriends, and hanging with the bikers who couldn't get enough of us. Choo Choo's was like the Whiskey a Go Go of Tucson. All the famous rock bands played there; it was the cool place to be. I was such a junkie I even OD'd during that first month.

I was hanging out at Choo Choo's with a musician named Tony. I thought he was cool because he dressed and wore his hair like David Bowie and did a lot of heroin. I went back to his hotel room and asked him to shoot it for me. He had brown-colored heroin, what they used to call "Mexican Mud," the darker, the more potent. I was a little worried at how much he was cooking for me.

"Tony, it looks like a lot," I said.

"Nah, don't worry, you'll be fine." He was already high, and I trusted him.

"OK, but push it in slow."

He got the dope halfway into my vein when I told him I was getting faint, but he pushed the rest in deep anyway. I could feel the rush of warmth throughout my entire body, but I couldn't react and I knew I was going under. I passed out immediately and my new junkie friend Tony left me there to die. He must have called an ambulance before he split, though, because I woke up in the hospital a day and a half later. I went through the same naloxone treatment that MJ had, but my overdose was worse than hers. There was a breathing tube down my throat and a tube in my arm, and I felt so miserable I couldn't believe I was still alive. After another day or so, I was released without any repercussions of any sort—no cops showed up, no rehab programs were offered, no methadone was suggested, nothing. It was like a routine emergency room visit, as if I'd broken a bone. I went back to MJ's apartment where nobody had noticed that I was gone. They had no idea I had been in the hospital and almost died. I went right back to shooting dope, but MJ told me to stay away from guys like Tony. I didn't listen.

I started hanging out with another bad boy, who introduced me to a classier junkie style. He was so attractive to me, and had so much charisma. He reminded me of James Dean. He had more money than he knew what to do with. His wealthy parents had died in a car accident and had left him everything. He shot most of it into his arm. He continued to live in his parents' house, a stately mansion in the wealthiest part of Tucson, and he turned it into the scene of a nonstop party, even when he wasn't home. The bands from Choo Choo's went there after their gigs, and it was like living in the lyrics of a Rolling Stones' song. A big glass bowl on the coffee table was filled with powdered cocaine, and there were beautiful Waterford crystal plates and silver spoons on hand for people to do as much as they wanted, like sampling fancy hors d'oeuvres.

My first time there, he brought me into the opulent master suite and tugged on my hand to guide me into the bathroom. He had a real silver spoon that curved at the end and clipped onto the marble sink, and instead of the usual plastic setup, he had glass syringes—glass works! I was in awe and in love. He cooked some heroin and then said, "We're gonna do a speedball." I had never shot the combination of heroin and coke that everyone seemed to love at the time. It was deadly; the heroin brings you down while the coke pulls you up. "Are you sure I'll be OK?" I worried. "Of course," he said, and I believed him. He put the coke from the curved silver spoon into the needle with the heroin and shot me up. Suddenly there was a whooshing sound in my ears that was so loud I felt as if I were on a runway, standing in front of a jet engine. I was panting hard, barely able to hold any air in my lungs. He picked me up in his arms and carried me to the big bed. I could feel the blood rushing through my veins, and colors were flashing in my head like the pulse of a strobe light. I was terrified. I was on the verge of losing consciousness, but I did not OD. This went on for about five minutes, and then the heroin kicked in, and I was really high. We had sex all night, and not only was I fine, I thought the whole scene was pretty cool. I had to get some glass needles for myself, a curved silver spoon like his, and a classy velvet bag to keep them in.

I got high constantly, but about a month after I shot up with that dirty, used needle, against MJ's advice, I started to feel really fatigued all the time, no matter what drugs I was doing or how much sleep I got. I started to notice that my skin had a strange, pale color to it and I started having pains in my side. I didn't think much of it, figuring these were normal side effects of shooting heroin on a daily basis.

Around this time, Mike, the owner of the Rendezvous, invited Louise and me on a drug run with him and his girlfriend, who also worked at the house when they needed extra money. They had a couple of kids together. He regularly drove from Tucson to San Diego to buy large quantities of coke. He picked us up in his bright canary-yellow Camaro and off we went. We stayed in a fancy hotel suite, did lots of drugs, had sex with Mike, sometimes all at once, and partied nonstop. We went to meet his connection, a guy with a yacht, but I was getting so sick I stayed off the boat. When we got back from the pickup, Mike made a huge bull's-eye out of coke on the glass table in our suite, and even though I snorted a lot of powder, I was just getting more tired. I went into the bedroom by myself, and that's when everyone knew something was really wrong because I was usually a die-hard party animal, the last to stop. They took me outside to get some air, and when I stood next to Mike's yellow car, we realized that my skin was the same color.

"Oh my God, look at you, you match my fuckin' car! You have hepatitis!" Mike said.

I didn't know what that was, but he was right. I had contracted hepatitis B from the dirty needle I used at the drug house that day a month ago. "As soon as we get back to Tucson, you have to go right to the hospital."

"Am I going to die?" I was scared now. My eyes and skin were completely yellow. My tongue was white.

For the next two days I did as much heroin as I could but never felt much better. The other drug addicts around me, my twisted mentors, agreed that I had hepatitis and since there was no cure, it would run its course. They told me to drink a lot of orange juice, which I did, but I was getting worse. My stools were completely white, and I was so weak I could barely walk. We got back to Tucson, and I went to the University of Arizona Medical Center emergency room. The staff were mean to me; I didn't have insurance, and they were not paying attention despite my loud, obnoxious hissy fits and threats in the waiting room.

I had no choice. I had to call my father. I told him everything, except that I was shooting heroin. I said it was hepatitis A because someone told me that's the strain you get from drinking bad water, and he knew I had been in Mexico, so I figured he'd buy it. He was so worried. He told me to get on a plane and come right home. He picked me up at the airport, and we rushed to the hospital in a nearby suburb, where they admitted me immediately. My father and grandmother were so upset. "Oh my God, what does she have, Petey?" Grandma kept asking as she made the sign of the cross over and over again. None of this stopped me from trying to lie to them.

I was alone in my hospital room when the doctor came in and confirmed that I had hepatitis B. My liver had completely shut down, and was so far gone, he said, that the level of the bilirubin, something your liver is supposed to excrete every day, was off the charts. I asked the doctor to tell my father it was hepatitis A and naturally he said no. He told me he knew I was addicted to heroin, my blood was full of it, and they would give me some pills to withdraw and stay clean. He relayed all this to my father, who knew I was getting high, but never dreamed I would shoot a needle full of heroin into my arm, let alone do it long enough to get addicted. My father came into the hospital room and I tried to work my perverse magic on him.

"Daddy, they said I have hepatitis but it's probably the kind you get from drinking water. You know I made a lot of trips to Mexico, and—"

"You little motherfucker!" he screamed at me. "I know what the fuck you got. You got hepatitis from sticking motherfuckin' needles in your fuckin' arms! If I ever catch you with a motherfuckin' needle, I'm gonna break your arms and both your motherfuckin' legs!"

My father had never talked to me or threatened me like that. I was his little girl. I started to cry. "I don't know what happened, Daddy," I sobbed. And he just stood there, unable, I'm sure, to even figure out what to do next. He had been a functional coke addict for years and probably never thought of himself as an addict, even though he did it every day; we both knew that. But heroin was serious shit in his mind, and I could see how worried he was beneath his anger.

I stayed in the hospital for a full month. As I weathered the excruciating monitored withdrawal process, the doctors and nurses tried to get me to eat liver, but I threw a tantrum and called Grandma. I told her no way I would eat that; I would leave the hospital if they tried to force me. She promised to bring me lasagna. I started getting better, the yellow jaundice went away, I gained weight, and I was getting restless, a good sign. The doctor told me I had received treatment just in time and I was lucky he was able to minimize the permanent damage to my liver. He said if I had gone much longer, I would have died. But there was good news. If I didn't drink alcohol or do any drugs for a year, my liver would regenerate itself. It takes a year, but if I followed his orders, it would work. So I did, almost. I moved back home with Grandma and my father. I didn't want to die. I still went out at night, to clubs and rock concerts, but only smoked a little weed and religiously took all the vitamins the doctor prescribed.

I healed. After about six months, my liver tested healthy, just as the doctor predicted. I was bored and had no heroin friends at home, so I decided it was time to go back to Tucson. I picked up right where I had left off and soon I was strung out on heroin all over again. I moved back in with MJ and went back to work at the Rendezvous, hung out with all my addict and prostitute friends, and slipped right back into the life that had almost killed me. Another second chance was thrown to the wind, like the ashes of a dead dream.

We started going to biker parties and hanging out with the rough outlaws who threw them. Another girl from work took me to a big party on a biker commune. It was one of the coolest places I had ever been, way out in the desert, two hours north of Tucson, even farther out than the Rendezvous. There were tents and a big fire pit with a pig roasting over it, and more Harleys than I'd ever seen parked in one place. I loved hanging with the bikers and their old ladies, tripping and getting high all day, and counting the millions of stars in the desert sky. I had found my new tribe and once again jumped in with both feet, ready to learn how to live in the unforgiving desert heat of the days and the crisp, cold of the Arizona nights.

That night, I saw a guy who I thought was so fine I could not keep my eyes off him. He had long, wavy blond hair all the way down his back, a killer tan, tattooed body, and the bluest eyes, just like the clear desert sky. I was smitten.

I asked my friend Dee Dee, "Oh my God, who *is* that?"

"Oh, he's one of the brothers," she said, "a patch holder." That meant he was a full-fledged member of the biker gang.

"Can you introduce me to him? That's who I'm going to marry and whose baby I'm gonna have." Dee Dee laughed. I hadn't even talked to him yet.

His name was Scott, but everyone called him Scotch because he drank a lot of it. Bikers were big drinkers and coke addicts, but they did not like shooting heroin and hated junkies. Dee Dee introduced us and we hung out at the pig roast, but that was it for a while.

Then one day at work, Dee Dee said, "Scotch wants you to come back out to the bikers' place. He really likes you."

I started going out to the commune every day, and soon I was staying four or five days at a time. I'd ride into work with the other biker old ladies. Bikers were OK with their women working as hookers, seeing us as assets for earning fast money. We would work at the Rendezvous all day, then go back out to the commune, known to the bikers as West Hell, Arizona. The brothers in the gang went in on forty acres of land, bought it from a rancher, and made it their compound, far enough into the desert that they could do anything they wanted, including growing acres of sinsemilla pot. They were expert farmers and botanists, and made sure the pot was seedless for ultimate profit. We all worked on harvesting, pulling buds, and packaging them into pounds for sale. My assignment, after working all night at the Rendezvous, was to spend the days rolling joints by the hundreds to keep the brothers stocked for their parties. Our well-honed operation came to an abrupt halt when the DEA raided us. Many were hauled into jail, but the bikers beat the charges because the DEA moved too quickly, before we harvested the crop. So instead of being charged with possession and delivery of a controlled substance, they were only charged with cultivation. Probation was the worst sentence anybody got.

The bikers were dangerous, armed, and crazy, completely off the grid, a subculture of hardened outlaws who only trusted another brother. They had few rules, but heroin was completely off-limits. So while I was on their land, I couldn't do it. I started sneaking around, copping from the other hookers at work and doing it on the property in secret. If I were caught, it would be close to a death sentence. I knew I was playing with fire, and my sneaking around was only going to end badly, plus I was falling in love. So I got some morphine pills from MJ and because I was around people who were not doing it, I managed to wean myself off heroin.

Not long after we first got together, I moved in with Scott. There was no running water and most of us lived in tents. While I had spent some time living in a tent and playing hippie on Stock Island, this was a real community. As a city girl I was fascinated by what I saw as an earthy lifestyle, and I loved it at first. I'd walk through the desert to get fresh water from the well, adjusting to the hundred-degree heat during the day and taking showers under a special rig, buck naked out in the open. Like a little farm girl, I learned how to milk the cows and drank the milk fresh. I shot rattlesnakes with Scott's rifle. All the bikers had big dogs, Rottweilers and Dobermans, to guard the land, and I felt safe. Once a week, we drove the hour trip into town on Scott's Harley to pick up mail at the local post office and get dry goods at the store. I loved riding into the wind, hugging Scott from behind as we raced across the highway on his bike. It was like I had landed in the movie *Easy Rider*, and I was the star. I was a member of the gang now and even had a patch on my leather vest that said PROPERTY OF SCOTCH. I could barely remember my spoiled family life in Chicago. I did occasionally sneak back to MJ's to do a shot of heroin with her, but I knew that if I wanted to stay with Scott, I had to be happy with pills.

I discovered I was pregnant soon after I started living with Scott. We decided we weren't ready to have a kid, so I had an abortion. I was nineteen, and it would be my fourth abortion. My first pregnancy was when I was fourteen, in the days before *Roe v. Wade*. When I told my father, he had a fit, but no daughter of his was going to have a baby at that age. He knew a doctor who lied and said there was something wrong with the baby, so he could perform a safe abortion.

Now, even with the passing of a federal law, it was still hard to get a legal abortion in Arizona because public aid did not pay for it, so Scott had to take me to California, where it did. We went to Pine Valley, up in the mountains outside San Diego, with a bunch of other bikers and met up with another gang from that area. One of the women in that gang was on California public aid, so she gave me her medical card and I had to assume her identity. The bikers took me to the clinic, and I had the abortion. I was surprised at how depressed I was afterward, more than the other times. I realized I wanted that baby, not another abortion, and I decided I just had to get pregnant again to make it right.

Scott married me in the Tucson courthouse when I was seven months pregnant, and I was so happy. I was married with a baby on the way and so in love. I stopped doing drugs throughout the pregnancy (except maybe smoking a little weed) so my baby would be healthy. Scott even made me give up cigarettes! I was really looking forward to being a mom, but these maternal instincts made me yearn for Grandma and my father and Crickie. The night after we were married, I flew to Chicago. I was happy, and I wanted to be with my family, so I stayed for a few weeks before I went back to my husband.

My baby was late, and I was so ready. One hot afternoon on the way back from the well, a trio of big, vicious dogs from a neighboring biker camp surrounded me. Petrified, I thought they were going to attack. They started to show their teeth and growl, and not knowing what else to do, I screamed at them as loud as I could. They took off, but I screamed so loud and so hard my water broke, sending me into labor. I made it to the hospital, but I needed an emergency C-section. Before I went into surgery, I begged the doctor to do a bikini cut. I pleaded with him, saying I would never be the same if I had a scar on my beautiful stomach. It was not a common procedure back then. When I woke up I asked the nurse only two important questions: "Did I have a boy, and did I get a bikini cut?" The nurse said yes to both, and it was one of the happiest days of my life. Two years after I'd first laid eyes on Scott, I gave birth to his son. We named him Sean. He was a beautiful baby. I was given Sodium Pentothal, Demerol, and a morphine drip. I was in the hospital for two weeks of pure bliss. I kept crying about how much pain I was in and getting more drugs. I would turn over and eagerly bare my cheek for whatever they gave me, and before long I was doing dope again.

Right after Sean was born, Scott and I moved in with his parents. I did not want to go back to the commune because I was afraid that if anything happened with Sean we'd be too far away to get help. His mother was not fond of me. After about three weeks, I wanted my grandma. As soon as the doctor said the baby and I could fly, I went back to Chicago. We stayed in Oak Park with my family for about a month. Everybody loved Sean, bringing cards stuffed with cash, and I was more pampered than ever. Grandma was so happy, and my father was so proud. They bought lots of new baby clothes. The Pampers piled high. I began to realize how much I had been roughing it with Scott, and I wasn't sure why anymore.

I was finished with being a biker's old lady. In fact, the more I thought about what went on at the commune, the more I started to hate the whole idea. I thought about how the guys would go hunting and bring the deer back on the hoods of their trucks and string up the carcasses. The big, stern biker women would come out with their knives and go to work on the deer, slitting their necks, skinning them, and chopping away at the meat like it was nothing. "Here, grab a knife," they'd say, to which I'd reply, "That's OK. Um, I'm going back inside to take care of the kids, I'm good." There was no way I could ever skin an animal. I don't even like to eat meat. Just seeing that was horrific to me. I was OK gathering eggs from the chickens, but I could never kill one. On Thanksgiving, they chopped the heads off turkeys. One time a brother handed me a decapitated turkey to pluck. It was heavy and bleeding. I could not get the feathers off. The horrible scent made me want to throw up. At first, the commune was different from anything I had ever known, so it was interesting to me. I felt like I was living in *Little House on the Prairie*. But when the romance of the lifestyle faded, I was done.

That first time home with Sean as a baby, it was hard to leave Oak Park for Arizona again, but I had to get back to my husband. While I was gone, Scott decided to rent a trailer in South Tucson, a bad area, because he knew I was reluctant to go back to the commune with the baby or back to his parents' house. He even got a construction job. Since we weren't living on biker land anymore, I started doing heroin every day again.

I knew pretty early on that this little family scene was not going to work for me. The time I had spent back in Chicago when I was pregnant and then again right after Sean was born was like waking up from a weird dream. I was reminded of how much I loved the city, the excitement of partying in a big town, going to nightclubs, and the attention and pampering of my grandma and my father. I missed being spoiled. I got my hair and nails done, Grandma was waiting on us, and I was happy. I remembered how much I loved all kinds of music, not just the heavy metal that the bikers were into. I went out and danced to Michael Jackson and David Bowie. I rediscovered a part of me that I had left behind.

After two years of living out in the desert, then trying to be a mom and a wife in the trailer with Scott, I had had enough. I wanted to go home for good. I wanted running water and nice-smelling shampoo and Grandma there to take care of me and Sean. I knew Scott loved Sean and me, but he drank a lot and was still trying to keep up the biker lifestyle, going on runs with the gang for days at a time and partying with lots of drugs and women. I saw my chance when I caught Scott cheating on me. I was back in Oak Park before he could even think about stopping me.

After a few weeks, Scott tried to talk me into coming back to him, but my mind was made up. I started seeing my old high school boyfriend, David, and going out to nightclubs and concerts every night. My father rented a nice two-bedroom apartment in Oak Park for us. Grandma took care of Sean every day and most nights while I sold drugs or went out. I did not miss the commune, the bikers, or any part of that life. Scott tried to make amends. He turned in his biker patch and even sold his Harley to buy a plane ticket to Chicago, desperate to fix our relationship. During his visit, I left Sean with him and went out with my boyfriend. Later I went out to Tucson alone, trying one last time to make it work, and stayed with Scott for a week, but we hardly slept together. I knew then that we were done. I kept saying I was going to file for divorce but never got around to it. One day, I got a long-distance call from Tucson that changed everything.

It was June 6, 1981. I picked up the phone and one of the bikers was on the other line. I could not believe what he was saying to me. Scott was dead. I stood there in shock with the phone in my hand and started to cry. He was a healthy twenty-seven-year-old man. They had found his badly decomposed body inside the locked trailer he had bought for our little family. Our dog, Rommel, a gentle Doberman that we both loved, was in the trailer with him. It was impossible to say how long Scott had been there, and the cause of his death was not clear.

I was devastated. I took Sean to Grandma's and left him there for the night, then went to the liquor store and bought a bottle of Jack Daniel's. I went back to my dark apartment, washed down a handful of pills with the Jack, and sank to the floor. I remembered Scott's rugged face and his beautiful blue eyes, and I was mad at God for cutting his life short and robbing my son of his father. I felt a kind of despair I had never known, a deep anger and frustration because I knew there was nothing I could do. Scott was gone. Suddenly, I felt the full weight of being Sean's only parent. I felt completely alone.

The next day I packed up Sean, and we took the first plane to Tucson to claim the body. I stayed with Darla, my friend from the Rendezvous, and left Sean with her while I went to the morgue with a few of the bikers to identify Scott's body. Before we walked in, I reached into my purse for a handful of Valium and swallowed all of them to help me get a grip. I waited a few minutes for them to kick in. Since I had taken so many, I was soon high enough to get through this gruesome moment. It was a sight I will never forget. Scott's bloated, unrecognizable body lay on a slab placed on the floor in a clear plastic body bag. Sobbing, I fell down beside him and put my hand on his arm. The feeling of his cold and lifeless body is forever seared into my memory. There was little left of the man I had loved, married, and created a beautiful son with. When I left Scott, I always figured Scott would be there if Sean needed him, but no. Sean would grow up without his father.

After the morgue, we went to the funeral home to make arrangements, and I signed the papers with Scott's biker brothers at my side. They paid for his funeral and talked me into cremating his body. After the services, we strapped the leather bag full of his ashes to the back bar of the Harley Davidson that led a long procession of bikes, their loud motors cutting through the hot Tucson afternoon. I got on back with one of the other bikers, and we rode out of town to bury the ashes on the desert property where Scott and I had once lived together. My two-year-old son rode in a car with friends. I know in my heart that Scott died loving me and Sean more than I ever could have appreciated back then.

Scott's autopsy officially said his death was from "uncertain causes." He liked to get high on pills, he drank all the time, and he started getting high from "huffing," sniffing glue. When I went out to see him the last time, I found out that he had met a girl who worked at a pharmacy and was getting highly potent prescription opiates, like Dilaudid and Demerol—ironically, the very things he was against when we were together. Any of these things, alone or in combination, could have been enough to kill him if he OD'd. The autopsy was sketchy, but showed that his lungs were congested. I even told the doctor that he sniffed airplane glue, but back then little was known about its effects. I learned many years later that when a person is high on glue, the brain shuts down the trigger to take a breath and many glue sniffers literally suffocate. Another theory that played around in my head was that one of the other bikers, with the gang's approval, might have killed him. Scott still owned five acres of their land, even though he had quit the gang. The land should have been left to Sean. They had enough motivation to take him out.

One more theory surfaced about three years later. I was in Cook County Court in Chicago facing a forgery charge for writing bad checks. The lawyer my father hired called me aside in the middle of the proceedings after a little conference with the state's attorney.

"Come here," she hissed in an angry whisper and led me to the back of the courtroom. "You're lying to me! I need the whole truth right now."

I was baffled. "What are you talking about?"

"How did your husband die?"

I thought that was so odd. There was no connection between this charge and Scott. "I don't really know," I answered her honestly.

"Stop lying!"

"I don't know exactly how he died," I insisted. "Nobody does."

Then she dropped a bombshell. "The court is willing to let you walk. They are saying they want to show sympathy for you because they know your husband turned state's witness against gang activity in Arizona and was in the witness protection program before he died."

I was stunned, even more so when they let me go. On a plea, the court was offering me a sentence of six years, but instead let me walk out the door, no charges. I told my lawyer I didn't know anything about this, but she advised me to go with it. "We'll talk about this later," she said, "but for now, just play along. They're letting you walk based on some research they've done and as an act of mercy to you. They're saying you lost your husband because he was a witness for the state."

I went along and got out of what would have been my first trip to the penitentiary, doing my first real time. My lawyer could not get any more answers without digging, so she didn't pursue it. She told me we should leave it alone in case it was discovered that they had the wrong guy, that it wasn't Scott after all, in which case the charges would be reinstated. Even though I was baffled, I gladly took her advice. She also told me to stop doing what I was doing or I would end up in Dwight Correctional Center, but I went about my crazy life unfazed and more convinced than ever that I was invincible. I thought she was delusional to think that I would ever go to jail. I even drove out to Dwight in the middle of my case with one of my friends and had him take a picture of me in front of the entrance. I jumped out of his car and struck a pose in the headlights, using the photo to taunt the lawyer. "This is the only way I'm going to Dwight," I laughed when I showed it to her. That's how sure I was that with my family's influence, my father's money, and my special kind of luck, I would never, ever go to jail.

Every theory about Scott's death proved to be inconclusive. When I think back on that day in the morgue, looking at his body on a cold, gray slab in my Valium-induced fog, I don't even know for sure if that was Scott inside the body bag. The bikers were against me going to the morgue, but they said it was because they did not want me to see him. He had been locked in that aluminum trailer, in hundred-degree heat, for days. But I needed closure because we were having him cremated. I saw his blond hair but never really saw his face, or what was left of it. Part of me has always wondered if he's still alive somewhere, hiding under a false identity.

I went back to Chicago after the funeral. I was a widow and single mother at age twenty-two. But rather than slow me down, my new circumstances just fed my demons. I partied as much as ever and did even more drugs. I left Sean with Grandma, figuring that he would be well taken care of, so there was no harm in not being with him all the time. I knew firsthand how Grandma would dote on him, so I never felt guilty. My father was around, too, and tried his best with his own limited parenting skills to get close to Sean. He spent time with him but would get really nervous about letting Sean run around, worrying that he would hurt himself. I took Sean with me on some of my trips back to Tucson or flying to the West Coast, but at other times I left him with my father and my stepmother.

Sometimes my father's lifestyle got in the way, just as it had when I was a kid. Sean remembers seeing his grandfather's triple-beam scale being used to weigh coke bags. When Sean was about three, he was playing in my father's closet and spilled a big bag of powder all over himself. My father and stepmother, Pat, were so horrified that Sean would get a contact high and have a heart attack, they frantically but carefully tried to scrape the coke off his arms and legs without rubbing it in. Pat brought him back to my apartment so upset that she put him in the hall, rang the bell, and left. Poor Sean was crying as he tried to explain that Grandpa was yelling at him to stay still while they cleaned him up. When I asked Sean what happened, he told me he was playing in Grandpa's closet and knocked over a box of baby powder. Once I knew he was OK, I had to giggle to myself when I tried to imagine the scene.

My father spoiled Sean almost as much as he had spoiled me. He tried to be a good grandfather, as much as he tried to be a good father, without a lot to go on. I not only followed in his footsteps but was an even worse parent. I loved my children with all my heart, but no addict can take care of her kids for long. Many times when I was homeless and felt like I might die in the cold, I thought of my beautiful children, and knowing that they were all safe and warm and well taken care of helped me hold on one more day.

Instead of settling down after Scott died, I did the opposite. I hung out in punk bars in Chicago, sometimes working as a go-go dancer in the cage at the popular Club Exit, and was always high on pills or weed, loving the fact that I got to dance in that cage, a coveted spot. I had a group of friends that I did drugs with—some were old high school friends and some were new friends from the clubs. We were not doing heroin, but popped pills, snorted coke, smoked weed, and drank lots of cough syrup for the codeine high. We had a crooked pharmacist friend who was giving us Dilaudid and Demerol that we would crush and shoot superficially, not into a vein but just beneath the skin. That got me talking about how great heroin was and I realized I was missing it and wanted to turn these new friends on to some real dope. I was piquing their interest and mine was coming back as a real craving. One particularly boring night, I decided I was done trying to substitute anything else for what I really wanted.

"Fuck this," I said, after another swig of cough syrup. "Let's go get some dope, the real shit. I wanna show you guys what heroin's like."

One of my friends said, "You can get dope?! You know somebody?"

"No, but I'm about to." Unlike MJ who tried to stop me from even trying heroin, I was eager to turn my friends on to it.

I went to Humboldt Park, a community in Chicago known for gangs and drugs, a rough part of the city that most suburbanites were afraid of. But I was not like most suburbanites. It was after midnight. I stood on the street and started asking people who walked by if they knew where

I could cop, guys who looked the part of dealer or junkie. Soon, I had connections and was doing heroin every day again. My habit escalated, and once again I was pulled into the life of a junkie. My criminal career was about to begin.

# Part II

# Flirtin’
# with Disaster

# 4

# Second Nature

ONE DAY I FIND MYSELF driving around the city in my red Toyota, the first car I bought with legitimately earned money, early in my recovery. As always, the Rolling Stones are blasting on my CD player, my windows are down, and I'm smoking a cigarette. It's midafternoon. As I pass a grade school, I notice the kids getting out. I spot an older woman, probably a grandmother, holding the hands of two young girls. I'm reminded of Grandma walking Crickie and me to school. It's a bittersweet memory, a scene from another life. This is not a neighborhood where I usually work, but I often drive around other parts of the city just to see what's going on. This is a quiet, narrow street lined with well-kept brick bungalows, their tiny lawns perfectly groomed, flowerpots sitting on the front steps, a small grocery store and other shops dotted on corners, a deceptively calm setting. I know there is gang activity around here, but it's not my Cure Violence site.

Suddenly, the car in front of me abruptly pulls over. It comes to a screeching stop halfway into an empty parking space, making it hard for me to get past. Two guys that I recognize jump out of the car, one with a gun. I can see that he has it raised and is aiming toward what must be rival gang members standing about a half block away. A drive-by shooting is about to happen right in front of me. At that moment, I know I have to do whatever I can to interrupt this shooting. I stop my car, with the engine still running and the Stones still blaring. I open the door, jump out, and run toward the guy with the gun. All I can see in my mind is that grandmother and those two little girls, and I am ready to do whatever it takes to keep them from getting caught in the cross fire. It simply is not going to happen.

"Whattaya doin'? Get the fuck outta here!" I yell, as I stand directly in front of the guy with the gun. He's speechless. Every time he tries to aim past me, I move in front of the gun, the two of us locked in a deadly dance there on this quiet street on a sunny afternoon. "Get back in the car, get out of this area! You're not supposed to be over here!" I scream anything that I can think of, determined to defuse the situation. While I'm yelling at him, he's yelling disrespectful slurs at the rival gang members and taunting them by throwing up his gang's hand signs.

The other guy standing there watching his gang brother trying to shoot around me says, "Damn, Bianca, we didn't mean for you to see this!"

"Well, I'm seeing it! I'm here. I see everything. I'm everywhere! Get back in your car now."

While I move around to stay in front of the gun, I know that the rival gang members will start running in the other direction, more than likely to get their own gun. Rather than carry guns all the time and risk getting randomly stopped by the police and picked up on a gun charge, gang members usually hide their guns in a building nearby or even in a bush. I figure wherever it is, that other gun isn't far away and they will be back soon to return fire.

"OK, OK, damn, Bianca, we're leaving!" The two guys shout as they get back into their car and start to take off.

But I'm not done with them. I get back into my car and stay on their tail, laying on my horn as I follow close behind them. I turn the Stones off and scream out of the car window as I drive, "Get the fuck outta here! Keep going, keep going straight." I know that if a gang car drives through a neighborhood without making any turns, it's a signal to the rival gang that they are leaving the area. But if they take a turn, it means they are going deeper into the hood, not drawing back. As we approach a cross street and the choice is to keep going straight or turn right, they decide to turn.

"What the fuck?" I think, as I pull my car onto the wrong side of the street, floor it so I can pass their car, and then cross in front of their car, forcing them to either stop or hit me. They screech to a stop and I jump out of my car again.

"What the fuck do you think you're doing? I used to be a getaway driver. You're not shaking me, you motherfuckers! I'm following you till you get back to your own hood. There are kids out here. You're gonna kill somebody!"

"OK, OK, OK! Bianca, we didn't want you to see this!"

"We're past that! Just get the fuck outta here." I'm screaming like a maniac by this point, and I can see the shopkeepers coming out into the street to see what the hell is going on—more potential innocent victims, I think.

"OK, Bianca, get your car the fuck out the way and we're outta here," the guy with the gun says.

"No way, motherfucker. Who do you think you're talkin' to?" I holler. "Do a three-point turn and get the hell outta here. There's no police here right now, but you best believe somebody has called them. I'm trying to save you from going to jail. I'm trying to save somebody's life, yours included. Get the fuck outta here *now!*"

They make their U-turn as cars line up on the street behind us, unable to get past until they pull away. I follow them all the way back to their hood. Then I call Felix, one of my Cure Violence teammates, pick him up, and we return to the area near the school where the shooting was going to happen. We know we have to talk to the other gang members to defuse their desire to retaliate, because there is nothing more disrespectful than a rival gang coming onto their turf with a gun and throwing up gang signs. We talk to them until we're sure they have calmed down and then head back to the other hood to find the two guys I had chased out. I soon spot the one without the gun standing on a corner, so we pull the car over.

"Damn, Bianca," he says as soon as he sees us. "You know I love you, but, I mean, what the fuck?"

"Listen," I say, "I love you, too, but I'm telling you, do *not* go back over there. Stay in your lane. Do whatever the fuck you want to do over here, but no shooting! I'm not tryin' to get in your business. But stay over here, and they will stay over there. Too many people are dying."

He laughs and starts telling a few guys who have gathered around us what happened. "Man, you try to go in, do a drill, be low key, spray the block, and get outta there, you know? And there she is. I was tryin' to do a drill, and here's her behind us, beeping, screaming, jumpin' in front of the gun. What the fuck?"

"Damn, Bianca, you got more heart than me. I wouldnna did that!" one of the other gang members says, and they all laugh.

In hindsight, I realize the risk was enormous. Even if I convinced the guys I knew to put down their gun, the rivals could have returned at any moment and caught me with a stray bullet in the back. But that is not what I was thinking. I just wanted to stop it from happening. I did get a little talking-to from my supervisor and acknowledge that what I did was not exactly the smartest choice. Safety first is a real and necessary part of our training. But I felt that since I knew the guys, they wouldn't shoot me. And in all honesty, I would do it again. I have made many similarly risky decisions in the effort to stop bullets from destroying lives. I know I'm not stopping their war, but that day I kept one more person from getting shot. It was worth it to me. I don't think of it as taking a risk. I just react, and sometimes I'm the only thing between a kid and a bullet.

My work as a violence interrupter with Cure Violence has made me an expert in violence mediation and prevention. In that role, I travel around the country and the world speaking and training the staff when a new site opens. I have gone as far as Abu Dhabi to meet with terrorism experts and former ISIS fighters. What I have learned is that violence is the same everywhere. I make it a point to visit the hood in every city and country, and one thing remains constant: street is street. People who face extreme poverty and lack education also face an epidemic of violence. They see so much that they become numb to its effects. That is the point at which Cure Violence tries to step in and make it clear that there are other choices and better ways to handle conflict than picking up a gun and shooting. I see many high-risk individuals successfully change their thinking. But I continue to be shaken by how normal violence seems in so many communities. A drive-by shooting is an everyday occurrence.

Early one September, I am in Durham, North Carolina, helping a new site get up to speed, working to train the staff to use our database and helping with conflict mediation training. The office is in one of the row houses in the Mac, the slang name for the McDougald Terrace projects in Durham, right in the middle of the community, keeping the staff close to the people they serve and on top of the daily issues they face. After a long day of PowerPoint presentations and a full agenda of speakers, I'm ready to hang out in the hood, so I decide to go for a walk. It's a warm fall evening, still light, and everybody is out. Kids are running around, playing in the street. Grown-ups are sitting on their stoops, mothers stand in little groups catching up, balancing toddlers on their hips. A group of fifth graders are trading tricks with their fidget spinners. I stop to watch them.

"Wow, you're so good at that! I love watching you," I say, joining their circle. They look at me like most young people on the street do when they first meet me, thinking, "Who is this white lady and what does she want?"

One of the women from my team catches up with me. We have become close over the past few days. There aren't too many women doing this work, and when I find another, we always bond. "Bianca's cool," she says to the kids. "She works with us. She's one of the Chicago people."

"Yeah," I laugh, "whaddya actin' so stiff for? Give me a hug!" I have them laughing and joking with me, as I always do. The feeling of community and love that washes over me at moments like this is what makes my work so gratifying. Soon they are each trying to get my attention, to tell me something about themselves, or to show me one of the fidget tricks.

We talk and laugh for a while longer, and then I spot a stoop nearby, an empty set of stairs leading to the front door of a row house, so I sit down. I lean back to look at all the activity around me, to rest and just soak in the scene. So many people are out enjoying the afternoon, just like any other neighborhood I've been to anywhere in the world. One of the kids follows me, and we keep talking as he stands there losing his shyness and becoming my friend. A little girl, about five years old, and a little boy, a toddler, come out of the screen door at the top of the stoop where I sit.

"Oh my God, you're so cute!" I say. "What is your name, baby?" They walk around the porch, a little shy, but curious. The toddler stands next to me. We talk, and I make him giggle. The little girl walks back into the house. Another one of my colleagues has caught up with us and stands at the bottom of the steps with the older kid, getting to know him, too. It's a warm, sweet scene, and I feel so grateful to be there, to be doing this work. I take a snapshot in my mind, wanting to hold on to it. And then it all changes.

Without even a second's warning, shots are fired, bullets spray all around us. It happens so fast. We have no idea where it's coming from, but all I can think about are the kids, the baby standing next to me, the little girl about to walk back out the door, and the fourth grader at the bottom of the steps. People are ducking for cover, running in all directions, and screaming at each other to get the fuck outta there. My instincts kick in. I reach over to open the screen door and push the baby inside, then grab the fourth grader and pull him, stumbling up the steps, and push him inside, too. I scream, "Get the kids, get off the street!"

Just as quickly as it started, it's over. From what I can see, no one was hit, but the streets and the stoops have cleared. My coworker and I just stand there, looking at one another.

"What the fuck!" I whisper.

"I know," he says. "Man, we're still standing here. There's nobody else out here. Good thing you grabbed that baby."

For a second, we both realize how close we came, once again. But no police arrive on the scene. In fact, nothing else happens to even hint at what has just gone down. And I realize how anesthetized a community becomes to the most dangerous of situations when they happen every day. This is normal. No one calls the police. No one comes back out to see what's going on. The usual reaction is to go inside and stay there for a while. Keep your head down and be thankful you didn't catch a bullet this time. Nobody registers their shock because they aren't really shocked.

Throughout my life on the street, I see many instances of violence up close. I've been shot myself and have lived with bone damage from that bullet for more than twenty years. I had no concern for getting caught or killed. Now I take risks to help people and to try to stop the violence surrounding these communities. But I am never afraid. My heart guides me. I return to the streets I once walked as an addict and hustler because I care and worry about the people who live there. I loved the street life. Back then I took risks for all the wrong reasons. It would take me a very long time to understand the difference.

# 5

# Lawyers, Guns, and Money

FOR GOOD AND BAD, I WAS a crazy-ass thrill seeker from the day I was born. At the height of my criminal days, I was never afraid to try whatever I thought was necessary to get money and dope. When I decided to go to Humboldt Park to find a dealer, I didn't stop at copping the dope. I *became* a dealer and got in so tight with the Latino gang that ruled the territory that I partnered with a leading figure in the gang hierarchy and became a respected member. It all started the night I decided it was time to get back to my one true love, heroin.

I was living in a nice, respectable Oak Park apartment that my father had set up for me and Sean, who was an active toddler demanding a lot of attention. He spent most of his time with Grandma, while I spent my time doing what I always did, partying and getting high. I was in my punk phase, with a spiked haircut, torn tight black jeans, studded jewelry, and an abundance of black eyeliner and mascara adorning my tough-chick, do-not-even-think-about-messing-with-me sneer. I hung out at all the punk clubs in Chicago, but most often the hard-core Exit, where I would take my place in the go-go cage, dancing in drug-induced delirium. Many nights I was so high I forgot where my car was parked and even had it stolen once by some crazy guys who drove me home, dropped me off at my apartment, and then drove away in my car. It took me three days to track them down, and then my father had to intervene with just the right level of persuasion before they would hand over the keys. Having a young child and being back in the bosom of my family did not slow me down for a second. That night, when I finally got bored with weed, pills, and codeine, I was more than willing to do whatever it took.

Suburban twentysomethings with no idea of what really happened in Humboldt Park at night, none of them could believe what I was about to do, nor did any of them understand just how dangerous it was. Kris, one of my friends from Oak Park, came along for the ride. This was long before the days of the "Heroin Highway," a strip along the Eisenhower Expressway that every suburban kid who wants to cop drugs knows about. When "ready rock," the crack cocaine that came to Chicago from New York, became popular and abundant in the 1990s, the Heroin Highway became the go-to spot. But back in my day, really good heroin, Mexican Mud like I had in Arizona, was connected to all the Latino gangs. I knew where to go, but it took a lot of nerve for an outsider, a punked-out white girl, to go into Humboldt Park to find a heroin dealer.

We jumped into my Toyota Celica, the car my father bought for me after I moved back to Chicago. I had badgered him into buying it since the Porsche was long gone and now I had a little kid to cart around. With Kris in the front seat, I drove to North Avenue. We didn't know much about the Humboldt Park neighborhood, but I knew that the area surrounding the park was known for drugs. Humboldt Park itself was and still is an expansive, green, tree-filled park with a serene lily-pad-laden lagoon, magnificent old park buildings, and paved pathways that during the day were open to the usual park activities: women pushing strollers, family picnics in the grass, bicycles whizzing by, and men pushing the traditional Puerto Rican *paletas* carts, selling the ice pops that tempt all the kids, forcing their mothers to reach into tight purses. But at night, the park cleared out. Gangs from the surrounding neighborhoods claimed their territory, creating a war zone that was no place for anyone unaffiliated and unprotected. Yet there I was, a crazy white girl from the suburbs, ready to do or say whatever it took to cop dope. It was late, dark, and the streets were empty except for dealers, junkies, and hookers. I stopped the car a few times, rolled down the window, and tried to talk to someone, but they would not talk to me.

Finally, I told Kris, "Fuck this, I'm getting out of the car. You stay here. Don't be scared. If anything happens, beep the horn, and I'll come back." She had a look of sheer terror on her face, but I went anyway.

I got out of the car and looked around. In the dim streetlight, I could see that I had stopped on one of the worst blocks in that stretch. The buildings were dark and boarded up, with broken bottles and garbage strewn along the curb; it was an abandoned-looking section that I knew was hiding exactly what I wanted. I was completely intrigued and not a bit scared.

I saw a guy leaning against one of the run-down buildings, baseball cap sitting low on his forehead, a cigarette dangling from the side of his mouth. I walked right up to him and said, "Hey."

"What's up?" he asked as he tossed the cigarette to the curb.

"Listen," I said. "First of all, I want to tell you that I'm not the police, I have nothing to do with the police, I just want to cop some dope."

"What? Girl, I don't even know who you are."

"OK, I get you, but here, look at my arms," I rolled up my sleeve and showed him the evidence from my days in Arizona. "See the track marks?"

We went back and forth a few times. He was leery and didn't really want to talk to me, but I was not giving up.

"All right, come on. Follow me," he said as he opened a loosely attached door that led inside the building. The light in the hall was flickering, and I could barely see the worn-down, rickety stairs leading to the second floor. He was drinking Coca-Cola in a glass bottle that was almost empty.

"Come on," he repeated as he motioned for me to go ahead of him, a little impatient now.

"Who the fuck do you think I am?" I yelled at him. "You walk first. And leave the bottle out here." I did not want that bottle to become a weapon.

"Look, girl. You asked me for a favor. I didn't come ask you!"

"Well, this is how it's gotta be," I stood my ground.

My adrenaline was pumping, and I was so into this. I knew right then that I was going to cop, but more than that, I couldn't wait to see what was going on inside that building.

I could tell by the grin on his face that now he was entertained by me. I don't think he had ever had an encounter quite like this, with a person quite like me. He put the bottle down and said, "You know what? I'm going to play along. Are you happy now?"

"Yeah," I said. "But you go first and walk five steps ahead of me."

"Oh my God, what the fuck?" There was a mix of surprise and amusement in his voice, and while he wasn't letting me give him orders, he was going along. His name was Luis, and I liked him. I knew he liked me in spite of himself.

We made our way up three flights to the top floor. Down the hall, he stopped in front of a beaten-up apartment door and knocked. Somebody inside hollered, "Come!" and we walked in. A bunch of tough heavily tattooed guys in black jeans and T-shirts, just like I'd seen notorious gang "heavies" portrayed on TV, were sitting around the dingy apartment on a torn couch and old kitchen chairs. Beer bottles, a half-full bottle of Jack Daniel's, and overflowing ashtrays littered the table. A cloud of marijuana smoke hung over the room. The lights were low, and the windows were boarded up. I felt totally comfortable there. The wheels in my head started turning, figuring out how to get in on their action.

"Who the hell is this?" one of them asked.

"She cool, she cool," Luis said. "She's looking for some dope."

"What? How do you know she's not police, man?" They all looked at him like he was out of his mind.

"Trust me, she's not a cop," he said with such confidence even I was surprised.

I learned that Luis had brought me to the head dealer in the gang's main safe house, where large quantities of heroin were stashed. The other guys in the room were all gang members. I was in, but they started to grill me.

"What do you want?"

"What do you got?" I asked.

"Well, how much do you want?"

"How much do you got?"

"How much you willing to pay for a gram?"

"Well, how much is a gram?"

We went back and forth like this, and they were getting a real kick out of me. "I'm Sicilian," I kept telling them. They were genuinely amused; they were starting to realize I was not your average white girl.

"Wow, you got a lot of heart comin' up in here," one of them finally said.

"Look, all I want to do is cop," I said. "And if it's good, I'll keep coppin' from you."

They assured me it was and let me try some. I shot up in their bathroom, got really high, and bought my first fifty-dollar bag from a Chicago gang. I asked for a phone number, but they said no, just come back to the building, hang outside, and Luis would be there. I went back to my car where my poor friend had really started freaking out. I calmed her down. We went back to Oak Park, and I turned all my friends on to heroin. But I was still in that safe house in my mind, about to shape-shift into yet another life, this time a much more dangerous tribe than I had ever fallen in with.

I was completely taken with the whole scene in Humboldt Park. I knew I had just met members of a notorious Chicago street gang, and I wanted to be one of them. They had a safe house, a scale, and several coffee grinders covered in plastic. I didn't know at the time what the grinders were for, but I knew it had to be something I wanted in on. Over the next few weeks, I kept showing up there, copping more every time, since I now had customers of my own. I went from a gram or two to half ounces to kilos. The gang members could see that I was good for the money and had no fear. Soon, I was given a number to call and everybody in the neighborhood knew me.

Gangs back then had strict hierarchies. Everybody knew their place in the gang structure. They moved huge quantities of drugs, and there were rules about how to conduct business, who to trust, and the steep price of messing up. A few months in, I met the gang leaders, the female members, and the chief of the section that I was doing business with,

Pappo. From the moment I met him, I knew I had to get in on his shit. I was so drawn to him. He was older, about thirty or thirty-five, with close-cropped black hair, a black moustache, and a goatee. His pockmarked hardened face reflected the harshness of his years on the street, and to most people he appeared menacing. I knew he was a ruthless killer, but that intrigued me. He reminded me of Al Pacino's Tony Montana character in the movie *Scarface*. He carried himself like a total badass, and spoke as if scripted by Martin Scorsese. He commanded respect, and wasn't afraid of anyone. He was firm with his people, but also good to us and reached out to help whenever we had a problem. I knew he would never hurt me, and this combination of benevolence and vicious potential made me want to get inside his head. I was one of his favorites because he knew I was loyal. I knew that if anyone messed with me, Pappo would make that person regret it. A willing and eager student, I became his protégé. Pappo taught me how to handle the Mexican Mud heroin sold by the gang. It was a black tar substance and had to be cut with powdered lactose before it could be measured into bags ready for the street. Pappo schooled me on how to mix it just right and put it into the coffee grinder to create the potent powder. He made sure I wore a protective face mask and gloves before handling it. The whole operation seemed so clinical, I felt like I was working in an underground science lab. I sat at the round table, surrounded by brothers and sisters all wearing protective gear and working their own grinders. Plus, Pappo was a heroin addict like I was and always took care of me with an extra taste before I did my rounds.

Every so often, the gang would move the safe house, sometimes to an empty apartment with no furniture. I would call one of their phone numbers, and in a short coded conversation get the new address and arrange to come by and cop. I often had Sean with me, so I would stop and get him a Happy Meal at McDonald's, show up at the safe house, and sit him on the bare floor in the living room while I shot dope and took care of my deal in the kitchen. There was my son, playfully talking to himself and shoving french fries into his cute little face, just like any other toddler, while his mom did business with one of the meanest gangs in the city. That they didn't care if I brought my kid along but also left me something to shoot up while I made my pickup was a testament to how much they trusted me. Drug addicts were never allowed inside a safe house, just dealers, and most of the gang dealers didn't do heroin. But even in this culture, I operated outside the rules. I was special, and when I placed my order my contact would leave that little bag for me on the kitchen counter, knowing that often I was dope sick by the time I got there. There was nothing wrong with this picture in my mind. As long as Sean was happy with his Mickey D's, and I was getting all the dope I could handle, all was perfectly fine.

As I became a fixture in Humboldt Park, I made it clear to the gang that I wanted to become a member. Soon enough, they trusted me with their secrets. One of the brothers was wanted for questioning for some murders and needed a place to hide before they could get him out of the country. When asked by the chief, without hesitation I said he could hang out in my Oak Park apartment. He and another brother moved in, and I started holding large quantities of heroin. Now we were dealing out of my apartment. The cops began to catch on; one of the snitches who always seemed to be around must've ratted that the two brothers were staying with some white girl in Oak Park. I had no idea they were following me.

I had to go to one of the safe houses to pick up an order. Sean and I were there with about five other people. While Sean sat there enjoying his Happy Meal, content to sit on the floor and play with his little toy, the ATF burst through the door with a bunch of Chicago homicide detectives, guns drawn and ready to fire. It was a raid.

"Up against the wall!" they screamed.

"My baby!" I said in a total panic.

"Your baby's gonna be fine," one of them sneered. His tone was hardly reassuring.

They lined us up, hands against the wall, and started to pat the guys down. Sean sat there, wide eyed, quietly watching all of this unfold. A female officer showed up to pat me down. They started asking us questions about the missing brother. We all gave the same answer: "I don't know." They asked for our IDs, and I had to hand mine over. Two of the detectives took a look and moved to a corner of the room, heads together, no doubt putting this white girl from Oak Park together with what they had heard on the street.

"Take her into custody for questioning," they said.

"I don't know nothing!" I insisted over and over again while they were running a check on me. I had a warrant out for my arrest at the time, and of course it showed up. I had been writing fake prescriptions for months and didn't realize how much the cops knew about my activities. The warrant gave them grounds to arrest me.

"My baby, my baby! What about my baby?" I screamed.

"Your baby can't come to the jail with you. What do you want to do? Do you want us to take him to social services?"

"No!" I yelled back. Social services was the worst place I could think of, and I knew I would lose Sean if they got him.

One of the gang members stepped up. "Don't worry. I'll bring the baby by my mother."

Relieved, I said OK, so Sean went with him as the cops took me to the police car. I felt trapped. My motherly instincts kicked into overdrive. I wanted Sean back. I don't know how, but I talked the cops into stopping by the corner gas station right by the safe house to get me a pack of cigarettes. I was in the backseat handcuffed while the driver went into the store and the other cop stayed in the passenger seat. As I sat there, a gang brother walked by and saw me. He gave me a menacing look that said, "Bitch, you better not talk." I nodded my head to assure him that I don't crack like an egg. The gang had Sean, so I had to believe he knew what my nod meant.

At the police station, I used my phone call and got to my father. I told him my bail was $75,000, which meant I needed $7,500 bond to walk. I told him to send Pat right away with the money to get me out of jail. He kept asking where the baby was, but I told him Sean was fine. While I waited for my stepmother, the detectives started showing me grisly pictures of the homicide victims and grilling me about the guy they were looking for, the guy I was hiding in my apartment.

"Whoever did this needs to go to jail," I agreed. "This is horrible, and I hope you find him soon, but I don't know anything about any of this." In truth, I did not recognize any of the victims, whom I later found out were from New York and had no doubt messed with the wrong brother at the wrong time.

While I was in custody, the brother who had seen me in the cop car was busy moving the fugitive out of my apartment. We all knew how the cops worked. As soon as they had my address, they would get a search warrant. So the brother got him out, and by the time the cops showed up my apartment was empty. That didn't stop them from kicking in the door and tearing the whole place apart. They didn't find anything. Of course, I didn't say a word. I had learned from a very early age that you do not talk to the cops about anything, ever. They released me as soon as Pat showed up with my bond. Pat immediately wanted to know where Sean was. Was he OK? Who exactly had him? What was the address? I told her that the gang chief said he would bring Sean to his mother's and that they were Spanish. "Spanish people love kids," I kept telling her. Pat was livid, appalled that I really had no idea where my baby was, nor how to find him. After a few hours of driving around the hood, with me telling Pat, "Don't worry, I got this, he's fine, trust me," we finally ran into a brother who would take us to Sean. An older Hispanic woman, probably a grandmother, brought him out, and he was as happy as ever. They had even bought him a new outfit, which he looked really cute in. I shot Pat an I-told-you-so look, and she drove us back to Oak Park.

Now the gang trusted me as much as any of them ever trusted anyone. I had proved myself capable of dealing with the cops. I didn't fold or snitch, and that made me a real insider. I was ready to go through the initiation required to officially become a member, the final step. It was called getting "jumped in." I had heard stories about what this meant and was a little scared, but I wanted it so badly I was ready to do whatever they asked. I had found my true brothers and sisters. I had shown them what I was made of, and I valued their approval and inclusion more than anything. I wanted to make Pappo proud and was ready to go in as far as they would let me.

There were two possible ways to get jumped in. One was to "walk the line"; the other, to "go on the wall." Walking the line meant that other women in the gang would line up across from one another, and as

I passed through the line they would give me their best beating, punching me as hard as they could. Going on the wall meant that I would stand against a wall for three minutes while two gang members beat me up, and I could not move. The women members also had chiefs. My chief chose the wall for me and chose two other women to do the beating who were gang members I hung with. The rules dictated that they had to give me their best shots from the neck down, could not give me any breaks, and if they didn't bruise me, they would be penalized with a violation and their own three minutes on the wall. One of those women had become a close friend. The clock started timing the three minutes. As my friend was beating me, she repeated, "I'm sorry," with every blow she landed. I kept screaming, "Just do it, just do it!" It was the longest three minutes of my life, and I did all I could not to show it. I was badly bruised everywhere. My ribs throbbed. My shoulders and chest felt as if I had been stabbed multiple times, and my stomach and sides were burning. This experience was just as painful as being in labor and much harder to take without collapsing. But I was determined to show them I could handle whatever they dished out because I knew in their eyes it made me worthy.

When the timer went off, I was badly damaged but still standing. The report went back to Pappo and the jefes, the other gang leaders, that I handled it like a soldier: I didn't flinch; I took it all. So now I was a full member of a Latino street gang in Chicago. They would become my family for the rest of my criminal life, my partners in dealing large quantities of drugs, covering my back when I was in prison, helping me cop when I was locked up, and the only source of support in between prison terms.

Along with my gang business, I kept up my other criminal cons and hustles, some that I had started when I was a teenager, like robbing pharmacies and writing fake prescriptions. I still had a pill appetite to support, on top of my heroin habit, plus I had a lot of friends that were eager to buy pills from me, so that continued to be an easy way for me to make money. I could never have too much money or too many drugs. I relished finding new and thrilling ways to get more. While the gang became my main source for heroin and gave me the connections

I needed to deal extensively, sometimes as much as a half kilo a week, I still got a rush from committing crimes.

I robbed my first pharmacy when I was fifteen. I had taken a job at a big department store called Wieboldt's in the Oak Park Mall during the busy Christmas season when they hired high school kids for extra help. I was rotated from department to department, working different counters selling high-traffic gift items, like men's wallets, and ties, and women's scarves. One day, I was assigned to the perfume counter. I thought it was the height of sophistication, waiting on wealthy women from Oak Park and neighboring River Forest. I really thought I was the epitome of fashion and a serious businesswoman, demonstrating designer scents like Chanel No. 5 and Estée Lauder's latest offering. It was more fun than I ever thought a real job could be and I loved playing the part. At the time, Wieboldt's still had a pharmacy in the store and I discovered that the perfume department shared the same backroom as the pharmacy. When I went back there to hang up my coat, I saw a cabinet labeled "Schedule II Narcotics," which I knew translated into drugs like reds, Christmas Trees, and 'ludes. I felt like a kid outside a candy store. I knew I had to get into that cabinet.

My perfume counter had a glass case that was also locked, and every time a customer asked to see something in the case I had to go into the backroom and get the key, which just happened to be hanging right next to the key for the pharmacy cabinet. Once I tested that key to make sure it would open the drug cabinet, I knew I was going to rob the store. It was time for a strategy not only to take the drugs but also get them out of Wieboldt's without getting caught. I immediately shared this discovery with my friends, other rich suburban kids who had nothing better to do but pop pills all day and had the money to pay for them. I needed to be able to identify which drugs were which by their medical names so I wouldn't waste the effort by stealing stuff that would not get us high. Like masterminds in a complicated heist, we hung out together in one of our bedrooms and pored over the *Physician's Desk Reference* (PDR), the catalogue of drugs that every doctor keeps close by. One kid's father was a doctor, and we had swiped it from his desk. I studied the *PDR* to learn the pharmaceutical brand names for the drugs I wanted. I was meticulous and calculating, a fifteen-year-old criminal prodigy planning one of my first serious robberies.

I learned that reds were Seconal, Christmas Trees were Tuinal, and of course 'ludes were quaaludes. Soon I knew exactly what to look for in that cabinet. I continued to work for a few more days and did such a good job selling perfume that they kept me on that counter, right where I needed to be. Finally, the big day came. I had my boyfriend and another guy as accomplices standing on alert by the phone for my signal. There were security guards in the store, walking around throughout the day, so I could not just walk out of there with bags full of drugs. I had two large Wieboldt's shopping bags ready in the backroom, with fancy tissue paper to wrap my haul like a regular purchase. I called the boys and told them to give me ten minutes, then get in the car, park in the Wieboldt's parking garage, and come inside. I told them to come to the perfume counter, act like they were shopping for a Christmas gift for their moms, and pretend they did not know me. As soon as I made the call, I went to the backroom. I took a deep breath, quickly opened the locked cabinet, and scoped out exactly what I wanted. The pills were in large five-hundred- to a thousand-count bottles. I put as many bottles as I could fit into the shopping bags, covered them with the fancy tissue paper, locked the cabinet, and put the key back on the hook. My heart was racing, but more from the sheer thrill than from any fear. I nonchalantly brought the shopping bags out front and set them behind the perfume counter.

The guys showed up as directed and bought a bottle of perfume. I wrapped it for them as I normally would, and then asked, "Oh, would you like me to put this with the rest of your things?" I stuffed the perfume into the same bag with the drugs, said, "Here's your receipt, and have a beautiful Christmas," and off they went, arms full of my first perfect haul. My boyfriend picked me up from work as usual, and I never heard anything about it in the store, nor in any of the papers. I stole over ten thousand pills that day and knew that I had a very special talent. At age fifteen, in addition to barbiturates, I added stealing to my list of addictions. As we sat in my friend's bedroom that night, in his parents' Oak Park mansion, a rainbow of pills spilled across his bed,

I was already plotting my next heist. We made a lot of money selling those pills to the rich kids in Oak Park. We were in business; a lucrative little crime ring was born. Many pharmacies didn't have much security back then, so we broke in during the night through heating vents or back entrances that were easy to pry open with a crowbar. I became the getaway driver.

Our most ambitious attempt turned out to be the last for my little ring of thieves. We decided to hit the Walgreens on Rush Street, figuring this high-profile address would be well stocked. Two of us hid inside until it closed. This was before security cameras, laser alarms, or the steel barriers that are now pulled down over the pharmacy areas in most stores and locked each night. As soon as the coast was clear, we went right to the pharmacy and were now such pros that we knew exactly what to look for and on which shelves to find it. We grabbed barbiturates, opiates, anything that we wanted to get high on. But our mistake that night was so basic it was almost comical. As we filled Walgreens shopping bags with pill bottles, we were also popping them like candy, getting way too high, and realizing much too late that we did not have a plan for getting out of the store. In a drug-crazed panic, my friend picked up a heavy metal garbage can on display in the store and slammed it through the plate glass window right there on Rush Street. Just as we were making a run for it, a police paddy wagon pulled up. I ran through the alley, my heart pumping, fists holding tight to the shopping bags I had managed to grab, and I got away. My friend went to jail and did time. I felt bad, but I had learned that this kind of amateur heist was not for me. I needed to know the whole plan and to believe that I had a foolproof scheme. I was becoming the kind of criminal that would not accept failure. There had to be better angles, and I found more than one.

I started going to crooked doctors, those who I knew would write me anything I wanted. But not every doctor would go for it every time, and I was determined to find a better way, something that would not be a waste of my time. When I was seventeen and living in Tucson, I learned from MJ how to forge prescriptions for the codeine-laced cough syrup Tussionex. I took that skill back to Chicago.

I was in a pediatrician's office with Sean for a routine baby check. The doctor left us alone in his office for a few minutes, and I noticed a pile of blank prescription pads on his desk. I grabbed one, shoved it into my bra, and after the doctor was done with Sean I calmly walked out of the office, now armed with exactly what I needed. I went to the Oak Park Public Library and got a book on Latin to learn how to write in the language doctors used. Once again, I studied the *PDR* and learned the scientific names for the drugs, like hydromorphone for Dilaudid and meperidine for Demerol. I studied the shorthand doctors used to communicate the order with the pharmacist, like *b.i.d.* for twice a day. It was easy to replicate the barely legible scrawl of most doctors and, I quickly learned, just as easy to fool most pharmacists. I was taking a crash medical course, and I felt like a real doctor as I practiced how to do it. I began "cracking scripts" all over Chicago and the suburbs. Whenever I ran out of prescription pads, I would rack my brain to figure out where to steal more. I discovered through trial and error that hospital emergency rooms were the easiest place to get them. They always kept them behind the counter so they could write them quickly for discharged patients. So I would go up to the nurse at the admitting desk and put on my standard Oscar-worthy performance.

"Excuse me, excuse me," I would say, breathless with urgency. "My friend was just brought in. She was in a car accident, and I think she's in critical condition. I don't even know if she's still alive! Can you please help me? Can you find her, please?"

I'd give an elaborate Italian name and make the tears come, wringing my hands and getting more agitated the longer the nurse took to respond. To calm me down, the nurse would leave the counter to go and see if my friend had been admitted without being listed. That was my cue to reach over, grab a few prescription pads, stick them in my bra, and wait there, wiping my tears with a tissue. When the nurse came back to tell me my friend was not there, I frantically asked where else they might have taken her and once the kind nurse named another hospital, I would run out, shouting, "Thank you so much!" playing the part all the way to the end of the scene.

Early on, I was turned down a few times by suspicious pharmacists who could tell that the scripts were fake. One even threatened to call the police. At first I could not figure out why, but soon learned that every doctor was assigned a personal DEA number. If a pharmacist paid close attention and realized there wasn't one on my script, I was in trouble. As soon as I figured it out, I started going to doctors again for a multitude of contrived ailments: headaches, sinus pain, a bad back, whatever it took to get the doctor to write me a prescription; many times I think they would oblige just to get me out of the office. But this got me a DEA number, and I used it until a pharmacist showed even a hint of suspicion, at which point I would repeat my performance with another doctor to get a new DEA number.

This system worked like a charm . . . until it didn't and I got arrested. I had been arrested many times, but my father would always bond me out, and his connections would get me off. I went to court, got a lecture from the judge, and was released. I started to believe that I was untouchable.

I was dealing heroin with the gang and cracking scripts all over Chicago, but I had a voracious habit, and I always thought I needed more money. I was so hyper, even though I used heroin every day and did barbiturates on top of it. I loved the thrill of conning someone or finding a new way to make easy money. I added a new activity to my busy criminal agenda, jimmying open mailboxes and stealing from wealthy residences around the suburbs. I would pry open their mailboxes and sometimes hit the jackpot, finding their bank statements and a package of blank checks sent to replenish a checkbook. I forged checks and cleaned out their accounts. Skimming through the files of a friend's mother's real estate firm, I found account numbers and signatures of upscale residents who were trying to sell their houses or condos. I would use that information on forged credit-card applications, stalk their homes for the mail delivery while they were at work, and max out the newly issued cards until they were declined. It was identity theft before the term was popular.

I even managed to steal the identity of an African American woman. I found her purse with her driver's license and checkbook. She was a wealthy businesswoman with a very healthy bank account, and I had to get that money. I went to the mall, bought an Afro wig, dark makeup, eyeglasses that matched those in her picture, wore a turtleneck, and even put on nice leather gloves to cover my hands. I walked into her bank and withdrew more than $5,000 after perfecting her signature. I continued to make withdrawals for two days, but stopped before things got too hot.

In the finest department stores, while getting the clerks to run around and wait on me, I liked to pretend that I was a rich trust-fund kid. I shopped my greedy heart out. Sean had the best designer clothes, little Izod shirts in every color; I had all the designer handbags, perfume, and shoes I could ever want. As my exploits began to add up, the FBI developed a growing interest in me. I had no idea they were paying any attention. But for a long time, they got nowhere since whenever I got arrested my father got me off. They couldn't make anything stick. The FBI only chases down a sure bet, so they continued surveillance until they had enough to put me away. I was becoming a notorious person of interest, but they could not nail me. I felt untouchable and in many ways, I was. I stumbled onto my most ambitious scam yet, what I considered my criminal masterpiece.

It began around 1981, in collaboration with Mark, a friend since eighth grade. Mark is still like a brother to me, and since he's gay, he's one of the few men I've known whom I never slept with. We got high together many times over the years and were about to become business partners. We were in our early twenties, and each of us had expensive habits. I was still dealing for the gang, but I was consistently on the lookout for another way to bring in more cash. I wanted schemes that were worth the effort, with bigger payoffs. Many times I rejected petty crimes because they were "too short" for me. If I was going to bother, I wanted the money to be big. Mark loved to move around and had traveled all over the country. I had been wanting to go to Tucson to visit MJ, but was low on cash and didn't want to ask my father, when I happened to mention it to Mark. I asked him how he was paying for all the flights he took. He had a job, but I knew he wasn't making enough to cover these trips. He told me he wasn't paying for the tickets. I was intrigued.

Long before e-tickets, massive computer databases, passwords, and tightened security measures, the airlines had an option they called TBM (tickets by mail). When you booked a flight over the phone, the agent at the airlines would ask if you were coming to one of their many ticket offices located all around the city to pick up the ticket in person or if you wanted it mailed to you. When you asked for TBM, the ticket agent asked how you wanted to pay for the ticket. If you said check, they mailed you the paper ticket without having any payment in hand. Mark told me the round-trip tickets would arrive at his house with an invoice and a stamped preaddressed envelope to mail the check back to the airline. But all that took time, not to mention the time for the check to clear and for banks to communicate with one another. It's hard to imagine that any of this could work in today's world of high-speed interactions and digital transactions, but everything then was much slower and computers were relatively primitive. Mark figured out how to time it just right so he could order the tickets, fly out, spend a few days at his destination, and fly back, all before the airlines realized he hadn't paid for the tickets yet. He had a collection of PO boxes where he'd receive the tickets he'd order using fake names and IDs. When he got to the gate and boarded the plane, he had a ticket in his hand, and there was no way to check if that ticket had actually been paid for, nor did anyone ever try. Mark took his trip and returned without ever sending in a check. And nothing ever happened. My manipulative brain clicked into full gear. I was ready to jump in.

I called Piedmont Airlines, a regular carrier flying out of Midway at the time, and booked a flight to Tucson for Sean and myself. Mark decided to come with us. Ordering the tickets over the phone, I danced a perfect dance, pretending to be naive about how it worked, asking whom I should make the check out to, and being so appreciative of the convenient TBM option. We timed it precisely, had a nice visit with MJ, did heroin together every day like old times, and then arrived back in Chicago before the nonexistent check could clear the bank. No money ever changed hands. I was hooked.

Mark and I took a few more trips together and had some great times. When Sean was with us, we looked like a perfect little family. During one trip, we were hanging out at O'Hare, ready to go, when Mark asked me if I realized that an airline ticket is like cash when you trade it in for a different ticket, even on a different airline. I knew it was possible to exchange tickets between airlines, essentially paying for a new ticket with an unused ticket, but didn't see how we could turn that into real cash. The catch was that on every printed ticket there was an FOP (form of payment) noted and on ours the word "check" always appeared. The printed tickets had a pale green background and a small box that held the FOP description. We knew the airlines never cross-referenced to see if the original check noted in the box had cleared before they issued a new ticket. But we couldn't be sure they would be that lax before they paid out in cash. We had to figure out how to change the FOP on the ticket from "check" to "cash." Sitting in my apartment in Oak Park, high on barbiturates, Mark and I weighed all the angles and together hatched a plan.

We made another reservation on another airline, TWA, for the same destinations and close to the same cost as the tickets we already had on Piedmont, around $900 apiece. There was a higher cost for the new reservation, but the difference was minimal, so our out-of-pocket was only thirty-two dollars. This time we went in person to exchange the tickets. We stood in line and acted like a married couple. I gave a stellar performance as I explained that we had to postpone our earlier trip and rebook our flights because my husband had a death in the family. As the ticket agent typed in our information, I continued to spin my elaborate tale about how devastated we were over the death, but we were so ready to get away and thank you so much for your help. She kept clacking away on the computer keyboard while I kept tap dancing, ever adept at the choreography of a good hustle. When asked how we were going to pay for the new tickets, I told her we'd use the old Piedmont tickets and pay the remaining thirty-two-dollar difference in cash. She issued the new TWA tickets, I handed her the cash, and Mark and I confirmed exactly what we had suspected. A gaping, gorgeous loophole emerged. The computers at the time could only accommodate two lines of information in the FOP box, so on the new tickets the original "FOP—Check" now showed up as the OFOP (original form of payment) and was moved down a space, while the new FOP right above it showed up as "Cash" because we had just paid cash for the small difference from the old tickets. Bingo. One more exchange, and both lines would say cash.

We waited until the next day and made another reservation on another airline. Back in line at O'Hare, another ticket agent clicking away on the computer, another Oscar-worthy performance, and a new ticket was issued for a mere difference of eighteen dollars. I could barely contain myself when I looked at that ticket and saw, "OFOP—Cash," and "FOP—Cash." It worked.

We waited until the end of the next business day for the final test. Back at O'Hare, we stood in yet another line and gave yet another ticket agent the same song and dance about needing to change our flights. She politely listed all the options: reschedule for another time, reissue the ticket right now, or exchange the ticket for cash. Careful not to appear too eager, I worked every minute, explaining that my aunt was dying and we simply could not leave, nor could we possibly anticipate when we would be able to go again, so I concluded that cash would probably be the best option and once this trauma was all over we would rebook. I apologized as the ticket agent once again hit that computer keyboard. Mark and I figured that waiting until the end of the business day would mean that the airlines had plenty of cash on hand to pay out, and we were right. Back in those days, a network of pneumatic tubes was used to send paperwork and cash from one location inside the airport to another, like they used in a bank. I came to love the whooshing sound as the container was dropped into a hole and sucked into the tube. The agent took our old tickets, filled out some paperwork, stuffed it all into the plastic container, and sent it through the tube. *Whoosh.* Soon enough, another whoosh heralded the payoff and the thrill of success; I would get butterflies in my stomach every time I heard it. The ticket agent took the container out of the tube, opened it, and I saw all that green coming out, hundreds, fifties, twenties, as she counted out nearly $2,000 into my open hand. In my mind we had just split the atom. We were fucking geniuses.

This set off a whirlwind of criminal activity that played out like the movie *Catch Me If You Can*. Mark and I worked this scam for almost two years, perfecting the timing and upping the amounts through trial and error and eventually burning through the airlines based at O'Hare. We figured we were pushing our luck if we repeated the pattern too many times with the same collection of airlines at the same airport, so we cracked it at Midway International Airport in Chicago and even did a few exchanges at Meigs Field, a single-runway airport on Lake Michigan right in the middle of the city that was used for private jets. But after many months, we started to worry that we were getting hot in the Chicago area; a red flag could show up on one of the exchanges, and the airport security would be on to us.

One day, Mark said, "You know we can do this in any city. There are five airports in L.A. alone."

"Oh my God, get me a list of every airport across the country!" I said.

We started taking extensive road trips, sometimes driving, sometimes flying. I was so convinced of my own brilliance and saw myself as such a success by this time that I insisted we ride to Milwaukee in a limo to exchange tickets there. We stayed in L.A. for ten days to work the five area airports, discovering how to book increasingly expensive flights by going first-class and adding multiple legs to the trip to drive up the ticket costs: Chicago to Denver to San Francisco to Tucson and home again. Many times the helpful airline agent would suggest a deal to save me money on the ticket price, and I would have to come up with an excuse to make her book the costliest flights. I would tell her it was a business trip and I had to max out my expense account for the quarter or I wouldn't get the same amount next quarter, and thanks so much for your help but please just book it at the original price. Sometimes this could mean as much as $5,000 on one exchange.

At our peak, Mark and I could take in over $20,000 a day by moving from airline to airline, airport to airport. During one call to order tickets, the agent asked me if I would also like to book a hotel and rental car. I said, "Sure!" and we figured out how to work that angle without ever paying a dime. We stayed at the finest Hiltons and Hyatts all over the country, and drove luxury rentals, like a Lincoln Town Car or a sporty Mercedes, from one airport to another. Mark would never allow me to drive because I was so messed up on Halcion (triazolam) all the time, in addition to my daily heroin habit. He was into speed and coke and could drive all night. He eventually started shooting speedballs with me and developed a heroin habit of his own.

Many times I brought Sean along. I would insist that we stop at sightseeing destinations like the Grand Canyon, the Alamo, and the Petrified Forest. I wanted my son to see America. At the Petrified Forest, I stole a piece of bark from one of the ancient, highly protected, off-limits trees. Sean saw me do it and said, "No, Mommy, don't steal that!"

"Oh, Sean, don't worry! Just be quiet, it's fine," I yelled at my sweet, earnest, six-year-old boy. He stayed quiet as we came to the exit gate, but I could see how scared he was. The park ranger stopped the car and asked if we had anything from the park. I hesitated, but I looked at my son's innocent face and for once in my life, I couldn't lie. I said, "Yes, I have this small piece of bark. I'm so sorry."

As I handed it back to the ranger, my son smiled with relief. Sean was subjected to more bad scenes than any young child should ever see. Many times we'd stop to eat in a restaurant, finding the nicest one in town, but I was always so high I could barely keep my head up, while Mark would be so hyped up on coke that he wasn't really hungry. We would sit there, out of our minds, and encourage Sean to "go ahead, honey, order whatever you want." Once, I literally passed out, with my head falling onto my plate. Sean started to cry and told the waiter, "Mommy doesn't feel good," while Mark hissed at me to sit the fuck up and tried to get us out of there in one piece. We were a perfect little dysfunctional family.

We always managed to travel first class, and most of the time avoided public scenes by living on room service and traveling in taxis or limos. I went to the hotel gift shops and designer boutiques to buy jewelry, perfume, candy, and toys for Sean. Sometimes I went down to the hotel bar to nurse a gin and tonic and pop more pills, and have weird conversations with the barflies, while Mark stayed with Sean, watching TV in the room. Before I left I would tell Sean he could use the phone to order anything he wanted to eat, call Grandma, whatever he felt like doing. I would come back to the room so high, toss all the jewelry on the bed, squeeze out of my tight designer jeans, and pass out wearing a hotel monogrammed robe. Even in my worst drug-infused stupor, I insisted on the best of everything and Mark, in his own altered state, went along. We booked hotel suites with king-sized beds and marble sinks. We burned through the cash almost as fast as we made it.

As we learned how to work more than one exchange at a time, I became an organizational whiz. My time at the Options Exchange had taught me how to work numbers and keep many balls in the air. I fancied myself a high-powered businesswoman, like a lucrative Wall Street broker, keeping track of which tickets at which airports were ready to exchange for which step, always careful to keep it all straight. I had to keep track of the different PO boxes we had in suburbs all around Chicago, where tickets were coming in every day, and make sure that when we did an exchange we used the right one of the many fake addresses and IDs that Mark and I were accumulating, knowing we had to change things up to avoid getting too hot. Mark and I even joined the American Association of Retired Persons—AARP—under assumed names so we could have the ID numbers they issued. Whenever I needed to change my name and get a new ID, I would get a blank lease form, fill it in with a new name and fake address, get it notarized by one of my father's friends, and then go to the library claiming to be a new resident so I could get a library card based on the fake information. That gave me the two pieces of proof of residence required to get a state-issued ID, but I still had to deal with getting my picture taken at the DMV. Mark and I stumbled upon a way to clear that hurdle.

Sitting in a bar one night, Mark met a guy who worked for the secretary of state, handling applications for driver's licenses at the DMV. It turned out that he was working his own scam. He told Mark that if he ever needed a fake ID, he could get him one for $300. We used the guy many times, standing in line at the DMV where he was stationed as one of the first people you'd interact with, responsible for verifying your paperwork and sending you on to the driver's test. But instead of paperwork, inside our envelopes he found his cash. He would stamp our application forms, complete with fake names and addresses, and send us on our way. We did this over a period of a year or so and the guy kept raising his price; by the end, we were paying $700 a pop. But it was the cost of doing business to us. We were making tens of thousands and we had a pile of fake IDs.

Occasionally, we would have no choice and the airline would not have enough cash on hand, so the ticket agent would have to issue what the airlines called a "draft," a money order. Sometimes the draft would be for $5,000 or $6,000, and we could not risk taking it to a bank where they might check on such a large amount, fake ID or not, and come up with something on one of us that we didn't even know about. So we started cashing the drafts at a currency exchange where just presenting an ID that matched the name on the draft was enough. They never checked anything, but I wanted some insurance anyway. I became friends with the agents at one place, and soon they would just take the draft and give me the cash without checking an ID.

I understood, almost by pure instinct, that the true art of the con was to make people comfortable with you by sharing the details of your life. The unsuspecting agents at the currency exchange were happy to see me coming and excited to hear about my adventures. They hung on every word, a welcome distraction from the monotony of their days, and they assumed that I was legit—in fact, would never have believed otherwise. I was a neighborhood friend who did regular business with them and had great stories to tell. That was all they wanted to know. And I never stuttered or got flustered, whether it was conning my friends at the currency exchange or the ticket agents at the airlines, or the guy at the car rental when we returned something late. Whatever it was, I gave a complete performance, totally high but unwavering in my confidence and control of the situation. The ability to talk my way in or out of just about anything was a gift and a curse throughout my life.

At the same time that I was working the ticket scam with Mark, I was writing fake prescriptions and dealing kilos of heroin through the gang. More than once, I was a mule, carrying drugs across the Mexican border and conveniently visiting a few airports at the same time. I was never afraid to do any of this. I weighed every possible scenario and had a backup plan, no matter how crazy, in case I found myself stopped at the border or collared by an airport security agent. My worst-case fallback was my father. I had complete faith that he would never let me go to jail; no matter how bad things got, he would rescue me. He knew I was into some heavy stuff but tried very hard to ignore it. One time I was at his apartment and noticed that he had a nice-looking hard briefcase, with a lock and lots of folders and pockets inside. I realized how much a case like this could help me organize my business.

"Daddy, I really need this briefcase. I'm looking for a job, and I want to look real professional and think if I had this case, it would really help," I said with total conviction.

"What? You are the only one I know who's been looking for a job for fifteen motherfuckin' years and still hasn't found one," he half-laughed as he shook his head. "Take the fuckin' briefcase!"

That briefcase became my bank, filing system, and Rolodex—everything I needed to run Bianca World, Inc. There were rows of airline tickets, organized by exchange dates and airports, pockets full of blank prescription pads, the *PDR*, contracts for rental cars, fake IDs, my entire business holdings. I even had a supply of pens and blank pads of notepaper. I kept it locked all the time and only Mark was allowed to have a key. When I had to leave town, I brought the locked case over to my father's apartment, and Pat, my blessed and clueless stepmother, kept it safe. In my mind, I was a real power broker and the contents of that briefcase proved it.

In one week's time, I might fly to L.A., work the ticket scam, drive over the border to pick up a load of Mexican Mud, drive back across the country, stopping at a few other airlines to exchange tickets, fill a fake prescription at a Walgreens here and there, drive back to Chicago, drop off the heroin at the gang safe house, and then return my rental car. Despite all the dope and pills I was doing every single day, I kept up an insane pace. I was a criminal tornado, crisscrossing the country, feverishly working my business.

Sometimes Mark and I would get home with so much cash we barely bothered to count it, Sean would be dropped off at Grandma's, and we would cop a couple of ounces of heroin and coke just for us. We stayed up for two or three days at a time, doing drugs and partying at my apartment in Oak Park. I was dealing at the same time and there were always people coming and going, some buying larger quantities than others. I would sell a small bag of heroin, or what we called a "spoon," because it was enough dope to fill a plastic spoon. We all knew that a McDonald's plastic spoon held a nickel bag of dope. Many times Sean would be sitting in the living room playing with his toys while I brought people into my bedroom, Dope Central, and filled their orders. He heard us talking about spoons all the time.

When I put Sean to bed at night, we had a little ritual that would help him settle down, and it always ended with me saying, "I'll love you forever, Sean, no matter what," and he would say it back to me. One night, my sweet five-year-old said, "I'll love you forever, Mommy, no matter what." Then he grabbed my shirt as I leaned in to kiss him good-night and in the most desperate little voice said, "Mommy, please no more spoons." I was shocked and my eyes filled with tears as I held him close, but I told him there was nothing to worry about. Mommy was just fine. On some level, I knew that my life was a reckless tornado of risk and self-destruction, but I believed I could stay above it all and would always protect Sean. I trusted that Grandma or my mother would be there to take him away from my world whenever I needed them. Sean would spend most of his childhood in their care.

Sometimes I left my own apartment just to get away from all the crazy junkies crashing there. I would transform into a punk queen, taking my spot in the go-go cage at Exit, so high on heroin and pills I have no idea how I even managed to stand up, let alone dance. I tore my fishnets for just the right effect, put safety pins in my ears, spiked my hair, wore the sheerest tops with no bra, never caring or even noticing if the top fell open, moving with the angry rhythm and screaming sexuality of Iggy Pop or the Clash or the Ramones while the crowded club pulsated along with me. It was complete abandonment and nobody could even talk to me I was so far gone. I danced until the club closed in the early hours of the morning, and then I would stop at the gang safe house to take care of some business and party a little with my friends. I stuck out like a neon sign in their hood, but they loved it. Then I would go back to my pad and rejoin the nonstop party, starting the cycle all over again. When we had to, Mark and I got our shit somewhat together and hit the road or took a flight to work the ticket scam.

Throughout all this, my father was paying my rent and living expenses, with no idea that I was making thousands of dollars a week and shooting it up my arm. But he wasn't stupid. He saw the nice clothes I was buying for Sean and all the things I bought for myself, and he knew I was running something. He asked me every so often where the hell I was getting the money, but he really didn't press it too much. I think part of him wanted to figure it out and part of him didn't want to know. At one point I even worked a few shifts as a cocktail waitress at an Italian restaurant owned by one of his friends just to keep his suspicion at bay. I waited on the mob guys who frequented the place. It was easy, fast cash; they overtipped me because they knew I was Pete's daughter. That kept my father quiet for a while. Every scam was cranking on every front, and I was a whirlwind of dysfunction that kept defying the odds. I was dancing on the edge of chaos every day, and it was exactly where I wanted to be.

During the same time, I followed all the big rock bands and had backstage passes to their concerts. Crickie's godfather was a big concert promoter in Chicago and, as my sister would say, I stole him from her because I got close to him so I could take advantage of his music connections. He got me VIP passes to any concert I wanted, anywhere in the country. I would time my airline ticket exchanges in other cities to catch a band I wanted to see. I was a regular backstage at Chicago's premier venues: the Aragon Ballroom, the Riviera, the Park West, Chicago Stadium, or the Rosemont Horizon, hanging out with the Who, Aerosmith, Billy Idol, the Psychedelic Furs, the Pretenders, the Rolling Stones, U2, and so many more, partying in their hotel rooms all night, sleeping with whichever one of them wanted me, doing their drugs, and having the time of my life.

One of those crazy times may have helped save me from some of the ravages of heroin abuse, like contracting HIV and getting AIDS. It was the night I met and partied with Iggy Pop. He was playing at the Park West, and naturally I had a backstage pass. I was thrilled to be so close to a guy who was best friends with David Bowie, the greatest rock star in the world at the time. I adored Iggy and his newest album *Party*, and especially the song "Pumpin' for Jill." That song drove me insane. I followed Iggy and the band into their limo after the show and went to their hotel suite. I sat on a couch, realized I had a bad headache, and started rubbing my temples. Iggy asked me what was wrong, and I told him. He said he was really good at getting rid of headaches, so he gave me a neck rub as I sat there almost out of my mind with excitement.

He really did make me feel better. I said, "Thanks, Iggy," and he said, "No, call me Jim." We never slept together but we had a great time talking. I secretly wanted to keep calling him Iggy.

It was 1981 and he was a notorious heroin addict. This tour was his big comeback after David Bowie had gotten him into rehab and helped him salvage his career. So there in the hotel suite, partying with the band, I did not want to do any drugs in front of him. I kept going into the bathroom to snort heroin, and I was sharing with the other band members, until finally Iggy followed me into the bathroom.

"What are you doing?" he asked. "I want some."

I hesitated and said, "Um, I'm snorting coke."

"That's what you're doing?"

"Well, and heroin," I confessed.

"Give me the heroin," he said.

"Didn't you stop getting high? I don't want to be the person who gets you fucked up again."

"Yeah, I went to rehab. My friend David sent me to Mexico."

"Bowie?" my completely starstruck self forgot about my concern for Iggy relapsing.

"Well, yeah," he said sarcastically. Like, who did I think he was talking about? "I'm fine," he reassured me and honestly, I would have done anything he asked.

I had a vial of heroin because even though I shot up most of the time, I did not do that when I was in groupie mode and partying with a band. It just wasn't cool. I handed him the bottle and started to hand him the straw, but he just took the bottle and gave me a weird look.

"Don't you want the straw or, here, I have a spoon?" I was confused.

"No, no, no. I'm cool. I don't need a straw," and with that he made a fist, poured some powdered heroin from the bottle onto his thumb, and quickly snorted it from there.

"Wait, wait, what did you just do?" I had never seen anyone do that and I was shocked.

"I snorted some dope," he said with a little grin on his face.

"You just poured it there?" I still couldn't believe how simple it was.

He did it again, looked up at me, and said, "My friend Keith showed me how to do that."

"Richards?" I said, my jaw dropping.

"Yeah," he said so nonchalantly that I was embarrassed to have asked. But I was so excited I could barely manage to stay cool. I decided right then and there that I was going to snort heroin like Keith and Iggy did, and from that day on, I never used a straw or a spoon again and only used a needle when I was shooting a speedball. I owe a debt of gratitude to Iggy for teaching me how to snort heroin so easily and possibly avoiding the deadly fallout from used or dirty needles that has claimed so many addicts' lives.

Every night was an adventure for me in the early 1980s. These were the highest of my high times, but they would soon come crashing to an end. The first time Mark and I realized that the FBI was onto us we were in the Denver airport, asking for a second reissue, one that would get rid of the "OFOP—Check" designation. But the ticket agent was diligent and insisted she wasn't authorized to make the exchange. Suddenly, we were up against someone who was actually doing her job. I tried arguing with her, explaining that I had paid for the ticket with a check and the check had cleared, but she was having none of it. I had to assume she was red-flagging me on the computer, so I walked out. Mark was happy to just let it go. "We have a million tickets to exchange," he said. "Just leave it."

But I could not drop it. I was too stubborn. Mark and I got back into the rental car. "I want you to drive around Denver and let's look for an old-school pharmacy."

"Why?" poor Mark made the mistake of asking.

"Just shut up and do it," I yelled at him. "You'll see." I was laser focused on getting that cash now; nobody was going to say no to me. Sean was in the backseat, asleep and, thankfully, oblivious.

We drove around for a while until I spotted the right place, a mom-and-pop five-and-dime store. I knew they would have what I wanted. I found the Maybelline makeup display, and sure enough they had the classic pale pea-green eye shadow that was no longer the hippest shade, but I knew it was still a staple with some older women. From the moment I saw the paper airline tickets, that green background had reminded me of this eye shadow. I knew that if I tried to alter the airline ticket by erasing the word, "Check," I would also erase the green background. Now I had what I needed to doctor the ticket without a trace. Back in the car, I easily erased "Check," took out the green eye shadow, ran my finger over it and colored in the white spot that was left, blending it in so it was just right. I made Mark drive around until we found a public library. He and Sean waited in the car while I went in, found the room where they let you use a typewriter, and simply typed "Cash" over the green eye shadow. It was perfect. We were going to get our $4,000.

"You're on your own with this one," Mark said when I got back into the car. "Don't worry, I'll take care of Sean when the FBI locks you up."

"We'll see," was all I said as I waited for the typewriter ink to dry.

We couldn't go right back to the airlines and had to make sure that when we did, there would be a different ticket agent on duty. To kill time, we went to visit my late husband's family so his sister and step-mother could see Sean. After Scott died, I had stayed in touch enough to know where his family lived. I was planning to stop by briefly anyway, because I had used their address to have some preordered tickets delivered there so I could keep up with the exchanges while on the road, something I did with friends all over the country. Scott's sister had the package for me when we arrived at her house. We dropped in, stayed the night, and had a nice visit. They were really happy to see us, especially Sean. The next morning, we went to the airport with my newly doctored ticket from the day before. There was a new agent behind the desk. I gave her the ticket and as I hoped, she put it into the magic plastic tube. *Whoosh.* Soon the cash appeared. I tried not to be too smug with Mark, but I had stumbled upon a new and even faster way to turn tickets around. We left for Tucson and I settled into the front seat of the car, took a handful of pills, and felt like I was on top of the world.

When we got to MJ's I called Scott's sister to let her know, as promised, that we had made it and all was well. That's when she told me in an alarmed voice that the FBI had been to her house looking for me. She didn't know anything—so she couldn't tell them anything—but now I knew they were chasing us. An eight-month-long cat-and-mouse game began. The FBI didn't have much on me because I was constantly changing the spelling of my name, using fake names and addresses on driver's licenses and doing most of this unchecked. But they managed to get closer and closer, until one day they showed up at my father's apartment.

I had used his address for a FedEx ticket delivery, and when I went to pick up Sean after another road trip, he told me I had a package waiting there.

"Oh, thanks, Daddy, I'll take it," I said.

"It's from Piedmont Airlines," he said, suspicion in his voice. "What the fuck is the airline sending you?"

"Daddy, what is wrong with you?" I answered, my voice dripping with innocence. "I'm going to Florida—look," I shoved the tickets under his nose. "I'm going to see Crickie, remember?"

"This is some bullshit, I just know it." He was smarter than I ever gave him credit for.

"Oh, Daddy, you always think that. I saved up all my tips from the restaurant, and I'm going to see my sister!"

"If I hear any bullshit from this I swear to God I'm gonna break your fuckin' legs!"

*Yeah, yeah,* I thought to myself, *the standard threat.* I knew he didn't mean anything and I was confident that he would never find out about the ticket scam. Even if he did, he would get past all his usual bluster and bail me out as always.

Soon, his suspicions were confirmed. He was asleep at the time, since he got home in the morning after being out all night, dealing drugs, and hanging with his guys, and he slept most of the day. As kids, Grandma and Pat would often shush us because he was such a light sleeper. "Be quiet and let the poor man sleep, he's been working all night," they would say. This day it was the same routine. There was a knock on the door, and of course, Pat, ever polite and innocent, opened the door. Two men stood there and flashed their FBI badges.

"Is this the Bianco residence?"

"Yes, it is." Pat would never think of lying or asking who they were, or why they wanted to know. "Come in."

"We're with the Federal Bureau of Investigation. We're looking for an Angalia."

"Oh, yeah, that's my stepdaughter." Pat had no idea what was going on. Sean sat on the floor playing with his toy cars.

"Is she here?"

"Oh, no, sorry. She's out. Is everything OK? Did something happen to her?" Pat started to get worried.

"We just want to ask her a few questions."

"Oh, sure. Have a seat. Can I get you guys a cup of coffee?" Pat was ever the perfect hostess, even for the FBI. The two agents took a seat at my father's kitchen table and started asking Pat questions.

"Do you know her date of birth?"

"Sure. August 12, 1958."

"How about her social security number?"

"Oh, I have no idea, but maybe I can find something that has it. Do you want me to look?"

"That would be great, and do you have a picture of her?"

"Oh, sure, we have lots of pictures of the whole family. Let me get the coffee started, and I'll go look."

She did just that, and when she went into the bedroom and opened the closet door, she woke my father up. He walked into the kitchen and said, "What's goin' on here?"

"Oh, it's OK, Pete. They just want a picture of Ang," Pat said, still holding a few photos in her hand.

The FBI agents were still being polite and apologized for disturbing my father, but told him they were investigating some illegal activity.

"Do you have a warrant?" my father asked, wide awake now.

"No, sir, we don't. This is just informal, we're asking some questions, and we need a picture."

"Get up!" my father yelled at the two agents sitting there, waiting for their coffee. "Pat, put the fuckin' pictures down. You two get the fuck outta my house and don't come back without a motherfuckin' warrant!"

"Sir, we're the FBI . . ."

"I don't give a fuck who you are! Get off my property."

"We're looking for your daughter, and we're going to find her."

"Good," my father said, and pointed to Sean. "You know what, you see that baby right there? That's her baby. When you find that fuckin' whore, you tell her to come and get her baby. I haven't seen her in days, and I got her baby, so tell her to come and get her fuckin' baby!"

He knew exactly where I was. As soon as they left, he called me and gave me hell over the phone. "I knew there was some bullshit with those tickets. I knew you were doin' something. I knew it!"

"Daddy, it's going to be OK," I told him as if there was absolutely nothing to worry about. But I knew I had just dodged a bullet. I had to stop the ticket scam immediately. I called Mark, and we agreed things were too hot. We never cracked another ticket exchange, and neither of us ever did time for that scam. But the FBI continued to follow me for a very long time. What I learned from their visit to my father was that, up until that day, they didn't know exactly who I was. I had managed to change my name just enough to keep them guessing. They would follow the ticket trail whenever I had tickets mailed somewhere, including to my father's apartment, and interrogate my friends at that address, but they didn't know what I looked like, and they couldn't get enough to find me and charge me. A name like mine would show up in a forgery case or a name I had used before would be part of a fake prescription report, but they could never pin me down enough to actually follow my movements because they didn't know what I looked like, where I lived, or who I really was.

Over the next three years, I knew the FBI was out there, looking for something on me, but I never worried about it, and other than stopping the ticket scam, I didn't change my activities. In fact, I took it as a challenge. I still thought I had the kind of luck that could not fail me. What else would explain my father waking up just in time to stop Pat from giving them my picture that day? My father made sure that I stayed out of jail just as he had since I was a teenager. I thought of going to court as an occupational hazard, nothing more than a brief interruption to my busy schedule. I lived in a nonstop cycle of getting arrested, getting bonded out, securing a continuance on my case, getting probation, getting arrested again, and the cycle continued. It never slowed me down.

But the incident with the FBI had rattled my father, and once again Pat tried to intervene. In what would turn out to be a last-ditch effort, she convinced him to get me into a twenty-eight-day detox program attached to MacNeal Hospital in Berwyn, a suburb next to Chicago. My father told me if I didn't go, he would get custody of Sean and cut me off completely.

I had so many hustles of my own going—selling drugs, writing bad checks, and embezzling from stolen bank accounts—that I wasn't worried about the money, but I did not want to be cut off from my son, so I agreed. I loved Sean more than anything in the world. I never dreamed that heroin could take my baby from me. Confident that I could work around any rules this clueless place might have, I started making plans that would guarantee my utmost comfort and access to whatever I would need while in the program. I insisted that my father get me a single room, knowing that a roommate would make it impossible to do things my way. I checked in and had to undergo three days of monitored detox on the hospital side. I was about as miserable as I could be. But I had been dope sick before, and I knew I could make it.

After three days, I was moved into my private room, and I immediately called my dealer. Once a patient was admitted, there were no daily drug screenings like there are in most rehab programs now. Apparently, back then this fledgling industry was not yet wise to the ways of most addicts; facilities even allowed visitors to sit with you, unsupervised, in your room. My dealer came the next day with a dozen roses, wearing a nice suit. I shot up in my room, and we had sex in my bathroom. He came to visit every day, always with roses and another bag of heroin. I had no trouble doing the twenty-eight days like that, and even though I was getting high the whole time I was away from the daily madness that my life had become. I was sleeping at night, eating well enough to gain fifteen pounds, and I came out looking healthier than I had in months, so my family was convinced that I had turned the corner. But I went right back to my dangerous, out-of-control life. Sean continued to get bounced between my grandma and Pat. Even in my drug-induced haze, I knew they would take much better care of him than I could, so as far as I was concerned everything was right with the world.

With the ticket cash flow coming to an abrupt halt, though, I had to step up my other activities. I kept writing fake prescriptions and forging stolen checks, and I started opening checking accounts in every bank around the Chicago area, writing bad checks until I got a notice of an overdraft. That was like free money to me because back then you only needed five dollars to open an account, and it took more than a week for the bank to realize that I was passing bad checks. Many of these crimes were much easier back in the days before massive computer databases and photos on every type of ID. I went through banks like blind dates, moving on as soon as the relationship stopped working.

I kept dealing drugs with the gang, confident that, without a picture of me, the FBI could not physically follow me. Then I stumbled onto a new hustle with a gang brother. Bobby was in jail a lot. He was a big guy and was always getting arrested on gun charges. One day at Grandma's I got a collect phone call from jail. It was Bobby asking if I could go pick up some coke and weed and bring it to the jail. I didn't hesitate: "Sure, tell me where." He told me where to pick up the package and to meet a correctional officer who was working with the gang. The connection who gave me the drugs also gave me some cash for the CO, Javier.* Javier would take the cash for himself and bring the drugs into jail when he went to work. I immediately saw many advantages to this hustle. Cash was changing hands; that always meant there was an angle to pursue. And there was a personal angle, too. The husband of my youngest sister, Dina, my mother's daughter with another husband, was in the same jail as Bobby, in the same division, and needed protec-

---

* For the sake of privacy, his name has been changed.

tion, so I told her to come along with me and we could ask Bobby, who was a gang chief, to watch out for her husband.

Javier flirted with me from the moment I met him. I gave him the money, he took the package, and it went off perfectly. Bobby called me the next day asking me to keep it up. Back then, the correctional system was full of holes. Inmates inside always had a lot of cash. Bobby sold the drugs inside, put cash in an envelope that he was allowed to seal, and sent it to me like a regular letter. (Inmates today are not allowed to seal anything that is mailed from inside prison before it is searched.) Bobby was sending me a cut, but I would not keep it because I wanted to stay in good standing with him and the gang. Instead, I went to the currency exchange, got a money order, and mailed it back to Bobby, so he could put it on his books, knowing that would reflect well on me. We had a good thing going on, but after about the third time I realized that since it was coke and weed we were dealing, I could get it for free from my father, make more money for Bobby, and keep some for myself. As always, I figured out how to twist things to my advantage.

Javier's persistent flirtation turned into an afternoon together at a sleazy hotel on Cermak Road, right down the street from the jail. He was still married, so we began an affair. I wasn't in love with him, but I thought he was a good bet because he had a steady job and was a crooked cop. He decided he didn't want me to be involved in smuggling drugs anymore, so I stopped. Bobby sent me a letter from prison telling me to get away from Javier, that he was bad news, but I didn't listen. I should have. I found out that Javier had the same hustle going with many inmates, was ripping them off, and was snorting coke all the time when I thought he was just a drinker. But when his wife finally left him and took their two kids with her, he asked me to move in with him, which I did. I told him from the beginning that I was fighting several pending cases and that one of them could send me to jail at some point, although I didn't really believe it. He didn't care. I lived in his three-bedroom apartment, continued to snort heroin or shoot speedballs every day, and kept up with all my hustles. I settled right in, partying at night while he was at work, getting high with my friends in my new place, and hanging out with him when he was home. But this little domestic scene was short lived. After so many years of cheating the devil with hustles that never should have worked, my long overdue serious day in court was finally coming. One of those pending cases was actually going to stick.

Javier drove me to my sentencing hearing. I had been to so many court proceedings just like it, but for the first time in my life, I was scared. My lawyer told me that the state's attorney was talking some serious time, three to four years, and we were running out of options. Before that morning in court, I started making plans to leave the country and told my father what I was going to do.

"Daddy, I will ride this baby to the end, but I am not doing that kind of time. No way! Before they sentence me, you're going to give me money and smuggle me into Mexico," I screamed at him. To me, four years was a life sentence. "Then, I'm going to get a new passport in Mexico and smuggle myself to South America. I have to leave the country!"

"Listen," he said calmly. "You're in trouble for writing some prescriptions and bad checks. It is not the end of the world. Why would you go through all that and ruin your life forever? You will never be able to come back, and you really will never see us again."

I tried appealing to my grandma, thinking she would be heartbroken that her baby would be in jail. "I'll never see you and Sean," I sobbed. "I can't imagine making you come all that way to see me at the penitentiary. Oh my God, Grandma, what am I going to do?"

"Whaddaya cryin' about?" Grandma almost laughed. "You're not the first one in our family to go to the penitentiary. I've been to Joliet to see Uncle Tony, I've been to the county jail, you name it. I don't care where I have to go. That's your family! You can handle it."

So I decided I could do it, but there was no way I was doing it straight. On the way to court, I told Javier to take me to the gang brothers. I bought several bags of heroin, and then we stopped at a friend's house to shoot up. I drank two bottles of methadone, about 180 milligrams, that morning, too. It was a hedge against the withdrawal I knew awaited me and the dope sickness that would take over once I was locked up. Having been on methadone before, I knew it would help. I got so high I could barely keep my eyes open in court. I honestly don't know how I didn't overdose that day. When we got to court, my mother was there, Pat was there, my father and Grandma and Aunt Louise were all there. They kept telling me I was so brave and that it would be all right, just hang in there. Instead of being ashamed of me, they actually seemed proud that I was facing the music head-on. Ironically, the one and only time my father had refused to bond me out on one of the charges I was facing that day turned out to be the final straw for the state's attorney. Pat had convinced my father to stop bailing me out, insisting that I would never learn and never change as long as he kept saving me. My poor father never thought I would end up in the penitentiary because of the one time he decided to get tough. Pat told me later that the first week I was sent away, waiting in Cook County Jail to be shipped out to Dwight Correctional Center, my father spent every day lying on the couch, drinking heavily, and beating himself up with guilt. But I never blamed him for anything. I was too smart for that.

I floated into the courtroom, holding on to Javier's arm, so high that even if I wanted to freak out, I couldn't have. I struggled to hold my head up as I sat in front of Judge Himel, a judge I had seen before. I liked him, and he seemed to like me, but this time there was only so much he could do. My lawyer told me I was fucked, so I should throw myself on the mercy of the court and just hope for the best. And that's what I did. But it wasn't enough for the state's attorney. He started listing my aliases, hoping to anger Judge Himel even further and push for a stronger sentence.

"Your Honor," I cried, "I've been married. Those are legitimate names. This is not fair."

Judge Himel decided to wax poetic and shut the state down. "What's in a name, gentlemen? A rose by any other name is still a rose."

I smiled and felt as if I had won him over, but then he said, "However, I am fully aware of your problem with Piedmont Airlines, Angalia. I have been contacted by the FBI, and they have agreed that as long as you get at least four years, they are willing to back off."

I would learn later that the FBI still didn't have enough on me to get me into federal prison. If they had, they would have let me do my state time and then stepped in to put me away at the federal level, but they didn't have a strong case, so they had to settle for what Judge Himel could and had to do. The judge explained to me that the law had changed, and if you are out on bond on a felony and you commit another felony, which I had done several times over, upon conviction, those sentences had to be served consecutively, not concurrently. The three forgery counts carried two years each.

"My heart goes out to you, Angalia," Judge Himel was completely sincere. "This is too much for your first time. I believe that if I could let you go right now, you would leave here and never commit another crime. But my hands are tied. In addition to the four years you've already received from the previous court's decision, I sentence you to two more years, running consecutive to those sentences for a total of six years in Dwight Penitentiary." Throughout all this I could hear my grandma's outbursts of "Mamma mia!" I couldn't turn around and see, but I knew she was looking up to heaven and holding her hand over her heart. I heard my mother say, "She's so brave! I'm so proud of her for turning herself in." My mother told me later that my father had to get up and leave the courtroom because he couldn't take it. He came back just in time to hear my sentence.

When Judge Himel's gavel hit the bench, it echoed like the closing of a trapdoor. I was horrified. My heart and my mind went into a free fall. I could hear my mother and Grandma wailing "Oh my God!" as they put me in handcuffs and led me away. I looked back at my family, saw the pain on my father's face, and realized he was powerless this time. The devil was at my heels, and my life had just taken a very bad turn.

# 6

# In and Out and In and Out

THE INTAKE PROCESS AT COOK COUNTY JAIL was a drug-hazed night-mare. I was held there until being shipped to Dwight Penitentiary. The conditions at Cook County were horrible, a shocking process designed to systematically break your spirit and teach you how to submit. And it worked.

Intake started at receiving, a large cage called the bull pen placed in the middle of a configuration of correction officers' desks. A big cardboard handwritten sign was taped to one of the desks: THIS IS NOT BURGER KING AND YOU WILL NOT HAVE IT YOUR WAY. Women who had just left court were held in the bull pen, some in street clothes and some in prison uniforms. At any given time there could be a hundred women squeezed into that cage waiting to be processed and then moved upstairs to the cell tiers. From the moment I entered the bull pen, I struggled to keep my wits. I was wearing my favorite black designer jeans and a powder-blue sweater I had bought on a shopping spree with my sister at Saks Fifth Avenue. As always, I was wearing several valuable rings given to me by my father, including a ruby and an emerald. One of the women, wearing a county inmate's uniform, could see that I was green and had never been past intake before. Since I always bonded out, I had never gotten beyond the holding area. I had no idea what I was in for upstairs. She tried to talk me out of my rings right there in the cage.

"Hey, you know they're not going to let you bring your jewelry up there, right? If you give it to me, I'll be able to sneak it in for you. Then I can give it to you when I see you upstairs." She had already been strip-searched and had just come from a day in court. But she had no idea who she was trying to scam. Even in my highest state, no one could ever put one over on me.

"Um, yeah . . . no," I said, thinking, *Who the fuck does she think I am?* I knew I looked innocent. I was still in my twenties, and that look had served me well, helping many times to convince a mark that I was telling the truth; now it was working against me. But I "knew game" on the streets and, like radar, it kicked in here.

"I'm giving my jewelry to the officers so they can put it in with my property, and my father will come pick it up for me. But, thanks!"

The intake process for division three at Cook County took all night. It started with a strip search, the most humiliating experience I had ever been through. Women in prison uniforms were taken out of the cage and sent back up to their cells. The rest of us were ordered to remove all our clothes while the female officers stood by. Any male officers walking past could also see us. If I hadn't still been so high, I might have really lost it and ended up in an even worse situation, like the psych holding area, a special hell I had only heard about.

Once we were all naked, we were lined up very close to one another. The guards shouted at us to raise our arms, turn around, squat, bend over, and spread our ass cheeks. The body of the person in front of me was inches from my face, so while I found myself in this degrading position, if I raised my eyes from the floor I would be staring into the completely revealed anatomy of the woman in front of me. The guards walked in between us, aiming flashlights at our exposed innards, checking for any contraband that might be stashed there. Some women tried to protest, crying that they were bleeding, having their periods, but there were no exceptions. We were so crammed in that the smell was unbearable. Some women had come directly from the city lockup after days of waiting for their court appearances and had not been given an opportunity to bathe. At one point I glanced up and saw a male officer stop and give us a quick ogle before he moved through the room. I tried to stifle tears of anger and shame but managed to stay calm, thanks to the dope still in my system. It was the longest five minutes of my life.

(The practice of group searches has since been halted at Cook County owing to a class action lawsuit settled more than fifteen years later, one that I was part of. I collected a $2,400 settlement while I was still in prison, as did thousands of other women. Strip searches at Cook County are now done in partitioned private cubicles with only female officers present.)

Once the strip search was over, we were led out of the bull pen, and forced to shower, a precaution against new inmates bringing in lice, or any other extra baggage. This is no longer done at Cook County because there are simply too many prisoners, and it would take too much time and cost the taxpayers too much. But back then it was standard procedure. I did not want to wash because I had sprayed my favorite Opium perfume all over my body and in my hair, hoping to block out the odors I knew would assault me in jail. But there I stood naked, shivering in the lukewarm water, with a guard watching me. She started barking orders at me.

"Get your hair wet." When I hesitated, she said, "Bitch, if you don't get it wet, we'll do it for you! Open your hand!"

She poured a small amount of unidentified liquid into my hand and told me to wash my hair. I was appalled. I had really long hair that I was proud to toss around and I used only the best products money could buy.

"Wait, what is this?" I asked. "I can't use that. My hair will be too tangled."

"It's for bugs!" she hollered.

"What? I don't have bugs!" Disgusted, I realized I had no choice as she forced me to dump the foreign substance on my head. There was no conditioner.

When I stepped out of the shower, they let me put my street clothes back on and moved me upstairs to a small dayroom. Then they assigned us each to a cell located down a long hallway with cell doors on either side. Once inside my cell, I was given a prison uniform to change into. I had to hang up my clothes and leave them on the door hooks, where they remained until I was shipped to Dwight, at which point all my personal belongings would be collected and put into a property bag for my family to retrieve. I found out from my cellie that Cook County had a place in the basement that everybody called Marshall Field's, a big closet full of clothes that other inmates had never retrieved on their way out. Inmates who were being released back to the street and didn't have the right clothes for the weather were allowed to go down there and pick something out.

The uniform was the foulest color I'd ever seen, a gold color I came to really despise. It reminded me of the gold jacket I had to wear when I worked as a runner at the Options Exchange when I was sixteen. I could barely comprehend where my life had taken me since. If I could, I would gladly trade this jumpsuit for that jacket right now. I had wet tangled hair, was wearing ugly uncomfortable clothing, and was shivering and locked inside a tiny room with a roommate I had never met, feeling completely alone. I wanted to cry, but all I could do was murmur, "What the fuck." Like most jail cells, the cold steel toilet was at the edge of the beds, which reminded me of the army bunks I'd seen in the movies. Because my father always got me out quickly, I'd never been stuck in a cell long enough for it to matter, but I was about to discover that taking a shit in front of your cellmate was one of the worst moments every day in prison; you never get used to it.

My roommate was not new to Cook County. She had been in this cell for a while, and was ready to give me the standard treatment for newbies. Everyone wants the bottom bunk, no matter what prison you find yourself in. But there was no way I was getting the bottom bunk right now. Whenever an inmate was on her own in a cell for a while, it was common practice to toss the top mattress on the floor and turn the top bunk into a mantle for things like family pictures and homemade cards from kids, arranged just so. I showed up late at night, after everyone had been locked into their cells, and my roommate was certainly not going to clear that space for me. I spotted the mattress on the floor and was relieved that I would be sleeping there. I was scared of the top bunk because I am such a restless sleeper and a clumsy person in general. I worried that if I managed to fall asleep, I might fall out. So sleeping on the floor wasn't a problem for me, but for many first-timers the bunk battle becomes their first power struggle with another inmate.

I threw down the small sheet and short itchy wool blanket given to me downstairs and tried to at least cover the mattress and myself. My roommate turned off the light. The window was covered in thick black screens and bars that let hardly any light in, barely a touch of sunlight during the day, and if no moon was shining at night, complete blackness. It was December 1987. The cell was freezing. I shivered in the dark, feeling trapped, but thankful for the massive amounts of heroin and methadone I had consumed earlier that morning. The drugs helped me finally fall asleep.

The glare of a flashlight shining in my eyes woke me. It was still pitch dark in the cell, and I was extremely disoriented. Sleeping on the floor, my head was right next to the toilet. A lieutenant was shaking me, kneeling down next to me with a female officer standing beside him with another flashlight. My roommate woke up equally disoriented. "What the hell?" she said.

"Are you Angalia Bianca?" the lieutenant asked.

"Yes," I mumbled, as my mind raced, thinking that my father must have pulled some kind of miracle and I was getting out; this nightmare was about to end.

"Your mother called," the lieutenant said, his voice oozing contempt. "She was very worried because it's so cold out, and she wanted to make sure you were warm, so here, I'm bringing you another blanket and a pillow." Nobody gets a pillow unless they've been in for a much longer time. It took a lot of wheeling and dealing among other inmates to score a pillow, and he was just handing me this one. The next day my roommate was stunned. "Who the fuck *are* you?" she had to know. Over the next five days, she would find out, since I loved to talk and she liked to listen. She even gave up her dayroom privileges to stay in the cell with me and hear my crazy stories.

I could almost feel my father's guilt radiating through the county jail's thick walls as he frantically tried to pull whatever strings he could to get me out. The best he could do was help my mother score me a blanket and pillow. I was grateful, but I still thought this might be just a bad dream, and maybe I was going to wake up back in bed with Javier. Even though I had been arrested plenty of times and spent more than a few nights in jail here and there, I had no idea what I was in for now. I fully expected to be quickly moved out of the hellhole that was county jail to my own private cell at Dwight. The other inmates set me straight pretty quickly. There were so many of us waiting to get shipped to Dwight, and they only moved people once a week, a busload of thirty at a time, so I was at the bottom of a long list. They laughed at me when I said, "Oh, no, I'll be going in a few days." Many women were held for months before being moved out.

I was despondent. Throughout my life, of all the horrible places in which I found myself, Cook County Jail was the hardest to endure. There is no movement anywhere, inside or outside the jail. Inmates are required to sit all day long without any exercise or time outdoors. All the windows are covered with the same dark screens, so you know it's light out but you can't really see daylight or anything outside. In the early morning hours, we had to get up, exit our cells, and then spend the day sitting on stackable hard plastic chairs in the dayroom or stay in our tiny cells. On the outside, I never got up before noon or went to bed before two in the morning, and this new rigid schedule was a shock to my system. The TV stayed on, tuned to the same channel all day long. Time stood still and the inability to move around freely was excruciating. Looking back now, I realize how hyperactive I have been for most of my life, but I always had enough drugs to calm me down and then knock me out. I had never been through this before.

As the drugs began to leave my system, I felt like I was going to jump out of my skin. Even with all the methadone I consumed before my sentencing, I started serious withdrawals on my third day there, with the inevitable stomach pain, vomiting, and the shakes and chills. The methadone was helping to make the withdrawals bearable enough, and having gone through it so many times before, I knew it could have been a lot worse. I learned from the other inmates that there was a secret distribution system within the walls of Cook County that helped women get over-the-counter drugs for minor ailments, like headaches, sinus congestion, and menstrual cramps. Inmates who were in tight with the nurses could score extra meds without having to stand in long lines or wait for the med cart that came late at night. I stood in line my first time and got a cold pill and a shot glass full of what they called routine A, something that was like NyQuil. It was used to alleviate heroin withdrawals, but it was not nearly enough to help me. Once I understood how things worked, I managed to trade that and get something stronger that I could snort right away. A lot of amateur prescribing went on, as we all did what we could to self-medicate and ease whatever pain we were in, hoarding pills and secretly trading them like kids with baseball cards. If you said, "I'm dope sick," the health worker would shove the routine A at you, and you could only qualify for methadone if you had already been on a program on the street, an angle that I had covered when I knew I was going in. (That is not the case anymore. Sympathy for dope addicts no longer exists in jail, and it is very hard to get relief.) They let me stay on methadone, but they immediately started escalating my detox by lowering the dose. By the time I got to Dwight, methadone wasn't allowed, so I went further into withdrawal.

Unable to accept what was happening to me, I called Pat every day, crying into the phone, "Tell Daddy to call the lawyer! I gotta get out of here, this is so horrible! You gotta help me."

In my worst moments of despair, the other inmates would try to console me with visions of Dwight and how much better it would be there. Some of those women didn't have out dates and had no idea when they were getting moved. They had to be looking at me with some envy, knowing that conditions at the penitentiary were much better. I'm grateful to them for trying to make me feel better. But they were quick to add that it would be a long time before I was shipped. That's just the way it was.

They were wrong. My father pulled whatever strings he had left, and I was shipped to Dwight on the next bus out, a Wednesday morning less than a week after I entered Cook County. My cellie was amazed and disappointed that I was leaving so soon. We had bonded, and I knew she would feel lonely without me. I tried to be strong and prepare for what was coming next as I took stock of my situation, but even this little piece of good news was not enough; I sank into despair. I was a twenty-nine-year-old heroin addict who had taken barbiturates and quaaludes like daily vitamins since I was in my teens, and I had done cocaine, LSD, and MDA hundreds of times. I had been a prostitute and a member of an Arizona biker gang, a member of a Chicago street gang, and a drug dealer. I had ridden in limousines and stayed in the best hotels. I was an accomplished thief and con artist, had beaten or outrun every charge ever made against me, gamed every system I came up against, and loved every minute of it. I had never been locked up for more than a day or two, and now I was petrified. I missed my family, especially Grandma and Sean, wondering when I would see them again. I felt something new and dark, an overwhelming guilt and sadness for what I had done to my beautiful boy. Sitting in that tiny cell, I remembered how I cried for my mother as a kid, when she left me, and realized that now Sean would do the same, and I couldn't do anything to take away that pain or comfort him. Feeling powerless made me more hyper than ever. Throughout my criminal career, I had complete confidence that I would never end up here. Now I was about to board a bus to spend the next six years of my life locked up and alone.

The day I was shipped to Dwight began at four in the morning. I was so anxious all night, barely sleeping, worried that I might not be on that bus. Inmates were not told anything ahead of time. We just knew that it was a shipment day, and we all hoped that our names would be called. From what I had been hearing, I doubted that my name would be on the list, but I could not handle this wretched place for another day, much less another month. I had to get out or I was going to lose it and things would get much worse. When the guards came to my cell door, I was asleep.

"Let's go, get your shit," a guard yelled at me, shining a flashlight in my face. "You're goin' on shipment. Move it!"

"Bianca, wake up, you're goin' on shipment, oh my God, I can't believe it! Wake up, girl!" My cellie was shouting.

"Um, uh, OK," I mumbled as I sat up and tried to wrap my head around what was happening. I was disoriented and became frantic. "What do I do? Where should I put my sheets? What about my blanket and pillow?"

"No, no, don't worry about that shit," my cellie said. "Just grab everything you want and stick it in your pillowcase. Hurry up!" I did what she said and left the new pillow behind for her.

The guards had thrown an ugly green jumpsuit on the floor. I could not believe I had to wear it, but my cellie told me to hurry up and put it on. It was three sizes too big and, with my hands shaking, I fumbled to zip it up and roll up the pant legs so I could walk. At the same time, inmates from other cells who had roomies shipping out started coming out into the hallway, ready to scavenge the stuff we left behind, anything new to ease the ordeal of a long stay at Cook County. I would be guilty of the same thing later in my prison career, coming to know all too well the desperation an inmate feels for a distraction from the monotony of being locked up for weeks on end. They all started shouting at me, asking for my stuff, especially the designer jeans and favorite powder-blue sweater I'd worn to court. My street clothes still smelled of the extra perfume I'd doused myself with before my sentencing, and I hated to part with this last bit of comfort.

"No, no! My family will come and pick this up. Can they do that?" I shouted at the guard.

"Yes, put the stuff in this bag and write your name on it. And calm the fuck down." The guards just wanted to get me moving.

I was pushed out into the hall and moved to a holding pen. The guards wanted to move everybody who was shipping out before their daily count on the tier to avoid confusion, so they hustled us out of our cells only to have us linger for hours in the bull pen before the bus arrived. There, I recognized a few women I knew in passing from the street, a couple I'd seen copping drugs, and a hooker I had known from the West Side, and while we weren't good friends, seeing even vaguely familiar faces helped put me somewhat at ease. I was not completely over withdrawals and really wanted to get moving, but the early morning rush turned into a tedious and uncomfortable hurry-up-and-wait situation. It was four cold, excruciating hours before the bus arrived.

Finally, the officers started the process of getting us on the bus. "Stand up, now!" they barked. "When we call your name, step out and stand here."

Never being good at following rules or standing at attention, I kept trying to lean on the wall nearby. The guards bullied and threatened me until I complied: "Stand up straight or we'll send you back on the tier, and you can wait for another shipment. Maybe you'll be called next month. Or maybe not."

Once we were lined up and ready to go, the guards handcuffed us together. I had to cross my arms in front of my body as they handcuffed me to the woman standing next to me, so the two of us were connected and would now be partners for the duration of the bus ride. Though it was a painful position to be in and the cuffs hurt my wrists, I thought, *If this is it, I can handle a little discomfort.* The guards shoved us outside where the temperature was minus eleven, bad even for Chicago in January, and we shuffled awkwardly toward the bus door. Some women who had been in Cook County for a longer time had managed to score DOC coats, but most of us were clad only in our thin jumpsuits. As I shivered, trying not to fall and pull my partner down with me, I wondered, *How the hell are we going to make it up the steps to our seats on the bus?* It was a white Blue Bird bus, much like a school bus, with windows at seat level so we could see the world going by. We managed to ease ourselves up the steps and into one of the seats. Then the guards appeared with a long chain. They strung the chain through our handcuffs, running it the entire length of the bus, essentially roping all of us together. They locked each end of the chain and did the same on both sides of the bus, so now we were all attached. Not only was there no way to escape, if there were ever an accident and the bus caught on fire, we wouldn't stand a chance. All I could think about was a TV show my mother loved to watch when I was young called *The Fugitive.* I watched it with her. The protagonist was a wrongly accused man on his way to prison on a train. The train gets into an accident, and he manages to escape, becoming a fugitive as he tries to clear his name. I tried to imagine what I would do if this bus crashed. Would I be able to get out? If I became The Fugitive, where would I go and who would help me?

The bus started to move and I struggled to calm myself and clear my mind. It was an hour and a half from Cook County Jail to Dwight Penitentiary. Looking out the window, I almost felt relieved as the bus traveled out of the city and into the countryside. I exhaled and for a brief time, stopped being afraid of what was coming next. The view along the highway gave me a bittersweet, peaceful feeling as we passed wintry scenery that I had never really paid attention to before. Even though central Illinois is as flat as a tabletop, the expansive terrain has a mesmerizing beauty, and at that moment I appreciated the wide-open space, fields that seemed to stretch to infinity. I wanted to be out there, running through the untouched snow, away from what was waiting for me in prison. As the trip dragged on and my arms began to hurt, I started to feel trapped again. I thought about Sean and ached to see him and hold him close. With my head turned toward the window, I cried as quietly as I could.

Pulling into Dwight prison in 1988 was not the same experience it is today. Before construction of the notorious X-House, a concrete fortress named for its menacing appearance from the air and built in the late 1990s to accommodate the exploding women's prison population, Dwight had a more serene, albeit institutional, look. The stately Victorian main building sat at the end of a long driveway and almost hidden behind it were eight "cottages" that housed the female prisoners. I remember thinking it was a quaint way to refer to the place where I would be locked up for six years. The main house was beautiful, a well-kept old building with interesting architectural details that you don't see in modern buildings. I was pleasantly surprised. *OK,* I thought, *maybe I can do this.*

The bus stopped in front of the main building, and the officers told us to stand as they unlocked the chain holding us together. We shuffled through the big oak front door and were ushered down to the basement for intake. By now it was about eleven in the morning, and we were weary. The basement was called the "bureau of identification." There were two desks with officers sitting and typing on computers, pulling up our information and adding to it as they called our names. The old-fashioned ink pad and paper were used to fingerprint us, and these were sent to the state police to double-check for any outstanding warrants. Each inmate was given a dental checkup, blood work, an eye exam, and a TB test. Next, the dreaded strip search. Still an unbearably humiliating experience, it was not nearly as bad as it had been at Cook County. Instead of a roomful of naked women shoved into a holding pen, two of us at a time were taken into a closed room. CO Winters was in charge that day, and she was a princess compared to the guards at Cook County, kind and polite and full of empathy. The search was quick and less invasive and I was grateful to be treated like a human being.

Once the strip search was over, we exchanged our ugly county jump-suits for a new uniform, a crisp buttoned-up short-sleeved white blouse and baggy navy-blue polyester pants, just like the kind I often saw worn by the old women in my neighborhood. (When I was out of prison, if I saw a woman wearing pants like those, I was tempted to tell her that she was wearing prison pants.) We each got three blouses, three pairs of pants, three pairs of socks, three pairs of extra-large panties, what we called Granny panties, and a pair of pajamas. All the clothes were made by inmates in prisons around the state. They were clean, the pants fit me, and it felt good to leave the ugly green jumpsuit behind. We even got a winter coat, taken from a pile of donated coats, the only piece of clothing that was not identical to everyone else's.

After all the intake procedures were finished, about six hours of standing and shuffling around from one area to the next, it was time for us to meet the warden. This was back when women's prisons were not overcrowded, and a little bit of civility still existed inside. We were spoken to like adults with hearts and minds. Today, there are so many inmates to process, clothe, feed, and monitor that the atmosphere is cold and harsh, more like a cattle roundup. Warden Jane Huck came downstairs to introduce herself and I instantly liked her. She gave us a speech about what we could expect and tried to put us at ease, as if to say this did not have to be the end of the world.

"We're here to make sure you stay close to your families and your children and that you find a productive way to use your time." She sounded sincere. But at that moment, my situation was really starting to sink in for me. I began thinking about how I was going to get the fuck out of there. Once I got off that bus, the crushing reality started to take hold, and I wanted out. I promised myself that I would find a way.

We were loaded four at a time onto smaller prison vans. When I got to my cottage, the guards took me in, and there were a few other inmates there to help orient the new arrivals. These were the "house girls." It was their job to help us get settled. Some of the long-timers had street clothes on. Under another rule that has since changed, you were once allowed to wear clothes sent by your family if you were classified as minimum security.

The house girls handed out bundles to get us settled: a nice wool blanket, not scratchy and thin like the one at county, two flat sheets and a pillowcase that smelled clean, an actual pillow, and a very small towel. The bundle also included an array of products in unfamiliar, unbranded packaging: trial-size bottles of shampoo and lotion, a tube of toothpaste, and a bar of green lye soap.

"I've never seen this kind of soap," I complained. The house girl told me that the soap and toothpaste were made in prison, and the shampoo and lotion were bottled there, too. I was appalled at the thought of using this stuff on my hair and skin and made no effort to hide it. She said I could eventually buy my own at the commissary, but not right away. "It's really good for washing your clothes and getting your blouse nice and white, too," she told me. I was repulsed.

I was still wearing my street shoes from court, white Capezio flats that I loved. I hated to let them go, but it was time. I was issued my first pair of what we called "white girls" in prison, white Keds that we were expected to keep clean. The house girls gave me another cleaning tip: lye soap and a little of the state-issued toothpaste was a great way to keep those white girls sparkling. I learned that there were many unexpected uses for the toothpaste, from treating acne, to hanging pictures on the cell wall, to fading heroin track marks on our skin. For a person like me who had never done chores or laundry or anything remotely domestic, I was annoyed that I would now have to keep my own shoes clean. But the biggest surprise was a plastic bag tied closed with six packs of cigarettes in it, half regular and half menthol, and ten packs of matches. The cigarettes, called Pyramids, were also made at the prison. I smoked menthol and quickly learned that I could trade my regulars for another inmate's menthols.

I was now ready to be taken to the tiny room that would be my new home, a small bare cell, just big enough for two inmates. I was assigned a roommate, but she wasn't there yet. I was put inside and left there as the door was shut and locked from the outside. Once again, I was alone. My heart and my mind were racing. The guards and house girls didn't tell me much about what to expect next, but I had been drilling other inmates for information all day. I knew that I had to stay in that room and could not enter the general population until they got medical clearance, the results of the blood work, the pelvic exam, the eye exam, and the dental check. I put my new belongings down and had a look around. The bunk bed was up against the wall, just like the one at county, but had much better mattresses. I sat down on the bottom bunk and bounced a little, listening to the creaking of the springs and thinking how nice it sounded. The room had actual windows, and you could see outside, unlike the perpetual darkness of Cook County. It was cold out, but the room had a radiator that was hissing heat into the tiny space. For the first time in a week, I was warm. I relaxed and realized how bone-tired I was. Along with all the products and cigarettes, I got a brown paper bag with my dinner in it: plastic bottles of juice, real fried chicken wrapped in tinfoil, little Styrofoam cups of fruit, and a real apple with peanut butter. I was so happy to have this food. I never ate at county, partly because I was dope sick and partly because the food there is unrecognizable and I was afraid to put it in my mouth. I didn't realize until that moment just how hungry I was. I devoured the best fried chicken I had ever tasted. I lit a cigarette after my dinner, and for a brief moment the weight of my sentence and the years I was facing lifted from my heart.

After I finished my cigarette, I put it out in the ashtray I had made using the tinfoil and the small milk carton. I made the bed, something I had never done in my life. The sheets were not fitted, and I had no idea how to make corners, so I did the best I could. With the blanket in place and the pillow in the pillowcase, I sat on the bed and felt comfortable, almost exactly as I did when I was in fifth grade and Grandma let me go to Camp Douglas. I put on the cute pink pajamas and almost had myself fooled into thinking this would be OK.

The next morning I opened my eyes and had to remember all over again where I was and what it meant. I was surprised to see that I had a roommate. I was so exhausted that first night and still had enough drugs in my system that I never woke up when she arrived. I lay in my bunk, trying to be quiet, and noticed things I hadn't the night before. The morning sun was streaming in through the windows, which made the cell feel almost cozy. This little room in a country cottage was nothing like the sickly, industrial-yellow cement-brick cells at Cook County. The windows, though barred, had cranks that could turn just enough to open them slightly outward. I stuck my hand in between the bars, opened the window with a loud creak at every turn and let in some crisp, fresh air without waking my cellie. I immediately craved coffee. But I had no idea if or how I was going to get it here. *They gave me cigarettes*, I thought, *so where's my coffee?* The door to the cell was a real door with brass handles, a small square window that allowed you to peer across the hall, and a small opening called the "chuckhole." This was a holdover from the days when Dwight was a men's mental health facility and the attendants would push food through the chuckhole, never opening the door unless they absolutely had to. The officers could open or shut it from the outside. In the early 1960s, before there was a designated prison for women, but as the ranks of female offenders were steadily growing, the state began using some of the cottages at Dwight to incarcerate women who committed serious crimes, and Dwight slowly transformed to a completely female facility. For many years, the quaint charm of the place was kept intact and by the time I got there, while some of that was falling away for practical reasons, it was still nicer than any other place I would be incarcerated. I didn't know it at the time.

On this morning, I stared at the chuckhole from my bunk and tried to will a cup of coffee to appear. My roommate woke up and we rested in our bunks, talking and getting acquainted. We had the usual conversation, complaining about being locked up and sharing a few details about how much time we had to do. But I couldn't hold it in another minute.

"So, do they bring coffee around?"

"What? Bitch, are you crazy?" She laughed out loud.

"You mean these muthafuckers don't bring coffee?" I was truly incredulous.

"Girl, you're in the fuckin' joint. This is intake. You're not gettin' nothing, not even a fuckin' candy bar. Be happy you got cigarettes."

"But I'm dying. I already got a headache."

"Well, if you're lucky the house girls will give you a cup when they're done with their chores. They usually make a pot."

Soon the house girls came around to read a list of our appointments for that day, standing outside the closed door and talking through the chuckhole. I was still in the midst of the intake process, so even though my blood work was done and I'd had the basic physical exam, I had to be scheduled for an evaluation with the prison psychiatrist, and I still had to have a Pap smear. Every new inmate did, so it took all day to get us through the intake process, moving from our cells to the exam rooms in the main building and back again. Without fail, each time a house girl came to the chuckhole to schedule something, I asked if there was any way she could get me a cup of coffee. I didn't realize that, even if she wanted to help me out, she would never say yes to such a blatant request. A house girl is still an inmate and couldn't trust any new prisoner to be cool and not tell on her. I was going about this wrong, but I would learn soon enough. And since I never stopped talking to anyone who would listen, I became friends with most of the house girls and the officers. I think they were somewhat entertained by me, so they eventually decided to trust me.

Even after all the tests and interviews were completed, my status was in limbo until I was completely cleared, a process that took about five days. That meant no mixing with the general population and no indication yet if I would be placed in minimum or maximum security for the duration of my sentence. The routine was supposed to be rigid, with twenty-three hours in our cells, and only one hour allowed out. But during that first week in intake, CO Knight showed us her softer side. When she came on for the second shift, she made an announcement. "OK, girls, we're gonna do rec in an hour. Be ready and I'll come open the doors."

My cellie and I were thrilled. This meant that we were not only getting out of our cell for a second hour that day but going downstairs to the dayroom. I hadn't been down there yet, and I was genuinely excited. To get there, we were led down a grand marble staircase, complete with brass railings, that wound its way to an expansive airy sitting room on the first floor. It was furnished with couches and a coffee table and even had a working fireplace. There were shuttered paned-glass French doors and rollout windows all around, letting in lots of light and creating an almost genteel atmosphere. The doors and windows opened out onto a terrace, closed off at the time since it was the middle of winter, but I could see overstuffed lawn furniture beneath plastic covers. The terrace looked out to a wooded area, and sometimes, when I stared hard enough from inside the dayroom, I would spot deer and rabbits. That first time, I was amazed. It was a charming setting and not at all how I imagined prison. We were allowed to bring our cigarettes and could sit and chat with whomever we pleased. The guards never wanted us to shout between chuckholes during our twenty-three-hour lockup, so I think they considered this extra hour compensation and hoped that we'd get our fill of chitchat in the dayroom. And while we did appreciate that time, we still shouted morning, noon, and night through the chuckholes. The meaner guards would threaten us all with tickets if we didn't shut up. If you accumulated enough of these disciplinary marks, it could mean restricted rec time or no commissary visits for two weeks, things that mean so much to an inmate doing a lot of time. But not much deterred us. We were always restless.

For now, I relished being in this elegant dayroom, free to smoke cigarettes and talk all I wanted. And to top it off, the most wonderful aroma in the world wafted in—fresh brewed coffee! The officers made an urn, and I was so grateful. I kept saying to whoever would listen, "Wow, this is so nice! I can't believe this is prison." Some of the other inmates agreed with me, but the house girls said, "Yeah, but just wait till you get to general population. Then you have to work in the kitchen or clean bathrooms or whatever they decide you should be doing all day. It's not so pretty. And you have to deal with a lot of other people all the time. This is calm now, so enjoy it."

There were other officers like CO Knight who let us out when they came on to their shifts, except the midnight shift, because after final count, nobody left their cells. I would be stuck in my cell after dinner, feeling restless and at a loss for distraction, when the officer just starting the middle shift would open our cell doors and say, "Come on, ladies, I'm gonna let you out again." Some gave us the choice to hang out in the dayroom, get in line to make a phone call, or even take a shower. Coffee continued to be a treat because inmates were not allowed to shop at the commissary until a week after being cleared for general population, even if you had money. My father had already sent money to my account, spoiling me even while I was in the joint, but I couldn't access any of it. But within that first week, I found a way around the rules. My mother was obsessed with a notorious inmate at Dwight named Patty Columbo, and as luck would have it, she was one of the house girls assigned to my group. Patty and her boyfriend had been convicted of murdering her wealthy parents and her brother in the hopes of getting the family inheritance. She was only nineteen at the time, and her boyfriend was thirty-eight. She was sentenced to 350 years. The sensational case had dominated the headlines in Chicago about a decade earlier. When I realized who she was, I gushed, "Patty, my mother is a huge follower of yours!"

"Wow. Well, I don't know how famous I am," she laughed.

"No seriously, my mother has been reading about your case in the papers for years. She can't believe a beautiful Italian girl would do what they say, and she hates that you're here. When she knew that I was coming here, she wanted me to find you and personally say hello and tell you how much she supports you. She's going to be so excited that I met you!"

"Oh, that's so sweet. Tell her I said hi."

"Oh, I will," I promised and then, seeing an opportunity, I said, "So, Patty, I'm dying without coffee. I have money in my account but can't go to the commissary yet. Do you think you could get me some coffee?"

"Sure," she laughed. "I got you."

The next day she brought me a whole bag of instant coffee. I realized that I could use the milk cartons left over from lunch, fill them with water, and line them up on the radiator at lights-out so the CO wouldn't see them. By morning, the water would be hot enough for a decent cup of coffee. I never got caught and managed to take care of at least one addiction.

After that first day at Dwight, I was cut off methadone and the torturous nights began. I could not sleep without drugs, and I knew this could last for a few weeks. I felt like a moth trapped inside a box. The lights went out at nine every night. Not long after that, the officers would walk through and shine a flashlight into the cell to do a room check. "OK, ladies, shake a leg, shake somethin', move somethin'," they would holler as they patrolled up and down the hallway, so they could see that you were in your bunk. My waking nightmare began right after they passed my cell. My mind raced as I relived my life, wanting all of it back. I missed Sean. Even though I didn't spend all my time with him, I always wanted him nearby. I would close my eyes and see his beautiful face and clear blue eyes, and my heart would ache. I just wanted to hold him. I knew I could not get through these nights without some kind of distraction, so before the darkness of the second night set in, I figured out a way to pass the time.

The only light that came in was a thin line from under the cell door. I spread my blanket on the floor as close to that tiny stream of light as I could get, lay on the floor, and, using a pencil I found and saved and the backs of pages I ripped from the Dwight Correctional Center handbook for paper, drew all night long. I had always loved drawing and painting. Now it was the only thing keeping me sane. I did this for two nights, and dragged myself through the days. On the third night, during her count on midnight shift, CO Knight flashed her light through the chuckhole. She could see that I was on the floor and moving.

"Inmate, are you OK? What are you doing?" she asked quietly.

"Oh, yeah, CO, I can't sleep. I never can," I whispered back, not wanting to disturb my cellie. Then a thought came into my head, and I blurted out, "Do you have anything you need done tonight? Is there any work I could do for you?"

She hesitated for a minute and then said, "OK, let me finish my count, then I'll come back and get you. You want to polish the brass?"

"Sure! I love brass!" I had no idea what that meant, but I would do anything to get out of that dark cell.

She came back, quietly let me out, and took me down to the day-room. She gave me the cleaning supplies and was genuinely amused to see that I had no idea how to use any of it. She showed me what to do. We chatted while I worked, and she gave me some advice.

"Stay out of trouble and get through your time, and you'll be OK."

"Yeah, I don't even know what happened to me, CO Knight. I took a wrong turn, but I'm so grateful that I ended up here with officers like you."

She laughed, "Follow the rules and you'll make it through this. Whatever job they give you, do your best and show that you're a hard worker and you want to do better. You'll be fine."

I think she really believed that, even as she was breaking a rule herself by letting me out after midnight. At the very least, we entertained one another. I was beginning to understand how to get by with the least amount of discomfort, and I was still in intake. Part of me knew I would be able to game this place for as long as necessary, even as I began looking for legal loopholes that might get me out.

This nocturnal adventure became a routine over the next few nights. CO Knight would let me work quietly on my own for long stretches while she sat in her office doing her paperwork. I polished the brass, learned how to buff the floors, dusted the furniture, and got through the night, lost in my own thoughts and soothed by the monotony of the work. She would get me back into my cell just before sunrise, and I might catch a little sleep—but sometimes I didn't and just kept going. On the day that CO Knight pulled the middle shift, she convinced CO Rose, who now had the midnight shift, to let me out, too. I was dressed and ready, practically standing at attention, when CO Rose got to my cell. A robust woman, she liked to eat and let me share in the spread she brought to work that night. In less than a week, I had done pretty well for myself and thought maybe doing this time might not be so bad.

I was medically cleared on the fourth day and allowed to walk to the chow hall instead of getting meals in my cell. My security clearance came down as "minimum," and I was told to pack up and move to area

C10, general population. I was not in a cute little cottage anymore but in a cell, in a long hallway lined with more cells. The doors to each hallway had bars, and you were not allowed to go from one hallway to another, but we did. If we were caught, we would be issued a ticket. The atmosphere was more institutional than the intake area. Instead of bunk beds, there were two small single beds on each wall, a stand-alone dented metal armoire with doors, a metal dresser with three drawers, a sink, and a toilet. My cellie was resourceful and had strung sheets in front of the toilet from the armoire to the wall to create a brand of privacy that was unusual in prison; I could actually go to the bathroom unobserved. She was at work when I got there but I already liked her for that. Instead of a chuckhole the door had a small window. My cellie had even made curtains for the windows. I unpacked and threw the sheets on my bed. I had stockpiled cigarettes because I knew it would still be a week before I could go to the commissary. I was sitting there smoking when my new roommate, Linda, came back from work.

"Oh, are you my new cellie?" Linda asked somewhat apprehensively. Every time an inmate got a new roommate, it was cause for concern because you never knew who you would be stuck with, sharing this tiny space, practically on top of one another. What was her crime? Would you be living with a person just out of the psych ward? A hardened criminal who had been in for so long she would do anything to keep herself amused, including messing with you and your stuff?

"Oh, hey, Linda. God, you've got it so nice in here," I remarked.

Linda was from Cicero, right next to Chicago. She was a drug smuggler, stripper, and dancer, so we had a lot in common. Sometimes when she played her music in the cell, she would start dancing and I thought she was cool. She was sentenced to nine years and in the process of appealing, so at first, she was careful about what she said to me.

"I'm a married woman and I've been framed," was one of her favorite refrains.

"Well, I'm actually guilty," I would laugh.

Linda loved my stories, and once we got acquainted she was more open with me. She lost her appeal and ended up doing all nine years, still swearing she was framed until the day she got out.

Eight years old with my five-year-old sister, Crickie, one year
before I started getting high.

LEFT: Twelve years old, already getting high, at Christmas with Daddy in 1970.
RIGHT: With Crickie, Christmas 1970.

The only photo I have with my parents
together, 1976.

With my father and stepmother, Pat.

Daddy and Pat.

LEFT: Sixteen years old at our family Christmas in Oak Park.
RIGHT: Seventeen years old, home from Tucson visiting Grandma, 1976.

Backstage with Roger Daltrey in Chicago right before I went on tour with the Who, 1975.

The Tucson years, strung out on heroin.

Jo, MJ, and I in Tucson. I'm the one with the hat and MJ's the one with the bangs.

Falling in love with Scott and hanging with the biker gang.

Scott, my biker boyfriend, before we got married, with our dog, Rommel, Tucson, 1977.

The only photo of Sean and his father, Scott, Tucson, 1979.

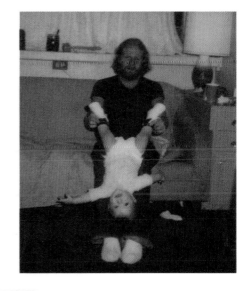

With Sean, visiting home in Oak Park, 1979.

My punk days, hanging out in Daddy's apartment, 1980.

My prize triple-beam scale, a gift from Daddy.

A visit with my beloved Uncle Joey before he disowned me.

Too high to open my Christmas gifts.

LEFT: Sean and my mother visiting me at Dwight Penitentiary.
RIGHT: My mug shot after violating boot camp parole.

With Grandma while I'm high on MDA,
early 1980s.

With Mark during the airlines scam.

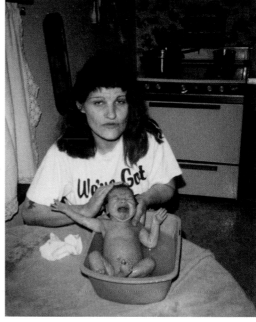

LEFT: With Sean on a break from chasing airline tickets.
RIGHT: Strung out and trying to care for my daughter Rachel.

With my Aunt Trisha in 1989.

Sean's eighth-grade graduation, when Grandma made me wear her sweater to cover my track marks, with Aunt Louise and Pat.

My prison gang leader boyfriend and I took this picture in the prison yard and developed it ourselves in photo class, Logan prison, 1995.

LEFT: Taken by my trick at the infamous Cove Motel in Cicero.
RIGHT: In my prison blue and whites during my last stint in the penitentiary.

My first room at A Safe Haven.

The picture of Sean that I hung in my first apartment after leaving A Safe Haven.

Speaking at the Traffick Free "Freedom Forum" conference, 2014. *Courtesy of Jaclyn Simpson Photography*

In the Sandtown neighborhood in Baltimore, 2016.

Sean and I with Chicago mayor Rahm Emanuel, who presented me with a Resolution for Bravery, July 20, 2016. *Brooke Collins, City of Chicago*

With Sean and his three children, my grandchildren, at Chicago City Hall, July 20, 2016. *Brooke Collins, City of Chicago*

Showing a young brother some love. *Courtesy of Jesus Salazar*

While I'm working in Little Village, Chicago, a young guy shows me his recent bullet wounds. *Courtesy of Jesus Salazar*

After two weeks on lockdown, first in intake and now waiting for my work assignment, I was getting restless and desperate for any kind of distraction. I made friends with anyone who would listen, told everyone my story, so everybody knew I was an addict, including the inmate across the hall.

"Hey, go to the med line tonight," she whispered one morning. "I snuck some weed in, and we can smoke a joint on the way, on the road."

Every night at eight o'clock the COs would let us all out at once and we would walk outside to the building where the pharmacy was. Only one or two of the COs watched us, and they didn't really pay much attention since we walked slowly and talked in whispers. It was a long walk, and it felt good to get outside for any reason. We found a place to hide and smoked the joint. I got really high, and it felt good. I could hardly talk when we got to the med line, I was laughing so hard.

I began to wonder when I was going to feel like I was being punished. I missed Grandma and I was dying to be with Sean. I did not want to be here. I wanted my freedom and my life back, but I did not feel like this was the unbearable hardship I had imagined. I was making friends, and here I was getting high. I kept my eyes open, as always, and I was learning how to get around the rules and avoid the officers' wrath. And while some of the other inmates could be mean and ruthless and tried to work me as if I were clueless, they quickly learned who they were dealing with. I had gone through the initiation for a street gang. I hustled with some mean and cunning con artists and had enough "conscious game" to spot a setup a mile away. It wasn't easy to put anything over on me. I was a quick study. I had figured out how to work the system, and there really wasn't much these women could throw at me that I hadn't seen before. I even knew quite a few of the inmates from the streets. It wasn't easy, and I hated being locked up more than anything I'd ever been through, but I wasn't intimidated. Within a few days, I was doing coke with the woman across the hall, shooting it with discarded needles she saved from her diabetic cellie. I had to wonder when this honeymoon period would end.

Linda worked as the assistant to the head of the kitchen, a mean CO named Susan.* She came back to our cell during that first week and told me I was getting assigned to kitchen duty, too. I was appalled. I could not do kitchen work. I had learned how to polish brass and shine the floorboards the week before, but I had no idea what to do with pots and pans. Grandma never allowed me into her kitchen and always chased us out if we even tried to boil water. The prospect actually scared me more than dealing with the gang or driving over the border from Mexico with a load of heroin. But since I had no choice, I showed up for my first day and reported to Susan. I was given another oversized jumpsuit to wear—this one was white and looked like a hazmat suit—and I had to tuck my long hair into a hairnet. Susan was loud and perpetually angry; everyone on kitchen duty hated her. Some would shout and call her a bitch when she turned her back.

"Bianca, get over here right now, I'm putting you on pots and pans," she yelled at me like a menacing drill sergeant as soon as I was suited up.

"Um, Miss Susan, I don't really know what that is," I meekly asserted, hoping that ignorance plus incompetence might be my ticket out.

"Get over there, NOW! The inmates will show you what to do."

I was put on a line of giant industrial sinks with a conveyor belt that led to a hooded dishwasher unit. The kitchen made meals for over a thousand inmates every day, three times a day. I had to start at the spot where the dirtiest, caked-on pots were endlessly stacked. I had no idea what to do first. My nails were long and polished since I had already managed to barter for supplies; I could not tolerate even the smallest chip. It was hot and steamy. I was disgusted by the smell and the look of what was stuck on those pots, and for the first time, I felt like I was being punished.

I had a pair of giant gloves, sort of protecting my nails, but making it even more difficult to grab and wield the giant blocks of steel wool I was given to scrape out the pots. I told myself I had to do this because I was in prison, so I legitimately tried to comply, scraping the inside of the pots while holding back nausea and doing such a bad job that the inmate next on the line kept shoving the pot back at me, pointing

---

* For the sake of privacy, her name has been changed.

out all the crap I'd missed. All of this was taking too long and slowing down the line, causing much frustration and shouting in my direction. Eventually, one impatient inmate changed places with me so now I was at the end of the line and had to rinse the pots. I was getting soaked. The other women on the line were trying to help and got to know me as the morning progressed; they thought I was hilarious. Miss Susan decided that we were having too much fun and that I had to get off the line. I was sent to mop the floor. She gave me an industrial mop setup with a wringer, something that I had never seen before, but I was afraid to ask, so I just went at it and got the floor so wet it became danger-ous to walk across. Another inmate, Marva, whom I knew from my cell section, showed me how to use the wringer. She was surprisingly nice considering she was in prison for murdering her twins. She had a lover inside who cheated on her and Marva became famous for serving her a dead rat. But she had patience, helping me more than once over those first few days, and I was grateful.

After several hours, I knew how to mop. My arms were aching, but I was settling in. I saw how the inmates worked the system, acting just busy enough to get by. As I got more comfortable with my sur-roundings, I started getting bored with mopping the floor all day and wandered off when Susan wasn't looking, venturing into the main dining room and sometimes even to the private dining room used by Warden Huck and other prison staff. I admired Warden Huck. To me, she was the consummate professional woman, in control, fair, and intelligent, but never uppity. I harbored a secret fantasy of myself as a powerful businesswoman, whatever that meant, and to me, Warden Huck was as close as I could imagine. Whenever I saw professional women portrayed in the movies or on TV, like Lois Lane in *Superman*, I always thought that's who I was really supposed to be—a go-getter, carrying a briefcase, drinking coffee, smoking cigarettes, doing important things. In reality, I had no idea how to be anything like that. Warden Huck walked the grounds and talked to the inmates all the time, knew our names, and made us feel like we mattered somehow. This was unusual then and is unheard of today. I managed to schmooze my way out of mop detail by the third week and got put to work in the executive dining room. All of this was helping me adjust as I tried my best to fit in and keep my mind from dwelling on what six years of this was really going to be like.

I was in my cell one night when an officer came to get me.

"Hey, Bianca, the warden needs you to go to her office right now."

"Really? Oh, God, what did I do? Am I in trouble?"

"I have no idea, but here's the pass. Do you know where it is?"

I had never been to the admin building, but I knew where it was. Part of me got excited, thinking maybe she was going to put me on work release. She liked me, and the way my sentence read, it was possible.

I got to her office and was sent in by the officer at the front desk. I found myself in one of the large old rooms from the original building. A long mahogany conference table took up the center of the room and was surrounded by antique wood furniture, including the warden's expansive polished desk. All this wood, plus large houseplants and a ficus tree, reminded me of Grandma's apartment in Oak Park, and I could see that the plants needed attention. While I had never learned how to clean a pot or use a mop, I did know about taking care of plants because I hung out in my uncle's flower shop when I was a kid and helped him prune and repot.

"Bianca, come in. Have a seat."

"OK," I said as I sat in the chair facing her desk, more nervous now that I was here.

"I have a dilemma. Your father has been calling here almost every day, so now they've got me talking to him. He keeps asking me how much money he has to pay for me to release you. I'm not sure that your father understands that we have no power. The judge sentenced you, and you have to do your time here. But he just won't believe me. He even sent a dozen roses for you, and I had to turn them away. We can't give you roses in your cell."

I started laughing; I couldn't help it. "That's my father."

"If I let you call your father, do you think you could talk some sense into him and tell him to please stop calling here? There's no amount of money he can pay us." He kept upping the amount, hoping to hit her price. I could just hear him, "How much is it gonna take? What do I gotta do? Who do I gotta call to get my baby out of there?"

Warden Huck handed me the phone with an outside line selected, and I dialed the hot dog restaurant. I knew he'd be there.

"Daddy?" I was so happy to hear his voice, I almost cried.

"Hey, I'm doing what I can to get you outta there." He sounded apologetic. I knew how helpless this made him feel.

"Daddy, it's OK. I'm OK. I'm with the warden right now. Listen, Daddy, you have to stop calling here because there's no way you can pay anything."

"C'mon, somebody's got to be able to get paid."

"No, there's nobody, Daddy. I'm in the Illinois Department of Corrections. This is the penitentiary. I have to do my time. The only way is an appeal."

"Well then, call that damn motherfuckin' lawyer. Call him, Ang!"

I realized at that moment that I had been in a daze, a kind of brain freeze for the past three weeks, trying to accept where I was and determined to just get along. "Bye, Daddy," was all I said, and we hung up.

Before I left the warden's office, I couldn't stop myself. "Warden Huck, my family owns a flower shop, and I know about taking care of plants. Would it be OK if I volunteered to work on your plants in here, because I can see they need pruning. I can polish the furniture and the brass, too." She smiled, thanked me for volunteering, and said she would set it up.

I left her office, went back to my unit, and called the lawyer. It was the twenty-eighth day since my sentencing, and you have thirty days to appeal. I had given up, reasoning that since my family had so many lawyers and knew all the inside maneuvers, there simply wasn't any way out of this. I was afraid to let myself hope and had not been in fighting mode since I turned myself in because I was so overwhelmed by this new reality. But this submissive person really wasn't me. I had never given up on anything without a fight, and after hearing my father's voice something in me snapped back. But I had to move fast.

The lawyer was hardly encouraging.

"Look, Bianca, there's nothing," he said when he answered the phone. "You fuckin' scammed people! You made a lot of money on the airlines, and you weren't even charged with that. So you're doing a little time. Deal with it."

"No," I insisted, "I'm going to appeal."

"Appeal what? You got the lowest sentence you could get."

"But they're consecutive. Why can't they be concurrent?"

"It's not gonna happen, Bianca. The law's the law. Just do your time and be thankful you didn't get more."

"All right, OK." I hung up.

That night in my bunk I could not stop thinking about it. *How did I manage to get so far in my criminal career? I'm smart and I'm a fighter,* I thought, giving myself a pep talk. *Why are you giving up now? You have to fight for your freedom.* The next morning, I woke up, found some paper and a pen in the cell, and wrote out my appeal in my own way: "To the Honorable Judge Himel, this is my motion to appeal my sentence of December 1987. I, Angalia Bianca, am filing this for your consideration. Thank you."

I had to mail it immediately to file on time. I still had the three stamped envelopes given to every new inmate during intake. That was the limit, and once your ID number showed up in mail processing for the third time, you had to wait a month before you could mail anything else. Eventually, I figured out how to get around that by using the IDs of lifers who had nobody to write to and never used their three envelopes; I just told my family to open anything that came from prison, no matter what name was on it. I was stuffing my appeal into the envelope and asking the CO on my floor how to get it into the mail when she told me that if I just sent it to the mailroom, it would sit there for days, plus I had to get it notarized to prove the date it was written because it could take a few days to get to the court. When I told her I only had two days left to make my appeal deadline, she wrote me a pass, and let me go straight to the prison law library where I could get it notarized and into the mail faster.

The staff at the law library looked at me as if I were an idiot. Not only had I handwritten this sad excuse for a legal document, but they had seen this kind of desperate move so many times and knew it was almost always futile.

"Look," I said to the librarian, Beatrice, known as Miss B to the inmates, as I was losing my patience, "I just have to get this request filed on time, then I can work on the real appeal."

"Yeah, whatever, I know how it works." She had to hold back a laugh. "I'll notarize it."

Miss B helped me make the three copies I needed to file, and off it went. Now I had to figure out the grounds for my request. I had to make a case. The next day I went back to the law library to ask the paralegals who volunteered there to help me. They were prisoners who were taking law classes, and oftentimes researching their own appeals. They were used to hearing stories of innocence from other inmates who had long sentences, tall tales of woe like, "I got thirty years, but I just drove the getaway car, I didn't know nothing about any drugs or guns. I was framed."

Most of the stories played like the same old tape, and even though they did their best to help us with details like the legal language and the proper way to file, they weren't all that motivated to dig deeper and remained careful not to hold out much hope of anything working or changing the court's mind. When I told them my long story of getting arrested, getting out on bail, accumulating warrants, and finally turning myself in, they confirmed the new law that made my sentences consecutive, not concurrent, and once again, I was told that there was nothing I could do to change my situation. They didn't find my case particularly interesting and probably thought I was being ridiculous and should just suck it up and do the time.

"Listen, I'll do the research myself. I just need to know what my grounds might be." I had made up my mind and nothing was going to discourage me.

"OK, whatever," one volunteer said. "I think your best bet is to motion to reduce and/or modify sentence. But you need an argument as to why."

"OK," I said, getting more frustrated by the minute. "Just tell me what I can read to figure something out. I don't know anything about law books or how to read one or what citations or statutes even mean. Just point me in the right direction so I can at least try. Please."

"We have about a thousand books, and you're welcome to take a look at any of them."

"But isn't there one that has something in it that can help me?" Desperation was setting in, but I was also getting angry, making me more determined.

"Look, honey, law books are filled with real cases and their outcomes. You gotta find a case that was similar to yours and was overturned and use the same argument."

I randomly pulled the biggest book I could find from the shelf and showed it to the volunteer. "What about this book right here?"

"That's *Black's Law Dictionary*, no case law, just definitions."

"Maybe I can just start there, and it will help me figure out the other books when I get to them," I sighed, feeling so lost and in over my head.

"Sure, honey, you can do that. You can't check that one out, but you're welcome to sit at the table and go through it. Maybe familiarize yourself with some of the terminology."

I thanked her and started my journey through *Black's*, with no idea what I was looking for in the gigantic, intimidating book. I felt like I was a witch looking for the right spell. I sat down and started with the letter *A*. I had to leave after a couple hours but went back the next day and the day after that, feeling the pressure to get the full appeal written and filed. By the third day I got to *E*, and a strange term caught my eye: ex post facto. Literally translated, it means "after the fact." The dictionary said, "If a state legislature or Congress enact new rules of proof or longer sentences, those new rules or sentences do not apply to crimes committed before the new law was adopted." I read the definition and almost shouted out loud right there in the prison library. It jumped off that page and into my brain like a hit of dope. I had found my loophole.

I started reading the Constitution to determine if any of my rights were violated as well, and concluded that I had received "ineffective assistance of counsel," a constitutional right, because my lawyer had not fully explored my defense options. If he had, he would have discovered what I did, that at the time I committed my crimes sentencing was to run concurrently. The switch requiring multiple sentences to be served consecutively happened after the dates of my arrests, and therefore my sentencing, as outlined by ex post facto law, was incorrectly imposed. Convinced that I was now as smart as any lawyer, I wrote up my own request for a modification of sentence. Now all I had to do was get myself back into court in front of Judge Himel, so I filed a writ of habeas corpus. I did all this without the assistance of the lawyer my father had paid. Instead, Aunt Louise had a friend whose son was just out of law school, and he agreed to help me. Mine was a real case, and he was eager to work on it. We spent many hours on the phone over the next two months plotting my court appearances and making sure I covered all my bases. Along with all that, I took it upon myself to write a letter to Judge Himel once a week. They were real tearjerkers:

> Dear Judge Himel,
> Your Honor, I know that I did wrong, and I have to be punished. I am so sorry. I cannot imagine the pain I am causing my young son with our separation, unable to see him more than once a week. I am convinced that once you hear my appeal, you will believe that my sentence should be modified, and I should be reunited with my beautiful boy.

I cried as I wrote the letters, just to be sure they sounded real.

While I obsessed about my appeal, I became convinced that my time in prison was going to end soon, and I started to believe that I would be out in a matter of months. This shift in my attitude made me more restless than ever and less able to cope with being locked up. I found myself taking more risks with other inmates to get drugs or to get out of my cell whenever possible. I fell into the trading and bartering wars that define life inside prison, working the other inmates to get anything extra or sometimes just messing with someone for entertainment. Grandma, my father, my mother, and even Uncle Joey were all sending me money, so I had plenty to bargain with. Drugs flowed freely, and I soon learned how to get whatever I needed or wanted to get high, sleep at night, and keep my head in a place that made the restlessness easier to handle.

My mother brought Sean to see me every week, but these visits left me feeling depressed and empty, which just fed my determination to get out. The first time they came, I was so nervous. I couldn't wait to see

Sean, but was embarrassed for him to see me here. He was eight by then and knew what was going on. I tried to help him see that I was fine and that this was not so bad. I even promised him I'd be home soon. My mother didn't believe that, but she seemed happy enough to come and bring Sean. She came twice a week, every week, once with Sean and once without him. Sometimes she would bring Grandma, or Pat, or Aunt Louise. I even managed to introduce her to Patty Columbo, and it was truly a highlight for my mother. Pat would smuggle special makeup, eyeliner, jewelry, and even hair combs tucked under her hair for me. I took whatever she brought and hid it in my crotch or under my tongue. My family was looking out for me in the joint, and it was always excruciating to say good-bye and watch them walk through the doors to leave. They weren't my only visitors.

I was regularly communicating on the phone with Javier, who was still my boyfriend, and he visited once a week, too. In the meantime, I had started having sex with one of the prison guards to get favors and special treatment. I set it up with him so that for fifty bucks he would look away when Javier would follow me into a nearby bathroom for sex. There were no cameras mounted on walls around every corner in prisons back then, so nobody paid attention, and in many respects the inmates ran the place. I didn't love Javier or even like him anymore than I did before I went to prison, but he was still useful, so I continued to make him feel good in exchange for the drugs and other contraband he smuggled inside.

I had been in prison for four months when the initial court appearance regarding my request for modification of my sentence was scheduled. I was not going to appellate court because I was not arguing a full appeal. As I was just arguing to change my sentencing, I would be going back in front of Judge Himel, and I was looking forward to seeing him again. Going to court was like a fun field trip, a break from the monotony and constraints of everyday life inside. The officers who drove the van were my friends, and they stopped at Burger King on the way and bought me lunch. I don't even remember being handcuffed on the way there, but I did have to be put in full shackles, hands and feet, when it was time to exit the van.

I was taken back to Cook County Jail, wearing a prison uniform this time and about to be put into the bull pen. I caught myself displaying the same kind of arrogance toward the other inmates that I'd encountered just months ago when I was so high I could barely hold my head up. I even remarked about how dirty it was in the cage and kept pleading with the COs from Dwight not to put me in there. They told me to calm down and promised to stay nearby, but they had no choice, and I had to stand in the bull pen with everyone else. I had become accustomed to being treated like a human being. Even though I was happy to be getting my day in court, the specter of being mandated haunted me. The judge could mandate a prisoner to stay in Cook County if a court appearance were pushed back a few days or another appearance were required shortly after the first one. Instead of sending you back and forth, they would squeeze you into a cell there to wait it out. Ever the drama queen, I kept saying I would kill myself if that happened.

In Cook County Jail, every inmate who is brought before the court has to have two county officers as escorts, in addition to the state COs who came from Dwight. I was their responsibility, too, since I was back in their jurisdiction. I had been arrested so many times that I knew many of the regular officers at Cook County, and sure enough, I knew one of the women who came to get me from the bull pen.

"Hey, Bianca," she seemed genuinely happy to see me. "Are you the one who keeps writing to the judge?"

"Yeah," I laughed. "How do you know?"

"Oh my God, you should have just seen him screaming at the state's attorney about your case!"

"Really? Why?" I didn't know if this was good news or bad news.

"He read one of your letters out loud to the whole court and everybody was almost in tears. When he got done, the judge yelled right at the state's attorney, 'You know what, the next time you motion to put one of these girls in prison, you better have gone down there to Dwight yourself to see what it's like.' Bianca, I don't know when I've seen Judge Himel so mad!"

For one of the few times in my life, I was speechless. I felt a slight pang of guilt and was glad the CO from Dwight had not been in the courtroom to hear that because in reality things weren't so bad there and I had actually come to like some of those responsible for keeping me locked up. I walked into his courtroom and stood quietly while he delivered his opinion.

"Bianca, I have been reading your letters, and I am so moved. You are an intelligent girl to have filed this request with limited access to resources or support. We'll continue this in two months, you've got a few more arguments to make, and there will be responses from the state that you will have to answer. So, I will see you again soon enough."

That was it, and I went back to Dwight. I was impatient, but I knew this was going to work. The back-and-forth with the state began. I would be notified of the state's rejection, and then I'd have to make a rebuttal and three more court appearances were scheduled. By that time, I had been at Dwight long enough to be allowed to wear my own clothes, so I got to dress the part, and it gave me such confidence that I could practically taste freedom. I had written to my aunt Louise asking her to send me a pretty dress to wear in court when I got off. In my mind, it was already happening. She sent a pretty powder-blue long-sleeve cotton dress that made me appear sweet and innocent. My hair was clean and shiny, conditioned with the expensive products I bought from the commissary. My makeup was perfect, and I was ready for the world. During transfer and while inside the bull pen, I still had to wear a thick brown leather belt with metal loops attached to it where the chains from the shackles around my ankles and my handcuffs were tethered. But this was removed before I went in front of the judge.

I stood there for my third appearance, looking respectable, and I knew I had won. Judge Himel said I would be released as soon as the paperwork was ready. This time, when his gavel hit, it was like fireworks going off just for me. I had to go back to Dwight, but would be out in two months. I ended up with a two-year sentence, nine months of which I was required to serve. I got my new calculation sheet in August with my out date set for October. I left Dwight victorious, feeling more untouchable than ever. And it was not a moment too soon because I was four months pregnant from my visits with Javier, who never used a condom.

The drama inside prison was like a nonstop soap opera, and the adrenaline was a high for us. We were constantly whispering, gossiping about who got caught giving a guard a blow job, or smuggling in drugs. If we saw any inmate with her eyes pinned, pupils tiny from being high on heroin, we were all over her because we wanted in. Now I was one of the main characters in this drama. I discovered my pregnancy before I won in court and started to panic about getting caught. My periods had been sporadic for years owing to my heroin addiction, a common side effect, but when the nausea started and my breasts were suddenly a cup size bigger, I realized what had happened. My cellie and I began plotting ways to hide the pregnancy and were working on a plan for the delivery of my baby if it came to that. I was so worried. The penalties for getting pregnant inside were steep, including spending a mandatory year in solitary confinement, which also meant losing a whole year of time served, and they would take the baby from me. While I kept insisting that I would win my appeal and be out before it mattered, my cellie and other friends insisted we hatch another plan, giving them some distraction and a reason to laugh. I had to hide the pregnancy so the mean inmates would not catch on and snitch. The haters were always lurking, ready to get revenge for some imagined slight or privilege that they felt you didn't deserve, and to keep the drama going. Some took everything you did as an affront to their very existence.

In the chow hall, a few started saying things like, "Girl, I never noticed how big your tits are. What's up with you?"

"It's this damn state food, man. I'm putting on weight," or, as we always said when someone gained weight inside, "I'm havin' a state baby."

"In your boobs? I don't know."

It was no secret that inmates had sex with the male officers who worked inside Dwight. It was a way to barter for favors and get a little relief from the harshness of being there. A pregnancy would be a bit of excitement to spice things up, so if it was at all possible, the other women wanted to know. I put them off, but it got harder all the time. My clothes were getting tight on me, so I had to borrow from the other cellies. We formulated all kinds of crazy plans in case this pregnancy went to term inside. One of my friends worked in the laundry, so I asked her to sneak a towel back to my cell every day, thinking we could start making diapers. I had another friend who worked in industry, where they made things from metal, and I asked her to smuggle a needle and thread and safety pins. I even asked one of my friends in the kitchen to figure out how we could sneak extra milk to my cell if needed.

At one point, one of them asked me, "What is this 'we' shit, girl?"

"Look," I said, "we're havin' a baby, all of us!" And since I was generous and they liked me, they were ready to go along.

I talked about giving birth in my cell without a doctor, figuring women did that all the time in the old days and most of us had kids, so we basically knew what to do. We all watched TV. You cut the cord, wash off the baby, and hand it to the happy mother. I even started making a schedule so we could share taking care of the baby and keeping it quiet so the COs wouldn't find it. We could hide it in the dresser drawer. Every time one of my friends thought I was crazy, I would just say, "Don't worry, I'll fuck the officer, it'll be fine." It gave us all a little adventure to concentrate on, making the time go by faster, and that was always a good thing. By the time I was released, I had stockpiled about twenty towels and boxes of safety pins in between my mattress and bed frame and was fully prepared to have a baby in prison.

Javier picked me up on the day I was released, and I went to live with him again. I waited for my baby to arrive, and never worried about getting caught again. I had beaten the state prison system. There was nothing I couldn't do.

# 7

# No Direction Home

I FELL RIGHT BACK INTO my old life. I started doing heroin within days after my release from Dwight, even though I was pregnant, and soon realized that I had caught a habit again. I did not want family services to take my baby away if she was born with drugs in her system, so I stopped and went on methadone. But Javier had a crack habit and sometimes I smoked with him when he was home. He was still a good bet. He had a steady job, but was as corrupt as any law officer could be, selling drugs and juggling various ongoing extortion schemes inside county jail. All of this combined gave him a decent income. I was still collecting social security checks from Scott's death, one for me and one for Sean every month. But even though that meant I had my own cash, I still couldn't stop the urge to hustle for more.

Within weeks of my release, I was dealing with the gang in Humboldt Park. As soon as Javier left for work, I would take the El to Damen Avenue where Pappo, who was still the leader of our chapter, and his girlfriend picked me up. Javier was working the night shift, and I was, too. Pappo and his girlfriend were my best friends, and I felt closer to them than my family. I had learned a lot from Pappo, becoming his protégé before going to prison. I was a quick study and willing to do anything he asked, still deeply loyal to him and all the brothers. I would have died for any one of them. I had one of my gang sisters tattoo the gang symbol on my left hand. Pappo taught me everything I knew about gang life, how to do business, and surviving on the street. He was a hero and role model to me.

But there were factions within the gang, members of the Nation that had problems with him and the way he was dealing drugs. It was rumored that Pappo had stolen cocaine from another brother and was losing ground inside the organization, falling into disfavor with too many other members. The gang had actual bylaws, many pages that addressed every facet of gang business and members' behavior. Unlike today's gangs in Chicago who have lost their leadership and become scattered and autonomous, the gang had a strict hierarchy and clearly defined penalties for the slightest departure from the rules. And they were ruthless in the punishments they could assign. Pappo was a heroin addict and dealer, both behaviors that broke written laws, even though heroin traffic was a big part of the gang's economy and he ranked high within the organization. The laws were written back in the 1950s when gangs were first formed, and their purpose was more political in nature, to "promote prosperity and freedom through love and understanding," to quote the bylaws, and to solidify the community, a noble plan that did not work. Eventually, the laws became irrelevant and were referred to only when they suited the gang's purposes, especially when it was time to get rid of a brother who was no longer in good standing. Then the laws were suddenly valid and unbreakable.

One early evening I got off the El and walked out to the corner of Damen and North Avenues where Pappo's car waited for me. His girlfriend sat in front. Pappo was in a dark mood when I slid into the backseat.

"Bianca, you know they're gonna kill me."

"No, Pappo, whaddaya mean? That's crazy. Who's gonna kill you?"

"The brothers got a hit out on me."

"Oh my God, no!" I was scared for him. "C'mon, man, how can we figure this out?"

"There's nothing I can do." He was resigned to it. "My hours are numbered, girl." I had never seen him like this before. But that was all he said about it.

We drove around, making our stops, laughing and getting high, having fun as we always did. I heard he'd been involved in that bad coke deal, ripping off another brother, but I figured he would outrun it, and I still trusted him with my life. As we drove around the Wicker Park neighborhood, his mood lightened.

"Hey, Bianca, I got some new dope, and it's really good."

"Oh, yeah?" I was hesitant because I'd gone on methadone to stay off heroin while I was pregnant.

"Yeah, you gotta try it."

"OK, let's do it." I didn't hesitate for long. It didn't take much to tempt me, and I figured just a taste would be fine. We pulled into Humboldt Park, and Pappo parked the car along one of the many streets that wind their way through the expansive tree-filled grounds. His girlfriend stayed in the car while we headed for a clump of trees near the pond, a secluded spot where we could shoot up. The sun was setting, and the sky was bright purple.

We got out of the car, took a few steps, and Pappo said, "Oh, shit. I forgot my piece."

"What? No, no, you need the gun, man. Lemme go back to the car and get it." I started to run toward the car, and he stopped me.

"Nah, fuck it, I don't even need it. Just fuck it!"

We walked into the park, across the grass, not far from the road. A car pulled up, screeching loud enough to make us glance back just as two guys jumped out and walked toward us.

"Hey, Pappo," one of them shouted.

As we turned toward the car, both men opened fire. I froze and watched as Pappo's body jerked with each bullet that struck him. He was still standing, taking hits in rapid succession and screaming, "Fuck you, fuck you!" with each hit. He reached out and took my hand as blood from his wounds sprayed over both of us. He grabbed my arm and turned me back around forcefully, even as he was being riddled with bullets. "Fuck 'em, just fuck 'em," he screamed as we turned our backs to the shooters, and he managed to take a few steps away from them as if we were just going to walk out of there. The shooters emptied their guns into his back, and his body jumped like a puppet on a string with each shot. The world around me stood still as I watched Pappo get murdered in slow motion. He fell to the ground, pulling me down with him as I screamed.

"Somebody call an ambulance! Now!" I kept repeating this until another car pulled up, and a couple brothers jumped out. They ran toward me and pulled me up and away from Pappo, toward their car.

"C'mon, you gotta get out of here, Bianca! Before the cops come."

"No, no, I can't leave him." I tried to pull away from them. I was in shock and could not think about anything but trying to save Pappo.

"There's nothing you can do. He's gone. Let's go!"

I was covered in blood, and they knew they had to protect me from a police interrogation. They dragged me into their car, and we drove off, leaving Pappo there, his life bleeding away, a dark pool seeping into the green grass as the sun went down in Humboldt Park.

The brothers took me home and left. I was still shaking from the shock. I had a part-time waitressing job, a condition of my parole, so I had to go to work. I took a shower, sobbing into the steamy water, got dressed in my work uniform, and threw my bloody clothes in the Dumpster in our alley. Javier could never know about this. He would throw me out or hit me, something he had taken to doing more frequently since I'd gotten out of the joint, even though I was five months pregnant. In his twisted mind, he thought I needed a little discipline. I went to work, but could barely hold it together. I kept hoping that Pappo had survived. I knew they had taken him to Mount Sinai Hospital, so every time I got a minute's break, I used the pay phone to call the hospital, but they would not give me any information. Finally, I lost it.

"I just need to know if he's alive! Did he make it?" I was so desperate; the hospital receptionist was starting to soften.

"Are you a family member?"

"No, I'm a very close friend. I need to know if he's alive."

"Um . . . I'm sorry, you need to contact the family, honey."

I hung up, and I knew that Pappo was gone. I felt angry and powerless and devastated. I knew all about the raw violence that fueled the gang and its loyalties, but had never been this close to it. And I knew I had to remain quiet. Why I wasn't killed with him I will never understand. Gang shooters usually don't want to leave behind a witness, but it was clear that the shooters weren't even trying to hit me. I had a reputation on the street and was known to live by the code of silence, but that felt like thin protection. Pappo's life was another bargaining chip in a complicated game that ruled the streets. I knew how to play, and for the most part loved the life, but I would never feel completely untouchable after Pappo died. It was rumored that the hit was ordered from inside the penitentiary, where other high-ranking leaders were doing time and running the business. They had grown tired of Pappo's transgressions and his heroin consumption, all of it bad for business and bad for the organization. So it was said that they put out the order for a hit and the call was answered.

The next morning, I was watching the news with Javier when he got home from work. The sensational story of an unnamed but high-ranking gang leader being gunned down in Humboldt Park was the lead; there was no mention of any others at the scene or any witnesses. Javier, a man who had no moral compass to speak of and who spent his life exploiting the criminal justice system, and anything else he could make a buck from, pointed to the screen and scolded me.

"You see what can happen?" He was gloating because he knew I was sneaking off to that neighborhood. "You keep hanging in Humboldt with those gang thugs, but I don't think you realize how dangerous it is. Believe me, I know. Those people are ruthless."

I sat there, trying to hold back tears. Javier thought I had no idea what I was dealing with, but I was actually more hard-core than he was when it came to dealing and mixing with the brothers. I had taken risks for the gang that would make him shudder, from transporting drugs across the border to selling them in Chicago's most dangerous projects. I walked the cruelest streets in the city to do the gang's business and never felt scared. He had no idea how deep my connections ran, and I was not about to let him know how much pain this hit had caused me. "Yeah, it's horrible," was all I could manage to say. In truth, I suffered more violence at the hands of Javier than I ever experienced with the gang. This man who hit a pregnant woman he claimed to love was far more vicious toward me than any brother I had ever known.

After Pappo was killed, I had a hollow teardrop tattooed under my left eye to represent mourning a death; a solid teardrop represents a murder. I stayed closer to home for a few months while things settled down. I was traumatized and thought I could try playing the role of mother and wife, at least my version of it. I even talked Javier into moving to the suburbs so I could be closer to my family, knowing Grandma and my mother would be more than willing to help with the new baby, as well as Sean. We rented a house in Berwyn, not far from where they still lived in Oak Park. When my daughter Rachel* was born, she and Sean started spending a lot of time with Grandma, but I would make sure they were home when Javier had time off. We even got married when Rachel was two years old. It might have looked normal for a minute, but it was hardly a Norman Rockwell picture. Javier was so crooked, internal affairs would come knocking at the door on a regular basis, asking me questions about my husband, trying to pin something on him. I would do whatever I could to look and act normal, bouncing our cute little girl on my hip and acting innocent. Once they told me about a police drug raid on the West Side of Chicago where one of the confiscated guns was his service revolver. He had sold it for drugs and never reported it missing. He would leave for work every day and tell me to call the lawyer first if he didn't come home or if he walked in and internal affairs was there to arrest him. He was smuggling so many drugs into prison and ripping off the gang members inside at the same time that he had no idea anymore how exposed he was. The other guards heard from the inmates that he was a target, so he was reassigned to tower duty because there was an inside hit out on him. The paranoia of getting caught hung in the air every day. That was the tone of our marriage.

As soon as Javier left for work, my drug addict and dealer friends would come over to the house where we did business and partied all night. I would make sure the place cleared out before he got home in the morning. Even though he was being watched by internal affairs, he judged me as if he were a perfect officer of the law and I were the criminal. At least part of that was true. I started dealing for the Kelly

---

* For the sake of privacy, her name has been changed.

brothers, well-known heroin dealers in Cicero. They were a big operation and kept me busy. I would drive to Cicero every afternoon, get high, pick up large quantities of heroin to sell, and make a night of it back at my house. I tried to keep up the appearance of being a housewife, even making dinner on Javier's nights off, having the kids around when he was home, deftly juggling two lives. But life with Javier was getting tougher. He had a bad drinking problem, along with a crack habit. He would get off work at seven in the morning, come home around eleven, drunk and high and angry. He started beating me all the time, even as I found out about all the other women he was cheating with.

I accused him outright one afternoon, naming the woman I knew he had just been with. He beat me like he had never done before, hitting me over and over again without holding anything back. Sean and Rachel were there.

"Sean, take your sister and go hide in the bedroom! Close the door. Run!"

"Fuck you, bitch," Javier kept yelling with every punch.

I managed to get to the phone and dial 911, screaming for help and spitting the address out before he grabbed me and hung up. The suburban cops showed up in a few minutes, and I thought I was safe. But before they arrived, while trying to defend myself I knocked his glasses off and they broke. Javier let the cops in, flashed his badge, and showed them his broken glasses. They decided I was the problem and arrested me for battery, not him. I had three broken ribs, was covered in bruises, and weighed less than 120 pounds. He was almost six feet tall and a hefty man, without a bruise on his body, but they took me to jail for assaulting an officer. We went to court, and he dropped the charges, having come to his senses, realizing that my father would do whatever he could to retaliate if I went to jail. Finally, there was a threat that Javier took seriously. He backed off. I stayed with my father for a few days, but went back home because I didn't want to lose my daughter and I had just gotten a serious taste of how powerful Javier could be just by flashing his badge.

But his reckless ways caught up with him, and my husband got shot one afternoon, behind a house in Berwyn. He was getting high on crack with an inmate who was out on house arrest. They ran out of drugs and called their dealer. When he got there, the dealer wanted what they already owed him before handing over any more drugs. Javier and his friend didn't have any money, and they started to haggle for more time and more drugs. The dealer pulled a gun and shot Javier. When the police arrived at the scene, he was unconscious and bleeding profusely, having been shot in the chest at close range. The dealer and Javier's friend pretended to be witnesses and told the cops a female shooter had driven by, stopped and opened fire before driving off. I was never a suspect with the police, but because of this story, some of Javier's family had their doubts. When the police interrogated the two so-called witnesses, they came clean and said there was no woman, no drive-by, and the dealer had done it in self-defense. The dealer got off by saying it was an accident. So while Javier lay in the hospital in a coma fighting for his life, the man who shot him was only charged with obstruction of justice for originally lying to the cops and illegal possession and use of a firearm. Neither of the men went to jail, and it stayed on the books as an accidental shooting.

I stayed by his side for the full three weeks that my husband spent in the hospital. At one point, the doctors wanted to pull the plug and take him off life support because he was in a coma, and his prognosis did not look good. But I protested because, whatever else he might have been, he was my child's father, and she needed him. So they kept him on life support while I practically lived at Loyola Hospital, Aunt Louise at my side. I felt bad that he was in such rough shape, but when he woke up, he was the same man I had grown to hate, as mean as ever. He was given the option to resign, and that meant the ongoing investigation surrounding him would stop. So he did. In the meantime, I moved back in with Grandma, who was now living with Uncle Joey. Rachel and Sean were happy there, and I was free to take care of my drug business. I wouldn't see my husband again for many years. He took his pension and hit the road, traveling all over the country. When I was in prison a few years later, he served me with divorce papers, and we officially split.

I continued to spend all my time in Cicero, getting high, selling drugs, and never coming home. The dividing line between Cicero and the city of Chicago is the broad and busy Cicero Avenue. Like other suburbs right next to the city, Cicero felt more like a part of Chicago than its own town. The area where I hung out was a string of pawn-shops, liquor stores, and run-down motels, with hourly rates posted under patchy old neon signs. I spent many hours in those rooms, turn-ing tricks or hooking up with one of the many men I just had sex with. Cicero belonged to a few gangs, and there was a lot of violence over turf and the drug business there. I became heavily involved with the Cicero gangs and spent less time with the Humboldt Park brothers. I fit right in, and they were impressed with my street smarts and obvious lack of fear. I became a successful dealer in Cicero, running with a new set of badasses and making a reputation for myself. I had been living with a man called Shorty off and on for months, and soon I was carrying his baby, my third child. He was a big dealer in Cicero; eventually, I took over his dope business and kicked him out. I never saw him again, and he never knew about the baby.

My family was beginning to lose patience with me. I would come home unannounced, stay for an hour or two to see the kids, and then leave again for weeks at a time. I started living with other junkies and dealers in apartments in Cicero that my father still paid for, turning tricks for extra money. It never bothered me to admit that MJ's predic-tion back when I was seventeen had come true. When she said I would end up a hooker on Cicero Avenue, I had laughed. For the most part, I was fine with how things had worked out. Javier was out of my life, my kids were taken care of, and I was having a good time. The dangers of being a woman in this game never held much sway with me. I knew I could be raped or beaten by a john; it happened all the time. But I assumed my instincts would protect me. I was wrong.

One night, I was standing on the street and a nice-looking black sedan pulled up. The man inside rolled down the window and motioned for me to come over. I knew he was a trick. Once we settled on the money, I walked around and got into the passenger seat. As soon as I closed the door, I heard all the locks click into place. He drove for a few minutes and then pulled over. I panicked. He turned toward me, and I could see that he was holding a gun. I told him he didn't need that, but he insisted that we were going to have sex and no money was going to change hands. I tried to get out of the car, but the doors had special locks, and I could not get mine to open. I was trapped. The man put the gun to my head and told me we were going to fuck right now or he would kill me. When I shouted "NO!" he hit me with the gun, pushed me down in the seat, and raped me. In the middle of it all, I begged him to wear a condom. He refused. When he was done, he started driving away and then threw me from the moving car onto Cicero Avenue. I was shocked and in a lot of pain. My head was bleeding, and I was overwhelmed with humiliation and anger. I had been roughed up before but had never felt so powerless. As much as any physical pain, I was wounded by the fact that my instincts had not kicked in to save me. I stopped turning tricks for a while after that but never told anyone because I did not want to admit to anybody, not even myself, that someone had gotten the best of me like that. I tried to put it out of my mind and carry on with my business.

I turned one of my apartments into a drug house, called a "tippin' spot" by junkies and dealers, meaning I was one of the busiest dealers in Cicero. People on the street would say I was "jukin," making a lot of money. This made the other dealers, especially the gang brothers, livid. Almost every weekend, like clockwork, a drive-by shooting would blow out my front window as the gang worked to scare me off. But I didn't even flinch. I just called the board-up service and ordered new glass. They came right away, since I was such a good customer, boarded up the window over the weekend, and by Monday the glass would be replaced. By Friday night, the whole cycle would be repeated, but I didn't care. I was making plenty of money. Ironically, the leaders of the same gang that was blowing out my windows were the ones supplying me with cocaine and heroin. Their guys could never know, because I was buying much larger quantities than they were—a quarter of a kilo (about nine ounces) of coke every other day—and turning it over much faster than any of them. The gang bosses were happy to keep me supplied, so long as it was on the down-low. Money trumps loyalty every time.

With another baby on the way and Javier's easy money out of the picture, I felt the need to up my income. I found a lawyer connected with an adoption agency who worked under the table. He got me a lucrative monthly payment with the promise that I would give them my baby when it was born. I had no intention of giving my baby away, but I kept it up for a few months, and, because I did it under another name, the lawyer couldn't find me, so I was able to scam him, too. At the same time, purely by accident, I discovered a new scam that worked like a charm, making me over $140,000 in about four months.

I was helping a friend work a home-improvement scam, going to houses, acting like he owned a construction company, and ripping off the owners once they gave him a down payment. I saw how this gave him access to people's homes and belongings and decided it was time for me to branch out on my own with an original twist. I followed one of his leads by myself, showing up at the home of an older man named Pete. I quickly realized that Pete was suffering from dementia and had a hard time understanding exactly who I was and what I was doing in his house. His wife was dead, he had no children, and he was living alone in a nice house in Logan Square, a Northwest Side Chicago neighborhood. I immediately saw an opportunity. I played it by ear, became Pete's friend, and that very first day I started working what I thought could become a gold mine for me. I found his checkbook in a desk drawer, and the balance proved me right.

"Pete, let's go for a ride," I said as he sat in his La-Z-Boy, staring at his television. "We're going to stop by the bank, and I need your signature. We have to take out $10,000 because you're having your bathroom fixed, and we have to pay the guys." This first time, I gave him a reason for the money in case he would remember anything. I really wasn't sure how he would react.

"I don't have any money," he said, and I knew that he had no idea what was going on.

"No, no, no, I have all the money," I reassured him. "I just need you to come with me."

He agreed, and we went to the bank. I wrote one of his checks for $15,000.

"Just sign here, Pete, and everything will be fine."

"OK, thanks." He did as I asked. The teller counted out the $15,000, and I knew we were off and running.

I kept this up over the course of about four months, and there was never a hitch. Pete came to know me and seemed completely at home around me. I was as nice as could be and actually got to like him and care about him, even while I was cleaning out his bank account. I have no idea who he thought I was, but he was never afraid of me, and I never treated him badly. I found his wife's jewelry and helped myself to the nicer diamond rings. We kept making trips to the bank, timed in a way that I thought would avoid suspicion. What I didn't know at the time was that whenever a customer withdraws more than $10,000 at once, the bank is required to report it. So the FBI was building a case on me again. The tellers were noticing that the same woman, more heavily pregnant each time, kept coming in with this old man who withdrew a lot of money. I was usually noticeably high, too.

One time, we went to the bank near closing time. Pete had written the check out to me, so he could stay in the car while I went in. The bank had put most of the money into the vault, leaving only small bills out for last-minute customers. When the teller saw the amount of my check, another $15,000, she told me it was too late to cash such a big check because they had put all the hundreds away and to come back in the morning. I insisted that I needed the cash right now and would take it in whatever size bills they had. The woman had to unlock the teller's window and lift it up to hand me enough bundles of fives, tens, and twenties to make the $15,000. Of course, this was a glaring red flag for the bank, and I should have known better, but I was operating on heroin logic. I didn't realize how many bundles it would take to add up to $15,000 in small bills. She kept handing the bundles to me and I could only fit so much in my purse, so I shoved them in my bra, down my pants, in my coat pockets, all while the other tellers looked on in disbelief. I waddled out of there completely oblivious to how this looked.

Between dealing, scamming the adoption lawyer, and embezzling Pete's money, I had so much cash on hand I needed a safe place to stash it. Though Grandma had moved in with Uncle Joey, I didn't spend that much time with her anymore, because I didn't need money. Over the last few years I only came around when I was really desperate, and Grandma always gave me whatever she had. Uncle Joey tried to protect his mother from me, saying there wasn't a calculator on earth that could add up all the money and trouble I had caused her. When I had a good scam going or I was dealing a lot, I never showed up. Now, I had more cash than I could handle and needed a place to put it. There was a painting hanging in Grandma's bedroom upstairs, and when I checked behind it, I discovered that the wall was hollow. I made a small hole with a hammer and began regularly shoving rolled-up hundred-dollar bills through it, so the cash was piling up behind the drywall, down by the floorboards. It was a perfect hiding place. I had about $50,000 stuffed inside my uncle's wall, and even though I started showing up at the house more often, Uncle Joey and Grandma had no idea what I was doing. My uncle didn't want me in his house at all, so I could only go over there when he was at work. I decided to spread the money around and left another $30,000 at my father's house. He knew something serious was up with me.

"Daddy, can you just hold this $30,000 for me?" I asked, running in as he and Pat were having dinner.

"What? Wait just a minute. Where the fuck did you get cash like this?" He yelled at me as I was getting ready to run right back out. I knew this would drive him crazy, so I came up with a handy answer.

"Oh, I'm sorry, I thought I told you. I went to the racetrack and hit the trifecta. Isn't that great? So can you please just hold this money, Daddy?"

He wasn't buying it, but, afraid to ask, he took the money anyway. "Don't tell me anymore. I don't want to know."

Whenever I had money, I was generous with it. Friends would tell me their troubles, like they had to bond somebody out or pay some back rent; they'd ask me for $4,000 or $5,000, and I would happily give it to them. There was no subtlety to how I handled my money. I didn't care what anyone thought. I even paid $17,000 cash for a brand-new Buick. The dealer hesitated for a minute, asking me where I got the cash, but he was happy to take the money in the end.

All this time Grandma was taking care of Sean and Rachel. I was getting close to having the new baby and continued my trips to the bank to get Pete's money. But I had a feeling that I was pushing my luck and decided to cash one more check and then call it a day with Pete. I figured it was better to quit before things got too hot, and one more haul would be the end.

Pete and I walked into the bank, as usual, and stood at the counter where you write checks and organize your deposit before getting in line. As I leaned on the counter, looking down at the paperwork, I sensed two people coming up behind me. While I was still looking down, a Chicago detective's badge appeared right under my nose and a voice quietly said, "Come with us, miss."

"What's this about?" I was the picture of innocence.

"We know you're stealing this man's money. Please come with us."

"What? That's crazy. I'm not stealing anything. Pete gave me the money."

I was gently but firmly hustled into the bank president's office, with Pete following behind me, as he usually did. They sat us down on a couch and asked Pete, "Sir, did you give this woman your money?"

After four months of going along with me, in and out of the bank, signing checks and never saying a word, Pete suddenly came to his senses. "Oh, no, officer," he said quietly. "I don't know this woman and never gave her any money."

*Oh, fuck,* I thought, *now he remembers something.* I sat there, my mind racing. I was wearing several of Pete's wife's diamond rings and the minute he said he didn't know me, I knew that getting caught with them could add home invasion to a potential embezzlement charge. I had to get rid of those rings. Every time the detectives turned their attention to something else, I slipped a ring off and stuffed it down into the bank president's couch until they were all buried there. I've often wondered if anybody ever found them or if there's an old couch still sitting somewhere with thousands of dollars in diamonds stuffed in between the cushions.

A rigorous investigation had been going on around my activities. The FBI had been working with the bank and the Chicago Police Department to nail down my identity. I found myself in the Chicago police lockup at Fifty-First Street and Wentworth Avenue, a high-security holding place for major crimes. I was seven months pregnant and strung out. It was even worse than the last time. I kept trying to convince the police that I was not a major criminal.

"Officers, I'm a prostitute, all right? He was my trick, that's it." I was ready to say almost anything not to be charged with embezzlement, but it wasn't working. The pregnancy worked in my favor, though, and was probably why they set my bail at a fairly low $100,000, which meant I only needed $10,000 to walk. So I called Pat, told her to bring the money I'd left at my father's place and to come bond me out. Sweet faithful Pat did exactly that, and I got out of jail after only two days.

I went back to my apartment in Cicero as if nothing had happened, dealing and getting high in between court dates. I did heroin the rest of my pregnancy. I was completely lost to the drug now and truly didn't care anymore. When I woke up the first morning out of jail, a police tow truck was outside the apartment, confiscating my car. The cops started coming around all the time, looking for Pete's money, and I started going to court. They appointed a special prosecutor to my case, not the usual overloaded public prosecutor. She was only in court for my case, and she wanted to nail me. She charged me with "financial exploitation of the elderly and/or disabled," because Pete had dementia. This was a serious charge, and I could have been looking at twenty years in prison.

Every time I went to court, the prosecutor demanded to know where Pete's money was. I would argue that I did a lot of heroin, and it was expensive.

"Your Honor, there's no way she could consume almost $140,000 of heroin in four months," the state's attorney argued.

"Your Honor, there's no money left," I answered. "I have a lot of friends. They're all heroin addicts, and I'm a very generous person. I have no money." I was determined to hold on to the money inside Uncle Joey's wall.

When I was about eight months along in my pregnancy, my old friend MJ came to visit me from Tucson. I was glad to see her and figured we'd have a good time, partying like we used to back in the day. Instead, MJ was shocked and ridden with guilt when she saw me. I was living in Cicero in an apartment that had become a trap house, with junkies passed out on the floor, gang members coming and going at all hours to buy drugs and hang out, and me locked in the bathroom for hours at a time, reminiscent of what MJ did in her own apartment years ago when I was a curious seventeen-year-old and she got me high for the first time. It was all too much for her. She actually used the phone in my apartment and called a rehab facility in Chicago, Haymarket, to get herself admitted. She got into a cab and went straight there. She has been clean ever since and now works with other addicts to help them get free of the same beast that almost killed her. I could not see what she saw at that moment. I was still blinded by heroin and the life I was living.

About a month after MJ left, in between court appearances, I gave birth to my third child, a daughter I named Christina. She was born with heroin in her system and family services would not allow me to leave the hospital with her, so I had to find a family member to take custody. My mother agreed to take Christina only if I agreed to come and live with her and to stay clean. Four days after moving in with them, I borrowed forty dollars from my brother Joe telling him it was for baby formula. Joe was my mother's son from her second marriage. I walked out the door and never went back. I did exactly what my mother had done when I was five, and she said she was going out for milk for my breakfast and never came back. But I knew Christina was better off living with my mother than with me, and plus, I could not wait to get back to Cicero. I had a lot of business to take care of and, of course, heroin was calling me. My sister Dina ended up adopting and raising Christina, and I would not see my second daughter again until she was twenty.

Even though my lawyer was able to use my pregnancy and then the fact that I had a newborn as reasons to extend my case, it was coming to a head and I was running out of options. He told me that I was probably going to get some serious time. I was starting to feel desperate.

"What if I return some money after all?" I asked my lawyer.

"Well, I think that would help," he said.

"Your Honor," I said when asked again about the money during my next court appearance, "um, I actually remembered where I put some of it and would like to return it."

The court immediately agreed that they wanted it, so they sent me with two Chicago detectives to Uncle Joey's house. Poor Grandma had no idea what was going on.

"Grandma, I need a hammer," I hollered from the top of the stairs, the two cops standing there with me.

"What the fuck are you doing?" Grandma screamed back.

"Never mind! Just get me a hammer right now."

"Joey's gonna kill you!" she said as she climbed the stairs and handed me the hammer. I started banging on the wall, tearing the wallboard open down near the floor.

"What the hell? Are we at Al Capone's house?" one of the detectives remarked.

"What am I gonna tell Joey? He's gonna kill me now!" Grandma was distraught.

"Grandma, just shut up," I screamed back.

All this drama was a good distraction, and I was able to pull some money out and push some back in while Grandma kept screaming and making the sign of the cross. I handed a big wad to the detectives, who counted it. They had $27,500, a little more than half of what was in the wall. The cop put the money inside his jacket, patted his chest, and said, "Hey, you know what I got here? I got a house payment." I shot him a dirty look. We left the house with a hole in the wall. Grandma went into action, quickly reaching into the wall to salvage the rest of the cash and hide it for me. She told my father that she made the hole in the wall herself by moving a dresser. He came and patched it up before Uncle Joey ever found out. Later on, when I needed money, Grandma would give me whatever I wanted.

My case was out of extensions, and it was time for sentencing. My last act of desperation was a real long shot. I applied for prison boot camp. This was a special six-month Department of Corrections program that was so rigorous and physically challenging that most men couldn't pass it, and women rarely even tried. But if you did manage to get through boot camp, you walked. The special prosecutor was reluctant to agree at first, but then she said that I was such a drug addict there was absolutely no way a degenerate like me would get through the program. I would fail and have to do all my time anyway, she predicted, so she went along, and it was put to the judge.

As he deliberated, the judge said, "I will take into consideration that you gave $22,500 back—"

"No, no, *no*, wait, Your Honor," I interrupted him. "That's wrong. I gave $27,500 back."

"Oh, I'm sorry, Bianca," he said as he reached for his reading glasses and checked again. "No, it says here $22,500."

"They ripped me off! The police ripped me off!" I couldn't believe that cop actually did it.

"Bianca, let it go," my lawyer said. "You stole it, they stole it, who cares? You'll be home in six months if you get through boot camp."

I was sentenced to seven years in prison or completion of boot camp. If I flunked out of boot camp, I had to do the seven in total. They immediately took me into custody, and I was back inside Cook County Jail.

I endured the entire Cook County intake process, and this time I was held there for two weeks. I had started myself on methadone a few weeks earlier when I realized that my sentencing was imminent, so I managed to get through detox a little easier. But this time around, there was no special blanket and pillow delivery in the middle of the night prompted by my mother's phone calls. Neither my mother nor my father made any extra calls on my behalf, and I realized just how estranged we were becoming. I had started paying for my lawyer, but in the middle of this case my father went into crisis mode. He realized that if they decided to investigate me further to find out where I was getting the money to cover a high-priced attorney, I could catch another charge since all my activities were illegal. That, on top of what I was already facing, could send me to prison for many years. So he paid my lawyer and later on would even send money to my prison account, but he washed his hands of trying to do more. Even though they still sent me money, most of my family was done feeling sorry for me. They were tired of being hurt and disappointed and no longer worried about trying to help me get out of jail. I had managed to alienate everyone but Aunt Louise, who would stay in contact as best she could throughout my life.

There was a waiting list for boot camp, so from Cook County I was shipped back to Dwight until a space opened up for me. I was there for another three months because the state had only recently allowed women to qualify for boot camp and the spaces were limited. I was lucky to even be on the waiting list. Before my time, to qualify for boot camp you had to be under thirty-five, sentenced to less than eight years, have no violent crime on your record, and no prior time in the penitentiary. A few months before my lawyer submitted boot camp as an option for me, the law was changed and would allow one prior sentence served in an Illinois Department of Corrections facility. So I had my spot on the list and didn't mind waiting at Dwight. In fact, if I had to be locked up, I was happy to be back there. I knew all the correctional officers, the house girls, and many of my friends from the first time were still there, so it was like a homecoming. I was back in cottage eight with CO Knight and CO Rose in charge, but this time I had to stay separated and in lockdown there because I was going to boot camp, so I was never moved to general population.

My cellie and I were both waiting for spots to open up, along with about twenty other women. I didn't have a work assignment and hardly got to move around at all, but I was allowed to shop at the commissary. Over those three months, I began to gain weight like never before, packing on almost fifty pounds. My body was so depleted from doing heroin every day that I was very thin when I first went into Cook County. Now my only activity was sitting around on my bunk at Dwight, smoking cigarettes, drinking coffee, and stuffing candy and snacks into my mouth out of sheer boredom. I lived on Little Debbie snack cakes, Snickers bars, Milky Ways, and potato chips. I spent at least fifty dollars a week in the commissary on junk food. I wasn't allowed to go to the chow hall for meals, so instead they were delivered to my cell. As I had nothing else to do and was so hyper, I ate whatever they gave me. If CO Knight let me out to polish the brass in the dayroom, I had to lie on the floor because my legs had become too heavy and squatting was uncomfortable. By the time I was shipped to boot camp, I was in the worst physical shape of my life, about to undergo the most difficult, relentless training a Marine Corps drill sergeant could dish out.

Finally, the day to get shipped out arrived. I was taken with one other inmate on the five-hour drive from Dwight to Vienna, Illinois, right on the Kentucky border. The officers let us smoke and eat along the way, like we were on a road trip, albeit chained and shackled and wearing bright canary-yellow prison jumpsuits. I watched the rural countryside go by and tried not to worry about what was coming next. We arrived at the Vienna prison, a men's facility that was also the intake hub for the Dixon Springs boot camp. The place was way out in the sticks, with nothing for miles around but woods and big empty fields. Once we got inside, they put us in a cage and the male inmates, some who had not seen a woman in months, stared at us. I was extremely self-conscious thanks to my newly acquired girth and didn't want any of these men to see me, so rather than flirt, I kept my eyes down and burned with embarrassment. We were taken from the intake cage to a van with about six men in the back and the women in the front. One of the prisoners was a former professional football player for the Miami Dolphins. As we settled in for the ride, I started asking if any of the men knew what came next. This prompted a locker-room-style, full-throttle pep talk from the football player.

"Listen up," he barked. "We're gonna get through this. Everyone look at me! Tough up! We're gonna make it, we're gonna make it. Fuck these guys, just fuck 'em." How he could look at me and even entertain this idea seemed absurd. But if I was nervous before, I was really getting anxious now.

The van pulled up and parked. Before we were let out, I could see a line of drill sergeants, correctional officers who were all ex-marines, in combat boots and full CO uniform, waiting for us. One of them opened the door and shouted at us to get out very quickly, one by one, walk to the officers standing up against the intake building, and wait to be directed. I lumbered out of that van as fast as I possibly could, but the officer kept shouting to move it. Every army movie I'd ever seen ran through my head. This was real, and I started to wonder what the hell I had gotten myself into.

The officers knew all about every one of us, why we were in prison, our entire criminal history, whether we were in gangs, all the things they could use to taunt us and try to mentally break us down, which was their mission, starting the moment we stepped out of that van. They never just spoke to us; they shouted everything. There was absolutely no talking back or asking questions without permission to speak, which was hardly ever granted. I never stopped talking, and now even one word would result in painful discipline. But my will remained strong, and that's the only reason I could even hope to survive what was coming.

"Get up against the wall! Turn around! Turn around!" They shouted this so many times that I was out of breath before they ordered us to stop. Then, each of us was taken by an officer and led inside for intake.

On the way in, the officers taunted us, yelling things like, "Your mama was a whore. Your daddy was a crack addict. And you're just a piece of shit." And to me, "Oh, here's the girl who stole all that money from the poor old man! That coulda been my grandfather, bitch."

When I tried to choke out "I'm sorry," they screamed almost in unison, "I didn't tell you to talk!" It was a lesson in submission, but not the worst thing I'd ever been through. That was still to come.

The first real trauma for me that day was getting a haircut. My hair was something I labored over, using only the best products to keep it shiny and beautiful. It was thick and wavy and had grown to my waist. I was proud of it. The intake area was one big room, with chairs positioned in the center for each inmate. I was told to sit in a chair. I could hear the buzz of the shaver. Silent tears ran down my face as I was given a crew cut. Every time I tried to turn and see how much hair was falling off, I was screamed at and told not to move my head. When it was over, my hair was about an inch long. I felt naked and humiliated. I realized a hostile takeover of my entire being had just begun. Part of the intake process was a physical exam with a nurse, and that's when the day's second trauma occurred. I was weighed for the first time in months and tilted the scale at 176 pounds, a number I never even hit when I was pregnant. The nurse said, "Don't worry, you'll lose it here."

I was taken to dorm three, where I took my first timed shower and was told to wash my entire body and shave my legs and armpits, something the women were required to do all the time. The water was turned off at exactly three minutes. If you were still soapy, too bad. Instead of full uniforms, new inmates were given combat boots and an oversized white jumpsuit that we had to wear for two weeks before getting a regular uniform, a blue blouse and pants. For those two weeks we were called "ghosts." The first order of business was a reading of the rules, including how to approach and address the staff, with special code words for even simple tasks. Permission had to be asked for everything, and if you didn't ask properly or address a CO the correct way, you were forced to do extra push-ups or laps around the track, or other grueling punishments like standing at attention in the hot sun for eight hours, unable to move even to keep the sweat from dripping into your eyes. You were never to say thank you or apologize. Instead, we said "*Hoorah!*" when responding to an order or a request. When we walked past an officer, we didn't salute, but we had to say, "By your leave, sir (or ma'am)." I felt like I was on a prison chain gang in Mississippi. The officers sounded like they'd seen the movie *Cool Hand Luke* one too many times, and those of us from Chicago actually had to work at not laughing out loud. It seemed so dramatic and over the top.

We learned that every day we were required to fall out for the morning run at 5:30. Since I was among the new arrivals, I only had to run three miles until I was in better shape; then it would be the full five miles. I thought the CO saying this was delusional. There was no way I could run one block, let alone three miles. I had never run anywhere in my life. And the morning run was one of two; the other run was at the end of the day, every day. The first morning I was horrified at having to get up. We were led to the huge outdoor track situated in the middle of Shawnee National Forest. There was nothing but trees for miles around, and I realized how hard it would be to escape. I told myself I could do this run and tried to mentally force myself around that track. After a few yards in the heat of the day, I was so out of breath I was heaving and getting nauseated. But the officers actually took pity on me, saw that I was trying, and in their own special way, said they would work with me, shouting things like, "Inmate Bianca, sling your fat ass around this track!"

The next four months was a series of missteps and harsh disciplinary actions that never really broke me but caused me so much physical pain I didn't think it was possible to hurt that much unless I was detoxing. I earned so many demerits and case notes that my stay was extended an extra thirty days, to five months. You were required to complete 120 days in boot camp within six months or you were thrown out and had to do all your prison time. Another extension and I could be back at Dwight for seven years. Most of the time I didn't break the rules on purpose. I just could never understand what the big deal was about trying to have a conversation. It was next to impossible for me to keep my mouth shut. There was absolutely no talking in the chow hall, where you were given exactly ten minutes to completely clean your plate and finish everything else that was on your tray. The portions were big, and the food was the best prison food I had ever had, but if you weren't finished in ten minutes, you had to squat, hold your tray, and consume everything that was left on it, including salt and ketchup packets, in one minute. Otherwise you faced grueling time on what was called the "motivation course," a series of physical challenges, climbing walls, climbing ropes, running up hills, all through the woods, in the humid Kentucky afternoon. Depending on the infraction, you could be out there for hours.

Only once did I willfully get in trouble, and it involved ice cream. When it was time for me to do the five-mile run every morning, it was so difficult that I started to plot a way to get out of it. I had managed to make friends with the officer who ran the kitchen, and when his assistant was released, I replaced her. This meant I had to report for that duty in the morning instead of the run, and I would make the sign of the cross every day when I heard the sound of runners on the track while I was inside the air-conditioned kitchen trying to get the other inmate to help me figure out what I was supposed to be doing all day. So I managed to get out of the morning run, not the evening run, but at least it was cooler out there later in the day. One morning I was working and a delivery truck arrived, which I had to help unload. Vanilla and chocolate ice cream were part of the delivery, along with peanuts and whipped cream, and I became obsessed with having a sundae. Once the delivery crew left, I found myself alone with what proved to be too much temptation. I got a Styrofoam cup and quickly filled it with both flavors of ice cream, nuts, chocolate syrup I'd found in the walk-in refrigerator, and a pile of whipped cream on top. I was in heaven, sitting at the CO's desk, my feet up, savoring every bite. Out of the corner of my eye, I saw a lieutenant walk in. "Ten-hut!" he cried. I jumped up, let the cup and the spoon drop to the floor, and with chocolate running down my face, kept my mouth closed tight, afraid to even swallow. The lieutenant paced in front of me as he contemplated what to do, torturing me with his silence. Finally, he said, "You might as well finish eating it because you are in deep shit either way." I was hit with a program review in front of the warden and superintendent, and my stay was extended for fifteen days. Why they didn't expel me I will never know, but I lost the job and was back out on the track every morning and every night.

Yet nothing could discourage me from breaking the rules. I tried to fake spit-polishing my boots by using wax I stole from the cleaning supplies, but I only waxed the tips of my boots, reasoning that with my uniform pants on, that was all that showed. When the CO lifted my pant leg it was obvious that I had cheated, so back to the motivation course I went. I tried to condition what was left of my hair with lotion I stockpiled in secret, got caught, and spent another three days on the motivation course. I even got punished for a racy cartoon birthday card from an old pen pal from Dwight featuring Dorothy and the Tin Man having sex. I had to read it out loud into a microphone in front of every male inmate and describe the cartoon. I got more time on the motivation course and another fifteen-day extension on my stay for something that wasn't even my fault.

But the hardest day in boot camp was the day I had to run the track carrying an eighty-pound log over my shoulder. I had been reassigned to a job in the tool shed and one day while working there, a male inmate came in and I recognized him as someone I knew from the West Side of Chicago. We were so happy to see one another that we exchanged a few surprised words before we noticed the captain standing in the back. He was furious and first told the male inmate to go to the track, pick up a log, and do ten laps. "Sir, yes sir," the poor guy hollered as he ran out the toolshed door. A few minutes later, while I was still standing at attention, I caught a glimpse of him running around the track shouldering an actual log. I figured there was no way the officer would assign the same punishment to me, but the next thing I knew, I was out there, trying to hoist a log of my own. There was no way I could run with it, so he let me walk instead, but I still had to do ten laps. It took until long after sundown. I had bruises everywhere, and every inch of my body was in pain. Many times, in the middle of these punishments, the officers would taunt me.

"Hey, inmate Bianca, how great would a pack of Newports and a cup of coffee be right now? All you gotta do is give up. Just say the word and we'll send your fat ass back to Dwight. You can sit on your bunk and eat Snickers all day."

"Sir, no sir!" I would shout, refusing to let them get the best of me.

"You know you're never going to graduate."

"Sir, then I'm leaving in a box, because I'm never quitting, sir."

And I never gave in. I got by on sheer will most of the time. I figured out how to do the hardest tasks, one time having to dig up a tree stump with a small shovel. Many times I would be out long after nine at night, finishing a set of push-ups or a few more laps around the track. The other female inmates told me they would be in their bunks after lights out and hear me counting off and feel so sorry for me.

I graduated as the most frequently punished woman to have made it through the program. I filled seven demerit cards, a new record. And even though I drove them a little bit crazy, the officers got a kick out of me; some of them even started calling me Private Benjamin, like Goldie Hawn in the movie. The nurse at intake was right; I lost over thirty pounds. The day of my discharge came. Each inmate was allowed street clothes from home to wear on the bus ride, and Aunt Louise had sent mine. As usual, she went all out. A huge box with two outfits, matching shoes, two purses, all wrapped in tissue paper, plus makeup, and hairbrushes arrived for me. The superintendent and the lieutenant in charge of the property room called me in.

"Bianca, does your aunt Louise know that we're putting you on a Greyhound bus, you're going directly to your family's house in Chicago, and you'll be on house arrest until your parole is over? Or, does she think you're going to Acapulco?"

I happily wore one of the outfits, and they gave me the money that my aunt had been sending that had piled up over five months because you can't shop in boot camp. I was ecstatic. We stopped on the way home, and I bought a pack of cigarettes. I felt great.

My brother Joe picked me up at the Ninety-Fifth Street bus stop and took me to my mother's house. My family did not really want me there, and they were so worried that I was going to take Christina, they didn't even want me to see her. I was clean, had completed boot camp, and my daughter wasn't yet fully adopted by my sister, who was officially her foster parent. I insisted that I wanted my baby back, and in my heart I did. I wanted to do the right thing, but I simply wasn't capable. I was always late getting back to my mother's house and causing the alarm to go off on the electronic monitoring device. I eventually cut the band off my ankle, so then I was AWOL and a warrant was issued for parole violation, but it took the police a few weeks to catch me. I started getting high within a week after being released. My mother's other son, my brother Rich, tried to give me a chance, letting me work as a receptionist for his carpet cleaning company, but I took twenty dollars from petty cash and my brother's car and drove to Cicero the first day on the job. I kept the car for over a month. I was arrested right before Christmas, and in less than six weeks I was back at Dwight. My family didn't see me again for a very long time.

# Part III

# Let It Be

# 8

# When Doves Cry

I MEET BOBBY AS HE'S RIDING his bike. He's an energetic teenager, still in high school, handsome and charming, and flashes the best smile in the world, one that captures my heart. He is all personality and has the kind of charisma that street swagger breeds, a combination of tough-guy posturing, a wisdom beyond his years, and a quick sense of humor. I soon learn that he is also a talented rapper. I just love him from the start and know I will do whatever I can for him.

On this warm summer day, he rides up to my car window and as I roll it down, I say, "Hey, are you Bobby?"

"Yeah, you're Bianca, right? My brother told me about you," he says.

I met Bobby's brother, Jesse,* a few months earlier. I was out canvassing the neighborhood after a shooting, handing out public education materials and talking to kids on the corners with my Cure Violence team, hoping to defuse the situation. Jesse told me about Bobby, still in juvie at the time, but about to be released. He wanted the crazy white lady who knew so much about the street to meet his little brother.

"So I heard you're pretty good with music," I say as Bobby sits there on his bike, sizing me up.

"Yeah, that's what they say," he shrugs, but I catch a glimmer of pride in his face.

---

* For the sake of privacy, both Bobby's and Jesse's names have been changed.

"Do *you* think you're any good?"

"Well, yeah, I think so."

"So, how can I check you out?"

He grins and tells me he has some videos on YouTube, so I look him up. I'm impressed with his delivery and his way with words. I can see his talent, but I'm not happy about his subject matter. Rap lyrics with violence as a theme, disrespecting and taunting other gangs, are not only unacceptable; they're dangerous. Lyrics that glorify guns and recount real gang shootings lead to retaliation that goes far beyond words and kids end up killing one another to defend their sense of honor. The accessibility of social media and the ease of making videos with smartphones have become ways to provoke and escalate a war already in full swing. I spend the next three years trying to convince Bobby that he should write different lyrics.

"Can't you write songs that don't disrespect somebody? That's what I want to see," I say to him.

"I got a lot of them like that. I'll show them to you."

"That's what I want you to put on YouTube. That could be your legacy."

He would just laugh, as if that was the craziest thing I had ever said to him. Nasty, volatile lyrics have become so popular and lucrative that record labels and music producers help support the proliferation of a rap genre that is literally killing kids. Some labels have even been known to hedge their bets by taking out a life insurance policy on a new kid when they sign him. Bobby is caught up in the promise of fame and fortune, unwilling to change the content of what he thinks will get him there. I know he's involved in a gang, and I know he needs to see other possibilities if I'm ever going to change his mind and possibly save his life.

I spend time with Bobby whenever I can, taking him out to lunch once in a while, like I often do with the kids I mentor. Whenever I see him on the street, I stop the car, call to him, and he always takes time to talk with me, flashing that devastating smile and leaving me laughing. We become close friends over the next three years. He knows he can count on me. But it's not enough to turn him away from life on the street. Bobby is a real street kid who loves being there, and I'm afraid for him, just as I am for so many young men engaged in the same cycle of violence.

There are two attempts on Bobby's life during these years. Both shootings spare him, but kill two innocent bystanders. After the second time, I call him. I want to talk to him, so I ask him to come out to lunch. Jesse comes with us. I'm so worried about Bobby that I tell him to turn his location off on his phone so nobody can follow him. I'm on high alert when I pick them up, taking the same kind of precautions I used to take when I was still in the life, trying to get away from other gang members or the police. I adjust the mirrors in my car so I can see all around me, keep it in drive, survey the whole block for people lurking in the alley, have the doors unlocked, and am ready to drive out of there as soon as they get into the car. Bobby thinks I'm crazy.

"Damn, Bianca," he laughs as I pull away from the curb the second they shut their car doors.

"No, no, no, listen. I am not getting my car shot up, or getting either one of you killed!"

But Bobby is every bit the tough guy. "It ain't nothin'," he insists.

"I'm telling you, you have to be careful. You can't assume nobody's coming back to finish the job." I'm trying so hard to get him to understand how dangerous his situation really is.

"Don't you worry, Bianca. I'm goin' to Georgia to stay with one of my cousins for a while."

"Will you be safe there?"

"Oh yeah, I'll just lay low."

I feel a little better, but I'm the only one who does. A few of my colleagues and others who know about Bobby's gang activities try to convince me that he's on the worst possible path. They are hearing talk on the street. The threat of Bobby getting shot again is very real, but I refuse to listen. I truly believe that I can save him. Even so, I always hug him like it might be the last time.

When he gets back to Chicago a few months later, we talk and he tells me some big news. A major record label is ready to sign him. He expects it to happen within the next month. He's living the dream, he says. I'm truly excited for him, but he's still out on the street, running with the gang, and his lyrics are as hard-core as ever.

One night about a week after I saw Bobby, I randomly wake up at 2:00 AM for no apparent reason. I smoke a cigarette, roll over, and try to go back to sleep. And then my phone rings.

"Bianca?" I recognize the voice. It's one of his friends. "Man, they just killed Bobby!"

"What are you talking about?" I say. "Where? How?"

He didn't know a whole lot at that moment. Bobby had been dropped off in his hood, but another car was waiting there. Somebody inside that car shot him in the back.

I am frantic. I try to call Jesse and Bobby's mother, but get no answer. I start to cry, but part of me is not convinced that he has really died. There is still a chance. I Google all the news outlets and check social media and find nothing. Maybe it's a mistake, or a bad nightmare. I fall back asleep for a couple of hours. But when I wake up, the first thing I do is check again, and there it is. Bobby is dead. I lose it. Though I have to go to the office, I cry all through my shower and all the way on the drive in. When I walk off the elevator on my floor, makeup dripping down my face from the tears, my colleagues are waiting, ready to help in any way they can, consoling me, hugging me, saying they know how much I loved him and how hard this one is for me. One of my supervisors says he can set me up with a counselor, but I just keep sobbing and saying I will be OK. I wander into my office like a zombie and sit at my desk. I am overwhelmed by the feeling that it was my fault; I did not do enough to keep Bobby alive. I rock back and forth in my chair and start hitting myself in the head, angry at my own inability to stop the inevitable. Another one of my supervisors, LeVon, is out in the hall and sees what I'm doing.

"Hold on, Bianca, hold on," he says as he comes into my office. "I know what happened, and I'm really sorry, but you know as much as anybody, that's what goes with the life."

"I know, I know, but I just—"

"Hold on," he says again. He can see how much I'm struggling. "Let me ask you something. What could you have done to save his life? Tell me what you could have done."

I immediately start sharing the irrational things going through my head. "Well, if I could have gotten him an apartment out of state or let him stay at my place, or maybe if I got him a job and he was off the street, or maybe if I had gotten him back in school . . ." These are all things that I know are unreasonable and just not possible. Bobby was a street kid. None of this was ever going to happen.

"Stop!" LeVon interrupts. And then he says the most important words I have ever heard in my professional life, words that I will have to repeat to myself many times: "Bianca, some people are destined to destroy themselves no matter what you do."

I start to protest. He repeats those exact words and then says, "Do you hear what I'm saying?"

I do hear him. I realize at that moment that he's right. There was nothing more I could have done. I did everything in my power to help Bobby.

I can't go to his funeral because I have to go out of town for work, so I do something I have done many times after we lose someone. I always feel the need to honor the dead in some way. I am in Upstate New York, near Lake Ontario. On my way to a morning training session, I stop at a florist, buy a dozen roses, and walk down to the pier. I look out over the dark churning water. It is like the void that Bobby's death will leave for me, for Jesse, for his mother, and for all those who knew and loved him. He was on his way to tasting his dream, but now he's been lost like so many others to the darkness of violence. I toss the roses into the water and watch as they disappear.

Bobby's loss still weighs heavily on my heart, even after everything I've seen and been through. I know how hard it is for his mother and family to cope; the pain never subsides. Sometimes, the only thing I can do to help is to grieve with them. I attend more funerals than I care to remember, and when another mother loses another child to the streets, there are no words, only a presence that says, "Here I am, one more person who loved your baby."

It is a hot day in July, one of those days when the entire city of Chicago seems to hit the streets. For some, it means outdoor cafés, family time at the beach, and balmy nights on fancy roof decks. For too many others in high-risk neighborhoods, a hot day in July means a spike in shootings and more death to mourn. I am at work when it happens again, and I get the worst kind of phone call.

"Bianca, they just killed Vee! He was standing right in front of his apartment, Bianca. He had his babies in his arms and their mama was right there, too."

"Oh my God! What can I do?" The second I say this, Vee's mother, the woman at the other end of the call, becomes hysterical.

"My baby! He's dead, he's gone!"

I can feel her pain and my own tears start. "Sandy, whatever you need," I manage to choke out. "What the hell happened?"

She tells me Vee was with his kids, a seven-year-old son and two younger daughters. Their mother said later that Vee had noticed a rival gang member walking by and told her they had to get the kids inside. She started gathering up their toys. Vee picked up his daughters and had his son by his side, trying to hurry them into the house, just as the guy came back and opened fire. He shot Vee right there, with his kids in the line of fire. Vee hit the ground still holding his daughter, as the guy ran off.

The kids were screaming, "Daddy, Daddy, get up!"

Their mother dropped the toys and ran to him. Vee was still conscious and said something to his son who was lying there next to him, unharmed but completely traumatized as his father's blood ran down the sidewalk. The little girls were crying and gasping for breath. Neighbors ventured out of their houses to see what had happened, watching in stunned silence as the ambulance crew closed the doors and drove away with Vee close to death. The horror of a father being gunned down with his children in his arms is beyond understanding. Vee succumbed to his wounds and died in the hospital about an hour later.

Sandy tells me all this over the phone as she goes from trying to calm down one minute to complete hysteria the next. She's living in another state and says she has to get on a plane to Chicago as soon as possible.

"How am I gonna bury another baby, Bianca? How am I gonna do it?"

"I'm here, Sandy. Whatever you need." That's all I can say.

We say good-bye and I feel my own shock starting to set in. Sandy has already lost a son to gang violence. I have known the family for years because I've been to court with them a few times, appearing on behalf of a third son, Vee's brother Cheng, helping to keep him out of jail and mentoring him. I worry now about his reaction to losing another brother, and I cannot fathom how Sandy is going to get through this loss, but I know I will be there for her.

I leave my office and immediately go to the hospital. I meet Vee's cousins in the waiting area, and they tell me he's gone. We cry together. Then I go to Vee's neighborhood. I know his guys are going to be angry and beyond consoling; this is not the time for mediation. All they can see is that a dude shot Vee with his kids in his arms. There is nothing I can say to any of them. We all loved him. I just want to be with them, hug them, and let them know I care. Then I head over to his sister-in-law's house nearby, and the same scene repeats, hugging and crying, shock and disbelief. Vee was not that active in gang business. He was trying to stay out of the way and focus on his kids. He was the last person we expected to get shot on the street like that.

Sandy calls me in a few days with details about the funeral. Gang-related funerals are not made public in the hopes of avoiding retaliation, but that doesn't always work. I have witnessed shootings at funerals many times, even at churches. I've seen caskets riddled with bullets while mourners duck behind the pews, adding to the horror and grief of a family's worst day. I tell Sandy I'll come to the viewing because I have to leave town for my job and can't make the funeral services. I get to the funeral home before anyone else, so I call Sandy just to let her know I'm there.

"Bianca, go ahead in. You don't have to wait for us."

"I can wait," I say, not wanting to intrude or be disrespectful to the family.

"No, no, no," Sandy insists. "I'm going to call the funeral director right now and tell him you're family. You go in and talk to Vee. Do whatever you want to do."

I try not to choke up as I ring the bell. The funeral director leads me inside. I ask where Vee is, and he points to a room. I slowly walk in and find myself alone with the casket. I freeze for a moment. I do not want this to be true, I do not want it to be Vee lying there. I walk to him and break down. I put my head on his chest and tell him I love him. I kiss his cheek, having asked Sandy if it's OK to touch him. She told me Vee loved me and yes, it's OK. I also asked if I could place a red rose with a card in his casket, which I do.

The family starts to come in, so I take a seat. When Sandy walks in I can see that she is trying to keep it together. She hugs me and says it will be OK. But when Vee's children come in with their mother, Sandy loses it. She falls across his body and screams for him to wake up. "Mommy's here," she keeps saying. The grief in that room is like a heavy fog, overwhelming us and making it hard to breathe. Vee's son is standing near me. He's trying so hard not to cry. I can see the contortions in his young face and I know he's struggling to be a big boy. It is too much to bear. I get up and walk over to him.

"Baby, do you remember me?" I ask.

"Yeah, I remember you," he whispers.

"It's OK to cry. It's OK," I take his hand.

"I thought it was fireworks. My Daddy had blood and fell. But he said, 'Daddy will be OK. At least I made the three of y'all.'" And with that, he finally starts sobbing, his little hands covering his face.

I hug him and then let his mother take over as I walk outside. I need a cigarette and join a few of Vee's cousins, out there doing the same. I keep thinking about Vee's son, already trying to be a man, trying not to cry in front of his daddy's casket. My heart aches for all the little boys and girls who will grow up haunted by memories of violence and loss, victims of a senseless, vicious cycle that plays out on the streets every day. It's their minds that I work to change, as they grow into high-risk teenagers ready to pick up a gun, caught up in the same endless war. I would meet their mothers in the penitentiary and hear the same stories over and over again, the same broken hearts trying to understand what happened to their babies. The women I met there have become my family; their children, my children. It didn't take me long to understand the devastating ripple effect that one bullet can have on a victim's family members, especially the mothers left behind to bury their children But it would take me many years of overcoming my own bad choices before I finally understood that violence is a learned behavior and can be reversed.

# 9

# A Rose on the Gray

I FOUND MYSELF CHAINED TO the seats on an Illinois Department of Corrections bus headed from Dwight prison to Logan, a coed facility even farther away from Chicago, to serve one year for violating my parole. This bus had an armed guard in a protective cage, higher security than I had ever seen before. I was handcuffed to another young woman named Sarah. I immediately noticed that she was wearing makeup, lipstick and real eyeliner, and I had to know how she'd managed it. She explained that she'd been in Dwight for over a year and was not coming directly from intake, as I was. We became fast friends, and she let me use some of her lipstick right there on the bus. I was really excited because there were male inmates at Logan, including many of my gang brothers. I knew they would look out for me, and I could make myself pretty comfortable. Within weeks, I was in a photography class; I was having sex with two inmates and even an officer in exchange for contraband and drugs; Aunt Louise had sent me my own clothes; and I was in great shape from boot camp, so I felt attractive again.

By this time in my criminal career, I had learned how to be "game conscious," on the street as well as in prison. I knew when someone was bullshitting me or trying to play me. I knew how to work the system, so I really didn't care about being locked up. Having sex in the library and bathrooms or giving a CO a blow job in an empty office would get me whatever I needed from the outside; the officers would keep up their end of the bargain since they knew that if any of us decided to snitch they would lose their jobs. It was easy for them to smuggle just about anything into prison, so I had everything I wanted, except my freedom. In Logan, heroin was so easy to get I even caught a habit again while I was inside. This was back in the day when inmates ran the prisons, and drugs and other contraband flowed freely throughout the joint. I had officers bringing me food and condoms from the outside. After having sex in a bathroom with an officer, I would say, "So what's our wife making us for dinner tomorrow?" And he would say, "I don't know. What do we want?" All of this was obviously against the rules and even a crime, but in those days prisons didn't have cameras placed around every corner, like they do today, so we got away with all of it.

Before I was shipped to Logan, one of the COs at Dwight said he was in love with me and started stalking me because I wasn't showing him enough attention. He worked the midnight shift on my unit and would come around to get me out of my cell so we could have sex in the laundry room. But he was getting really loose and clumsy about when we met up. I knew I had to end it. He might get fired, but I would end up in "seg," solitary confinement, for a year and lose all my good conduct time. At about the same time, I was told I fit the criteria for a minimum-security facility in Kankakee and could volunteer to transfer. There were no fences, no locked cell doors, and I even heard from another inmate that they had tablecloths in the chow hall. But instead of getting excited, I snapped and refused the offer. Even though it was a chance to get away from my stalker CO, I knew that a place without much action was not for me. I thrived on the drama inside prison, and I knew I would go crazy; time would pass too slowly without the constant gaming that made being in the joint interesting and exciting.

To get out of it, I said to my counselor, "The minute those people send me on the side of the road to pick up cigarette butts, I'm taking the first thing 'smoking' to Chicago." She immediately upped my security status from minimum to medium and had no choice but to ship me to Logan.

I had one bad moment during that first time in Logan. After Pappo was killed, I had drifted away from the Latin gang and concentrated my activities in Cicero. I was skipping gang meetings in Humboldt Park and got behind in paying dues. Now that I was in prison with both male and female gang members, I was held to the tighter, male standards. I acknowledged my gang brothers and sisters whenever I saw them, flashing the gang sign and calling out to them in Spanish, actions that were against the rules and earned me many disciplinary tickets. But in spite of that show of loyalty, word had come down from the leaders that I had dropped out of sight and shirked my membership responsibilities on the outside, so I was issued a violation on the inside. Because I had proved myself to be a stand-up individual and shown that I would never rat on anybody or disrespect the gang, they gave me two choices: I could go my way and be considered out of the gang—a rare occurrence because you can't really retire from a gang—but then I would be dead to them, which meant I could no longer acknowledge my brothers and sisters. They were like family to me, so I didn't want that to happen. The other option was to take the violation and get a timed beating by two other female inmates, very much like my initiation. I chose the violation and was beaten for three minutes up against a prison wall. It was excruciating, but three minutes on the wall felt like a small price to pay.

After a few weeks at Logan, I settled into a routine. My gang brothers would share dope with me since it was customary to take care of the sisters inside, so every morning when I got to school, I got two joints and two small bags of heroin. We sisters sold it for cigarettes and commissary items that were then put into what we called "the box," an area in my cell where I was in charge of stockpiling and distributing everything. This stash was then handed out to sisters coming into Logan so they would have the basics until they could shop at commissary themselves. I didn't need the stuff or the money because Grandma was still sending me money, even though Aunt Louise was the only one who continued to have any other contact with me, plus I had a few tricks on the outside that were sending me cash to keep me close for when I got out. Instead of selling the drugs, I bought extra stuff at the commissary to put in the box so the count was always right. I would smoke the joints every night with my cellies instead of selling them, blowing the smoke out an open window, laughing and having a great time. One of my cellies, Spunky, and I snorted the heroin. Most officers looked the other way. One time the prison went on lockdown for three days because of gang violence inside. The men were always making weapons. For those three days, drugs were unavailable. I went into major withdrawal, lying on my cell floor, throwing up and in so much pain that I decided once I got through that I could no longer accept the heroin from the brothers, so I just took the weed. I realized the heroin supply was too unpredictable in the joint and I did not want to go through that again.

I would take many other trips to Logan over the years, but this first stint was cut short. I found out that I had never gotten the six months of good conduct time subtracted from my original sentence in boot camp. In boot camp there was no allowance for good behavior. You didn't get any time off the required four months, even if it took you six months to complete it with disciplinary extensions, like I had. But, since I did graduate from boot camp, my good time for that sentence was now going to apply to my current sentence. The records department said I had to be awarded that time. So after about five months at Logan, while sitting in class one morning, I was told that I was being released the next day. I was heartbroken. I was having an affair with the leader of the Gaylords. I really liked him and didn't want to leave. He was in photography class with me, so we would have sex in the darkroom all the time. After a tearful good-bye to my cellies, I left the next day. But this time I wasn't on parole, so I didn't have to stay anywhere in particular. Except for Grandma and Aunt Louise, who gave me money and bought me new clothes, most of my family didn't want anything to do with me. I was back in Cicero dealing again, working the streets, and getting high. It was the start of many years during which my family would have no idea where I was or what kind of trouble I was in. And I was too high to care.

One day, I was driving around with a friend, and we decided to stop at the latest "tippin' spot" where I knew the best dope in Chicago was being sold. It was 1995 and back in those days, you could pull up to guys standing on the corner who were actually hawking their goods. "Park, park, blows, rock," they would call out to anybody who slowed down. A blow is a tenth of a gram of powdered heroin, what we used to call "China white," and a rock is crack cocaine. As if we were pulling in to buy tickets to a rock concert, they would holler, "Have your money out, unfold it, have it in order," and flag us through a takeout line. Every so often, someone would shout, "P's in the hole! Get little," meaning the police were coming. Everyone would scatter, and the cops would grab anyone they could catch and then leave.

On this day, the line was really long and as a white person obviously out of place in that neighborhood and no doubt buying drugs, I did not want to stand around for too long, since I knew that if the cops showed up, I'd be the first to be grabbed. I walked the length of the line, trying to figure out how to cut in, when a very handsome black man walked up to me. He looked just like the actor Wesley Snipes. I thought he was so gorgeous, I was almost speechless, a rare experience for me.

"Are ya tryin' to buy some blows?" he asked me in a deep sexy voice.

"Um, yeah, I want four," I answered.

"You want me to get you to the head of the line?"

Now I'm thinking, *He's cute, but he's trying to scam me. He's not ripping me off.* So I went into street mode and in my most badass voice, I said, "Yeah, if you get me to the front of the line, fine, but I'm not giving you any money."

"No, no, no," he laughed. "What's your name?"

"Bianca." I softened. I couldn't help myself.

"They call me Blue," he said. He took me to the front of the line and said, "Give her four blows."

I pulled out the two twenty dollar bills to pay and Blue said, "No, keep the money for next time."

"Oh, no, c'mon, what's the catch?" I wasn't buying this bullshit. "I want to pay for all of mine."

"No. Give me your number. I want to call you."

"I can't give out my number, you give me your number." I only had Grandma's number and couldn't give that to him.

I wrote down his number and he said, "Seriously, call me, awright?"

I just smiled and tucked the paper into my bra. When I got back to my friend's car, she told me he was the guy who owns the spot. She commented on how fine he was, and when I asked if he had a girlfriend, she said she had no idea, but a man that fine probably had as many women as he wanted. I thought about him on and off, but never called. I went about my normal life, running the street and getting high. Then, about a month later, I bumped into him again.

"You full of shit," he said when he saw me, flashing that killer smile. "I told you to call me, and you didn't call me."

"I was gonna call, but I was in county for three days, and I been busy!" I would catch an arrest here and there for prostitution or trespassing or attempting to buy narcotics, spend a few days in Cook County Jail, and then get released, so it was mostly true. "I promise I'll call," I said. He just laughed.

It would take another few weeks before I ran into him again. There was a heroin drought after a big raid in Chicago, and I was driving around with some friends looking to score. I saw Blue walking down the street and I pulled the car over.

"Blue, Blue!" I shouted, and when he walked over to the car he told me again that I was full of shit for not calling him. "I'm sorry. I meant to," I said. "So where can we get some dope? I really need some dope. I'm sick. What about your spot?"

"Nah, it's shut down for now. It's a drought, man."

"Well do you know where we can get some blows?"

"Yeah, I think so."

"OK, get in."

I was driving a Maserati that belonged to a friend's boyfriend, and I think he was a little impressed. He sat up front. The radio was bumpin' loud, and I knew there was something going on between us. Blue told me where to pull up, and I gave him forty dollars to score for us. When he walked away with the money, my friends told me I was crazy, that he was going to rip me off. But I didn't think he would, and I was right; he came back with four really good blows. I told him I would buy him a blow, thinking he was probably broke because of the drought. But he flashed a stack of money, and after we let my friends off, he told me he had scored a lot of dope.

"Let's go get a hotel room, get high, and fuck around," he said. So we did. We spent the whole night having sex and getting high, listening to music all night long. A big song on the radio was "Kiss from a Rose" by Seal, a huge hit in 1995. It wasn't really his kind of music, but because the lyrics really spoke to us, it would become our song:

> You remain my power, my pleasure, my pain.
> To me you're like a growing addiction that I can't deny, yeah
> Won't you tell me is that healthy?
> Baby, I compare you to a kiss from a rose on the gray.

It was the best night I'd ever had with a man. The next day, I drove Blue to his house. He lived with his mother. When he got out of the car, I could tell he didn't want me to leave. "Make sure you call me. I mean it," he said. I promised him I would. I got on the highway heading for the suburbs to return the Maserati, went as far as one exit, and turned back. I pulled up to Blue's house and beeped the horn. When he came out, I said, "Get in. I'm not going home. Come on. Let's just go." That started a twelve-year relationship that played out like the junkie version of Bonnie and Clyde.

We were both seasoned hustlers and heroin addicts, so we were each working our own criminal activities. I had moved to another area of Chicago and was not active with the Latino gang, even though I maintained my good standing. I had learned from what we used to call the "thoroughbred" hookers how to rob tricks without actually having sex with them. I was never "flatbacking," which meant having sex with any trick anywhere you could; I considered myself too smart for that. Plus, I was still robbing department stores and fencing jewelry and high-end perfume. Blue was a master pickpocket and knew how to spot a mark with a lot of cash. He even did armed stickups. For a long time, we just hung out together after doing our own things, sharing dope and complimenting each other on the haul. But Blue was a nonstop hustler, and there was never enough money for him, so we went into business together. He taught me how to pickpocket like a pro and shortchange people by asking for change on the street and totally confusing the victim. I would put my own spin on things and make a lot of money. In the beginning, Blue and I had so much cash that we stayed in expensive hotels for weeks at a time. When we got tired of that, there were always people on the West Side who knew Blue and who had an extra apartment because their mother died or somebody went to prison and, because we had so much money, we would take over the space, sometimes just living there, but most of the time turning it into a trap house, as well, so junkies came and went and we made money around the clock.

One of the motels Blue and I stayed in many times was on Cicero Avenue. It was a rent-by-the-hour flophouse called the Shamrock. The rooms made a ring around the parking lot, with balconies reaching out from broken sliding doors covered with filthy drapes. Your shoes stuck to the carpet, but we never noticed. The Shamrock was a favorite among pimps, hookers, dealers, criminals of all kinds. It was known as a go-to place for rocks and blows. I had robbed more than a few tricks there. Life at the Shamrock was crazy, with so much action going on all the time, plus constant police raids causing people to run from their rooms to escape arrest. One summer evening, Blue and I were hanging out in our room, the sliding door left open to let in the humid breeze, when I swore I heard my mother's voice through the mix of loud music and partying sounds coming from the other rooms. I ran out on the balcony, dressed in a flimsy top and hot pants, and there she was, sitting in her car with my aunt Trisha, her sister. Hookers and their tricks were walking by, people were buying dope right there in the parking lot, and my mother was clearly traumatized.

"Angela! Are you here? Where are you?" She shouted out, not knowing exactly where I was.

"Holy shit, that's my mother!" I said to Blue as I walked out on the balcony, right above her car. I ran down the stairs to the car window.

"Oh my God, what are you doing? Get in the car!" My mother was sobbing now. "Please get in the car!"

"Mom, Mom, Mom, I'm OK. These are my friends. Everything's fine. I promise." I tried to sound casual, but I could not calm her down.

"No, please come with me. Please, I don't want to leave you here!" She was getting so upset that she was starting to scare me. "Look at these people you're with. Sean wants you. He's calling for you. Come with me!" I just smiled and told her to call me and we could go to lunch someday soon, never thinking for a second how absurd that must have sounded to my mother, a woman who hardly ever went to lunch. I walked back up the stairs to my room knowing I wouldn't see her for a long time.

My life with Blue and the way we lived was everything to me. I would have done anything for him. At first, I was the more reserved one when it came to criminal activities. But he taught me every possible way to hustle and rob and con, from armed robbery to how to follow and completely clean out a wealthy "vic." I had robbed tricks many times on my own, taking them to a hotel, distracting them by drawing a bath, and then stealing their wallets and running out while they sat naked in the tub. More than once, I left a hotel room in my underwear, pulling on my clothes as I ran down the hall. Then, Blue and I started working together. I lured the vic into the room, and Blue would show up with a gun and rob him. We did the same thing right out on the street. Hanging around Union Station, Blue would spot a mark, and I would lure the guy around the corner with the promise of sex. Then Blue would stick him up. I couldn't help but feel bad for the vic when we did this. I worked hard to perfect what I called a "smooth stang," meaning that the vic never even knew I was stealing from him until hours later when he realized what was missing, his wallet or cash from a shortchange. To me, it was the art of theft, and I got a big thrill when it worked.

I learned so much from Blue, and I loved every minute of it. Mostly, I really loved *him*. I would have done anything he asked. It wasn't unusual for one of us to get picked up by the cops for something—drug possession or soliciting—and spend a week or two in lockup at Cook County, until one of us showed up to bond out the other one. When it happened to me, I would sit in jail and worry about Blue getting picked up, too. I worried about him not having enough dope, keeping warm out on the street, and not getting caught in a bad situation. I was so in love. I had never worried about anyone like that. As time went on, I took on more of his habits, doing things in public I never thought I would do, like drinking wine out of a bottle inside a paper bag right on the street. He would laugh when I said, "Blue, I can't do that. That's not ladylike." He was amused by my upscale manners, but before long I was as comfortable on the streets as he was.

When we had a car, usually stolen, I was the getaway driver for Blue's armed robberies. Once after taking a vic for a few thousand dollars outside the Greyhound bus station, the guy started screaming and chasing Blue when he realized what had happened. I was waiting for Blue under an overpass when he came running to the car and jumped in, screaming, "Go, go, baby!" We easily got away that time, but there were times when the cops actually chased us. One time, I was parked on Harrison Street, right outside the bus station, and I could see from the car that Blue was having a confrontation with a white guy. He pushed the guy down onto the sidewalk, and I could see that things were getting heated.

I pulled the car up to where Blue was standing and hollered, "Daddy, get in, Daddy!"

Completely out of breath, Blue slid into the front seat and said, "Go, go!"

I took off, flying down Harrison, screaming, "Who was it? Was that a vic or was that the people?" meaning the cops.

"Nah, baby, it was the people!"

"From the Greyhound or the Chicago police?"

"Chicago detectives!"

"Holy shit! Are they gonna come after us?"

"Hell yeah, baby."

Now I was flying up the street, trying to get to the Eisenhower Expressway and head for the West Side. But they have radios, so of course they were waiting for me up ahead, right before the on-ramp. As we got closer, I could see the detective's car parked with two cops standing outside it, ready to arrest us when I stopped at the red light coming up. At the same time, another cop car was right behind us. Blue put his hand on my leg and said, "That's it, baby. They got us. You did good, but we done." He was ready to get hauled in, and I knew he didn't want me to risk getting shot or having a bad accident. So I stopped at the light, but just as the two cops jumped out and ran toward my car, I decided I wasn't giving up that easily. "Not exactly," I said to Blue, as I floored it and sped up the ramp onto the highway. Blue was shouting, "Look atchu, girl! You driving, girl!" In my rearview mirror I could see all four lanes behind me had flashing lights, with a paddy wagon, two cop cars, an unmarked car with a siren on top, all getting closer. Up ahead, two state police cars were off to the side of the road, so they got in on the action. I could see the exit for Independence Avenue coming up.

"Fuck it, I gotta lose them, I gotta get off the highway right now." I was trying to be calm but the adrenaline was pumping.

"Baby, where the hell did you learn how to do this?"

"On TV! I watch TV, man." And it was true. I always wanted to be driving in a high-speed chase just like Starsky and Hutch.

I veered onto the exit ramp going so fast I don't know how the car didn't flip over. And now, all the cop vehicles in pursuit had to go down to single file to get off the ramp, which gave me time to figure out my next move. I kept going, crossing other streets that thankfully had no oncoming traffic and I got right back on the highway. The cops had to do the same single-file formation to get back up the ramp. I was getting closer to the suburban exits, and I did not want to get off outside the city limits. There's an old saying, "If you want to be a crook, stay in Cook," meaning stay in Cook County, because we knew how to beat the charges and work the system. The suburban police were known to be much stricter.

I decided I had to get off the highway again, so I took the ramp at Kostner Avenue, but the light was red, and cars were stopped there. I hit another car, pushed it out of the way, and my car spun around. Now I was facing all the police cars.

"Get out the car!" Blue shouted, so we both ran out of the car and kept running in different directions. I ran as fast as I could down an alley until I came to a burned-out building. I went into the basement, a dark place filled with rotting plywood and piles of garbage. I could hear the sound of the cops' feet on the floor above, mixed with the unmistakable sound of rats scurrying all around me. The disgusting odor almost knocked me out. I hid under some plywood in a far corner in the back of the basement, even though I saw a giant rat slink through the pile, its long thick tail disappearing into the dark. I almost stood and gave myself up, but then I thought, *OK, bitch. Go ahead, stand up and you'll be freezing at Eleventh and State,* because I knew they would take me to the lockup there. I crouched under that pile, holding my breath and staying still for over an hour. I could see the cops' flashlights and watched their feet, but I never made a sound until I knew they had left the building. Hours later I finally crept out from under the pile and made my way to Blue's mother's house.

Blue was already there. Though we had both gotten away, the cops had the car, which contained my purse and our clothes because we had been practically living in it. The cops picked me up a few weeks later and tried to get me to admit that I was driving. They said they knew I was the white girl who hung out with Blue, but I kept insisting that he had many white girls. "I'm not the only white girl," was my sole defense, and I stuck to it. I would have gone to my grave denying any involvement; as always, anything for Blue. The police eventually gave up and let me go because they had no proof that I was driving the car that day. But I came to realize that Blue and I were getting a reputation among the police as a notorious couple, always on their radar. An eight-by-ten photo of Blue hung on the corridor wall at Area One police headquarters at Eighteenth and State Street under the heading "Ten Most Wanted Quality of Life Violators." This was a category like public enemy number one that meant this person was always involved in crimes against the public.

We were infamous and lived on the run for most of our twelve years together. Our cash situation would go up and down, and we started living in abandoned houses on the West Side of Chicago. One of the strangest ironies of my life happened when we found an abandoned house on Fifth Avenue and Karlov. We called the neighborhood "K-Town" because the names of all the parallel streets started with a K.

The City of Chicago often boards up and marks abandoned houses with a red painted X on the front door to signal that they are unsafe, generally because of rat infestations and rotting infrastructure. The properties are owned by banks that don't keep them up or simply left by owners who have died without heirs or any relatives to take them over. Homeless people and drug addicts take over these places, usually picking one room to close off to the rats and fix up with a few comforts like an old mattress, blankets, and even some nicer touches depending on what could be scavenged. Blue and I had done that in the Fifth Avenue house. We fixed up a bedroom and would crawl in through the back door so the police could not tell anyone was in there when they drove by. We lit candles at night and kept the windows boarded up. It was almost cozy. We still hustled, sold drugs, did stickups, and occasionally one of us spent time in jail, but for a little while it felt like a home.

I knew that at one point in our history, my family had owned a home in K-Town, around Fifth and Karlov, but I thought it was the large wood frame house up the block. I eventually discovered that Blue and I had actually been squatting in the very brick house once owned by my family. Grandma, her husband, and their kids—my father, Uncle Joey, and Aunt Louise—all lived there in the 1950s. I confirmed this when I showed Uncle Joey a picture of the house many years later, and he told me that the bedroom we had lived in was Grandma's bedroom when she was a young wife and mother. I would sit behind the house and do heroin, hiding in the bushes so no other junkies would bother me, having no idea that I was crouching in the same alley where my grandma took her garbage and maybe walked with her kids so many years ago.

Blue thought he was invincible and took foolish risks to make as much cash as he could, sometimes making decisions that put us both in danger. He would steal drugs from other gangs and rip off other dealers, to the point of getting a reputation as a crazy, untrustworthy player. I once got caught up in the fallout from a bad deal and almost lost my life.

We were driving around the West Side with Blue's friend and fellow gang leader Carl. Carl had a lot of respect for Blue. They both ranked high in their branches of the gang; Blue was a "five-star Universal Elite 4-Corner Hustler," meaning he had a "glove" and the most stars possible. That gave him a certain amount of power over those under him. Carl hustled with us all the time and was driving us around in his car, with Blue up front and me in the back, taking us wherever Blue wanted to go. They had been out all night and had just picked me up so we could go cop. I couldn't help but eavesdrop as they bragged about their exploits from the night before. They had robbed a drug dealer, and one of them had shot the guy in the butt, so he wasn't hurt that badly, but the fact remained that they had shot another dealer. I was alarmed.

"It's OK, baby. Don't worry about it," Blue said. "You don't gotta worry about those fuckin' GDs," referring to the Gangster Disciples, a rival gang. Blue was always going to rival territory to cop and steal better drugs. But he was never scared, and he truly considered himself untouchable.

We pulled over to the spot where Blue said we would cop, and it turned out that it was near the spot where they had robbed the dealer the night before. As Blue got out of the car, I could feel tension, and I knew that something was going on. I looked around and saw a few guys walking quickly toward the car. They came right up to Blue and formed a circle around him. I jumped out of the car.

"Hey, let's go. What's going on?" I shouted, not sure what I thought I was going to do.

"Ang, get back in the car!" Blue yelled at me, so I did.

"What the fuck is he doin'?" Carl was still behind the wheel, but he was starting to freak out. "Get out, Bianca, and see what's goin' on!" So I jumped out again and Blue was distracted, worrying about me, as a couple of the GDs pulled their guns. Blue went to grab my shoulder and throw me back in the car. I had hair down to my waist at the time and just as Blue tried to push me back into the car, one of the GDs grabbed my hair and wrapped it around his hand. At the same moment, Blue jumped into the car, but I was pulled out by my hair and hit the sidewalk as Carl floored it and the car pulled away. It all happened so fast that I'm sure Blue was in shock and so was I. Now I was on the ground, and the GD was dragging me by my hair.

"What the fuck are you doin' with her?" one of the GDs yelled at the guy with my hair still in his hand.

"No, we got that asshole now. Blue loves this white bitch. He'll come back for her."

They forced me into an abandoned building a few houses away, still holding my hair tight, dragging me and pushing me into the basement. I was wearing an expensive white leather White Sox jacket my father had bought for Sean that I really liked—I had sneaked over to their house and begged Pat to let me borrow it, which of course she did. They ripped the jacket off me and forced me to my knees. The floor was littered with broken glass, and since I was wearing shorts, every time they dragged me a few feet, my knees and legs would get cut up. Someone would punch me in the face every few minutes. I could feel blood dripping from my lip, and I knew my eye was swelling up. I refused to cry, but I thought they were going to kill me and do who-knows-what first.

Word must have been getting around the hood. More guys were showing up, some of them shouting, "Man, what the fuck? You got a Vice Lords bitch!"

"Yeah, but that motherfucker will be back to get this bitch, and then we got his ass. He loves this white bitch." And every time he said the word *bitch* he pulled my hair tighter and punched me in the face. "We goin' to have some fun with this bitch first." Now I was sure they were going to rape me before Blue managed to get back, and probably kill me when they were done. But, stubborn as ever, I wasn't going to give them the satisfaction of crying or begging for my life, so I just took it. Finally, a younger guy walked in whom I recognized from the hood. I knew he recognized me, and he said, "Man, what ya got Bianca for?"

"Blue is comin' back for this white bitch, and we'll trade her for him," the guy said as he landed another blow to my face.

"What? What the fuck are you goin' to do with her? She don't know nothin' about what Blue does. He don't discuss business with her." He was one of them, so he knew better than to outright plead for my life, so instead he said, "Man, do you know who her family is? Do you know what the fuck is going to happen over here if anything happens to her? That's not an ordinary white bitch. You have no idea. Let the bitch go!"

"Fuck her and fuck her family."

"Man, you're going to make the block so hot," he kept trying to work it for me. "We don't need the police finding a white bitch here."

"Fine, bitch, get the fuck out of here!" the guy let go of my hair and I stood up with my hands in the air.

"Come on, bitch, get the fuck out of here," my rescuer was still acting like one of them, and I was so happy to follow his orders. But before I left, I had a stupid impulse.

"Wait," I shouted, "I want my fuckin' leather!"

"What, bitch?"

"Man, I just got you your life," the young guy whispered to me. "Fuck the jacket. You got about two seconds to get outta here before they change their minds."

I was so angry, but I walked out without the jacket. I was bleeding from head to toe, and my face and eyes were so cut up and swollen, I could barely see. Now that I could let my guard down, I started shaking and had trouble breathing. I stood on the street for a few minutes when a van came by, and I recognized a few junkies whom Blue and I sold to. They pulled over and said, "Is that you, Bianca?" They were scared but let me get in the van and took off heading back to Cicero. In the meantime, Blue and his brothers were gunning up to come back and get me. On the way, we saw them pass by in their car. The guy driving the van let me off at Blue's mother's house, and I did what I could to pull myself together. When Blue got home, he was furious. I knew somebody definitely paid for what they did, but I never asked.

Violence was part of our life and we were always aware of the danger inherent in what we did every day. I was a victim many times. Blue and I had gone to the projects to cop, but when we got to the sixth floor, we heard gunshots. "Run, run!" Blue shouted as we hit the stairs, moving as fast as we could. When we got to the sidewalk, I realized my leg was bleeding profusely. My adrenaline had been pumping so hard that I never felt it until we stopped running. I wasn't a target, but had been caught in the cross fire, hit by a bullet that probably ricocheted off the concrete stairs. I was bleeding so badly that it scared me, so I took a chance and went to an emergency room, giving a false name. They treated the wound, said it was probably a small slug, and I checked out against medical advice. I never had an X-ray and assumed that the bullet was still there, only to discover many years later that the bullet had exited my leg but left my bone dead and deteriorated. It would cause me a lot of pain before I finally had the bone replaced with a metal rod.

Whenever Blue would get picked up and sent to jail or the penitentiary, I would hustle twice as much so I could send him money. He did that for me at first, but stopped after a few years. I'd be lucky to get a card or a fifty-dollar money order twice a year. I refused to see that I was not as important to him as he was to me because I was so in love with him. During one of my later times at Logan, I was having a conversation about another inmate whose man was cheating on her on the outside, and I was appalled.

"That bitch is fuckin' my man outside while I'm in here," she said.

"Oh, God, how horrible," I said. "I'm glad I don't have to worry about that."

"Are you serious, Bianca? That's what you think?" One of the other inmates said in a catty voice, feeling the need to set me straight.

"Blue would never do anything to hurt me. There is NO way!"

"Blue is a real good-lookin' man. If you think that he's not fuckin' around you are out of it, girl. He's got a reputation, he's a leader, and he's got money. Do you really think these bitches aren't throwing themselves at him?"

"Oh, I'm sure they are, but he would never! He might play 'em and take their money, but he's not having sex with anybody else."

"You poor delusional girl, Bianca," they would laugh at me, but I never caved. I was sure Blue loved me and was as loyal as I was to him. "You're wrong," I insisted.

But they were right. I found out Blue was screwing around as much as he wanted and almost always had other women on the side. Even though I had sex with men inside, I felt like that didn't count because it was survival and got me things I needed. After I realized what was going on, our relationship started to decay, if it was possible for a junkie relationship to get much worse. But we were codependents in the most literal sense, and we continued to support our habits together. We even had two babies during that time.

Blue had children with another woman, and would always say, "Don't get pregnant now. We got a good thing going here." But he would refuse to wear a condom. He was with me when our son, Anthony, was born in 1996, but the authorities would not let us keep the baby, because he was born with heroin in his system. I was not in touch with my family anymore, but I knew that my mother would respond to this, so I called her, and she came. My mother once again stepped in, showing up in court to keep the state from taking one of her grandchildren. Over the years, I caught many cases with the Department of Children and Family Services (DCFS) because I was getting high while my kids were in the home. Even after they were gone and living with my family members, the police would still report me because I was a known junkie and criminal. Many of the same cops showed up again and again to harass me, determined to get me for something. I would tell them the kids were with my family, but it didn't matter.

I did not give up Anthony without a fight. My mother would let me take him for a week or two, and we'd stay in the projects with friends. Blue went to prison right after he was born. Soon I caught a case and got time, too, so Anthony was back with my mother and then in foster care with a family that really loved him. Many times Catholic Charities helped my family cope, and Uncle Joey worked with them and a social worker friend to find a family that wanted Anthony. My mother wanted to keep him, but she was getting older, still had to work, and it was just too hard for her.

I kept fighting to keep Anthony from inside prison. I managed to get us a court date and got Blue a special writ to get him into court from prison, too, so we could fight together to maintain custody, trying to defend ourselves against being declared unfit parents. I would have done anything just to see Blue at that point. When I realized the state was going to petition for a trial to take Anthony away from us, I was ready to sign him over. The court let me speak to the woman who had taken him as a foster child and who wanted to adopt him. She told me how much she and her husband loved children and how badly they wanted to raise Anthony. They had money and could give him a good life. She made me feel better about giving him up. I cried my eyes out in court but knew that this was the right thing to do. In front of the judge, Blue was adamant and kept saying, "No, we're not signing. That's my son!" I asked the judge if I could speak to Blue alone.

"Baby, let's be real. You might not get out for two more years, and I could be in for another year. Where we goin' with him? He deserves a life." Blue agreed to sign.

I was sobbing when I said good-bye to my baby boy and asked his adoptive mother, "If I ever straighten my life out, will you let me see my baby?"

"Of course," she said.

"Will you always tell him that I love him and I'm sorry I fucked up?"

"I promise," she said, and she was so gentle with me. I knew he was going to be OK. I signed the papers, and she adopted Anthony.

Blue and I were both back out on the streets sooner than we thought. Not long after, I found out that I was pregnant again. I decided to get clean so I would not have the same custody battle that we had just gone through with Anthony. I was out of the joint and decided to get into a detox program at St. Mary's. I really was determined to walk out of the hospital with my baby this time. Blue and I were living near the projects on the West Side, renting the first floor of a small house. The landlady lived upstairs. We tried to make a little home out of it—we had a couch, a recliner, a table, and a red rug to go with the black furniture. We still spent most of our money on drugs since Blue was still using, but we tried to make the place livable. Since I was trying to stay clean and getting bigger every day, I didn't go out much with Blue during my pregnancy. So he went out most of the time, sometimes gone for hours at a time, figuring I was home safe and he could bring me some fried chicken when he came back; that made me happy. I never worried about him, and for a short while things were calmer for me than they had been in a long time.

One night, Blue did not come home. When 5:00 AM rolled around and the sun was coming up I started to get angry. *Where the hell was he?* I fell asleep on the couch, but finally heard a key in the door.

"Blue?" I said.

"Damn, baby," he was panting as he flopped down onto the recliner, "I got shot. The police shot me."

"Oh, God, would you stop it! I don't even care that you didn't come home all night. Just go to sleep." I thought he was messing with me as he often did. But I sat up and could see blood oozing from his leg, right below his shorts.

"Who shot you?"

"The police!"

"Stop it, Blue." I honestly didn't believe him. "Really, who shot you?"

"The police shot me."

"What did you do?"

"Nothing!"

"Blue, the police don't just shoot people."

We went into the bedroom so he could lie on the bed and I could see his wound better. "What did you do? Why did they shoot you?" I was really scared for him now.

The way he described it, it genuinely sounded like an accident. I knew Blue would never try to provoke a cop; he would run before he would engage with a police officer. The cops had pulled him over, and of course, they had a long sheet on him so they drew their guns and tried to pull him out of the car. Blue tried to scoot out of the other side to get away and when the cop went to grab him, his gun went off and the shot hit Blue in the back of his leg, leaving a slug in the fleshy part of his thigh.

He was lying on the bed and starting to bleed a lot. I was beginning to panic. We couldn't go to a hospital, so it was up to me to get the bullet out. I had no idea what I was doing, but I knew I needed some supplies, like gauze, alcohol, peroxide, bandages, and some kind of a clamp to grab the bullet.

"OK, I'm going to Walgreens to get supplies, baby, so you don't get infected. And I'll get some whiskey, too!" Once again, I remembered what I had seen on television. On many episodes of *Gunsmoke*, Doc Adams had to remove a bullet from some hombre, and whiskey was important.

"I got blows, baby. Don't worry. Just hurry."

I ran to Walgreens as fast as a seven-month-pregnant woman could, grabbed as many first-aid supplies as I thought I needed, and got some whiskey on the way back. I put Blue's bloody clothes in a plastic bag. He was snorting blows, and I tried to get him to take a swig of whiskey, but he just yelled at me to get the damn bullet out. I poured peroxide right on the wound, watched it bubble up, and tried to steel myself. I could only imagine how much it must have hurt. Blue was holding his leg up so I could get to the wound, trying not to scream too loud.

"Blue, I don't think I can get the bullet with this clamp!"

"Just shove it in there. Just do it!"

"OK, but give me a hit of that whiskey!" I had never done anything like this and the feeling of his meaty flesh inside the wound was making me sick.

I dug the clamp into his thigh, through the gaping hole. I moved it around and suddenly felt the metal hit another piece of metal. I had it! I started to pull it out but lost hold of it. It took me three tries to pull the little slug out of his leg, with Blue screaming instructions at me, writhing in pain, and bleeding profusely. I closed the wound up with butterfly Band Aids and wrapped gauze around his leg really tight. Then I put the slug in another baggie and buried that in the backyard with his bloody clothes. I kept the wound clean, and he seemed to be OK.

After three days, I had to go out and hustle for cash, and while I was on the street a detective involved in the shooting who knew me stopped me and asked about Blue. The cop who shot him had to justify why his weapon was discharged, so they were determined to find Blue. They took me into custody. I didn't tell them anything, but while I was being held, the snitches in the neighborhood told them where we lived and they went to the house and arrested Blue. Because he had been shot, they had to take him to a hospital first. Blue told me later that the doctor at Cook County Hospital was so impressed with my work, he asked, "Who did this? They did a really good job!" Blue just said, "Yeah, my woman did it."

The cops needed evidence, so they were asking where his bloody clothes were, and I refused to say anything without his consent. So the cops let Blue and me talk in an interview room and he told me it was

OK to show them where the clothes were buried. I gave the cops the shovel and they dug up the clothes and the slug. Blue went to court and the cops jammed him, saying that he was a menace to society and had been in jail before. With so many things stacked against him, Blue went back to prison for some years.

Blue was in Cook County Jail when our daughter, Alia, was born. I was on my own and having trouble making rent on the house, so I moved into an abandoned apartment with my friend Porshia. This time, since I had detoxed while I was pregnant, they let me take the baby, but I knew I had no business trying to take care of her. Blue was not around to help me hustle for money, I kept living either in the projects with other junkies or in abandoned buildings, and I started getting high again right after she was born. I took her to jail to see her father a couple of times, but then I had a warrant out on me again, so I couldn't do that anymore or I would get arrested the minute I showed up for visiting hours. So I was on the lam for a few months with a tiny baby, but after that one last really bad Christmas Eve, out in the cold, dope sick, trying to feed her and keep her warm, I knew I could not take care of her. I called and begged my mother to let us stay with her, but when she did, I walked out with my baby a few days later and disappeared again.

I took Alia to a friend's house, a woman named Kari, who had actually taken me to the hospital when I went into labor and was in the delivery room when Alia was born. I knew she didn't get high, would take good care of the baby, and would never keep her away from me. After a few days back on the streets alone I caught another arrest for shoplifting and was in McHenry County Jail, but I refused to say where Alia was. My lawyer, after being pressured by the state's attorney, made a deal to get me three years, but only if I told where the baby was. The state's attorney was adamant that the baby had to be found, even though she had no legal standing or jurisdiction in Cook County, and when she brought it up in court, my lawyer shut her down. But he decided he wanted to help her find the baby, so to get me to talk, he acted concerned about Alia and got Kari's address out of me. I took the three years and was back at Logan. In the meantime, against attorney-client privilege, he shared that information with the state's attorney, who then called Cook County DCFS, which tried to take Alia. But I got to Kari first, called her from prison, and told her not to answer the door. I told Kari to bring Alia to my next DCFS court date, and I would ask the judge to let her be the foster parent.

When I got to court, I appeared in front of the judge, wearing prison clothes and the leather belt that kept my hands and feet shackled. This was a mean form of harassment, since they usually didn't make you appear in court like that. I saw Kari standing there holding my beautiful baby girl and couldn't help myself. I blurted out, "Your Honor, can I please hold my baby?" She said, "Yes, give the baby to Miss Bianca." They put the baby in my arms in between the chains. I held her tight, kissed her neck, smelled her, and when I saw that she remembered me, I started to cry. The judge would not rule that day to let Kari keep the baby and instead sent her to an emergency overnight shelter. Kari ran out of the court in tears, so hurt to lose the baby, and I was in a panic.

As the caseworker tried to wrestle Alia from my arms, she said sarcastically, "What am I supposed to do with this baby? Do you have diapers?"

"What?" I said, "I'm in prison! I don't have anything."

"Oh, great. What am I supposed to feed her?"

"Please don't give her peas, she hates them. And don't give her formula with iron because she gets diarrhea."

"I have dinner plans, and this is going to take all day now."

I cried as they ripped her out of my arms and could even see that the officers in court were feeling uncomfortable. Alia was clutching my hair, screaming, "Ma-ma, Ma-ma," and the judge got up and left because it was such a heart-wrenching scene.

I started fighting for Alia on paper, filing motions from inside Logan. I was relentless, especially when I realized after hearing the judge say it in court, that the state's attorney had provided Kari's address, something she was not supposed to know. I knew then that my lawyer had gone against privilege, and I had a case. It took me a year, but it went all the way to the Illinois Supreme Court, and I won. The state's attorney was terminated, and my lawyer got a disciplinary mark against him from the bar association.

It took about five months to get Alia out of the DCFS system. I found myself crying in court again, desperate to keep my daughter. I continued to write my own motions from inside prison, feeling certain that I could turn my life around and keep my beautiful baby girl. I did not want to lose another child. But after a few court appearances, I could see that so much was stacked against me, and I had to do the right thing for Alia. I did not want to be declared an unfit mother in a court of law and was ready to do whatever I could to avoid having that label for life. Once again, I managed to get Blue out of prison for a day in court, and we signed the adoption papers with Anthony's parents. I was so thankful that they could grow up together, but I wouldn't see them again until they were in high school. Anthony and Alia's adoptive mother kept her promise, and for that I will always be grateful.

Throughout all these years, I was in and out of Logan many times. Except for Aunt Louise, my family no longer stayed in touch and stopped sending me money. It was the final cut-off, but I was too far gone to care. Because I was generous on the outside, I was never without allies on the inside. I had a lot of street cred to fall back on. When I was in the joint, people I knew from the street remembered and were always willing to help me out. More important, they trusted me. I managed to hustle for what I needed, so I was never destitute when I was in the joint. During one of my later sentences at Logan, I discovered a whole new scam using the newly arrived Internet.

Another inmate told me about all the sex sites on the Internet. She said that all you needed was a picture of yourself and some titillating background info to go along with it and the sugar daddies would come out of the woodwork. She had found a man that was sending her money every month, a lonely horny old guy who was banking on seeing her when she got out, something that she knew would never happen since all the information she shared was false. I immediately saw bigger possibilities, way beyond one man, and started to put a new scheme into action. I wrote a letter to Aunt Louise, asking her to get Nicky, her grandson, an eighth grader, to look up the sex site called Secret Pen Pals, and figure out how to get me on it. Nicky printed out the application and sent it

to me so I could fill it out and send it in with the ten-dollar fee and
the cutest picture of me that Aunt Louise could find. I made the application as tantalizing as I could, sharing from my cell how I loved long
walks on the beach under the moonlight, soft kisses, and holding hands.
I added that I had made a few mistakes in life and was in prison. For
many, this was a turn-on.

Before long, I had created a booming business. The sex site posted
my information and mailed me twelve pages of men. I started working the list to get men who would bite and start sending me money
every month. Since nothing is private for long in the joint and I was
suddenly getting so much mail every day, the other inmates started
asking me what the hell I was up to. Getting mail is a very big deal
in prison and inmates desperately wait for every little piece of corre-
spondence like it is gold. When my name started getting called ten or
more times a day, they all knew something was going on. Those who
were not in my inner circle started calling me "Internet ho" and "mail
whore," nicknames I proudly accepted. "That's right. I am a ho, and
a good one, too!" I'd shout back at them, waving multiple envelopes
marked with a red "Received" stamp indicting that a money order was
inside. Never one to miss an opportunity, I expanded my operation and
got other inmates in on the action. I was organized, using a code of
variously colored highlighters to indicate the most profitable men, the
weird guys, or the sadistic creepy guys to avoid when sharing personal
information, so the other women had some idea how to best milk each
guy I connected them with. When a new inmate arrived, especially a
younger woman, her friends inside would come ask me to help her get
in on the action so she could make money and get settled in the joint.
It was a win-win all around. I had plenty of money to get by with inside
prison and would spend a hundred dollars a week at commissary, big
money in the joint. Once I even got a sugar daddy to wire me $1,500
on the day I was released.

Once again, I had found an angle that helped me survive. In the
middle of one of my later sentences at Logan, I remembered something
a lifer had told me years earlier, during my second stay there. "This is
probably the last time you're going to have money sent to you from

your family," she told me. "If you keep coming back here, they're gonna cut you off."

"Oh, God, what?" I answered, laughing. "Not my family. You don't know my family." At the time, I couldn't imagine it.

"Mark my words," she insisted. "You're lucky on the second time, but if you get to the third trip here, you won't get a dime from your family. It's gonna run out, honey."

Her words were prophetic. I was constantly in and out of prison over the years. Blue was doing serious time, and we became estranged. I left him for good in 2007. I finally realized the painful truth that he was never there for me when I went to prison and had always been cheating on me. I felt like the biggest fool in Chicago. Drugs got the best of him, too, and in the end we turned on each other. When he was in the joint and I was out, I'd stay in the projects with friends, other junkies who knew all about us. Everyone seemed to know he cheated on me all the time. I was embarrassed and angry, sometimes spending days sitting alone crying in the high-rise project's unlit urine-smelling stairway. Blue hurt me more than I could have imagined, and after a while my anger won out. I refused to communicate with him, coming to hate him almost as much as I had once loved him.

With Blue out of my life, I was completely alone and homeless with no one to help me with money or to have my back on the street. I saw gang members, kids, and even cops get killed on the street and in the projects all the time. But I had been a well-known hustler and gang member for so many years, and a lot of guys knew me as Blue's woman, so I could take care of myself and had a reputation as an individual who could be trusted, as much as any criminal trusted another. One time, after just getting out of the joint, I hooked up with a guy I copped for all the time, and he let me stay in his apartment and share his dope in exchange for sex. The place was full of gang members and dope dealers who hung out in the hallway, partying and getting into fights. One night, somebody decided it would be fun to play Russian roulette. I walked into the hall just as one of the players pulled the trigger and a bullet shot into the hustler's temple, killing him and splattering blood on the walls. Once again, I hit the streets looking for another place to sleep.

The years piled up, and my ability to stay ahead of the game dwindled. Each time I was released from prison, I was more and more alone. I had abandoned my family just as much as they had abandoned me. I had alienated Sean, lost my other children, and felt there could be no turning back now. I sunk deeper into heroin addiction and could not keep up the hustle beyond what I needed to feed my habit. Whatever game I had left went toward making just enough money to score dope for the day, get high, and pass out wherever I ended up. Now, all my friends were homeless and lost to addiction, just like me.

# 10

# A Hard Rain

I WOKE UP WITH THE SUN in my face. I had passed out in a stairway leading to the basement behind a shop on Halsted Street in Pilsen, a neighborhood on the West Side. This was my home now. I usually ended up in this alley or an abandoned building in the projects nearby with Carlos, another homeless junkie. The cold November night we first met we were arguing over drugs that a man had given us after we had helped him cop for himself. We both wanted the bigger half of the bag, but in the end we split it evenly and became friends. I never knew his last name. I just knew that Carlos and I shared the same struggle. We spent our days hustling whatever we could, only stopping when we could buy enough heroin to keep from getting sick. Sometimes we made better money, got really high, and would sit together for hours, talking and laughing until we passed out. Carlos and I watched out for one another, sharing our dope and promising never to let the other one OD and die alone in the alley. He would build makeshift shelters behind the buildings using whatever he could pull from the Dumpster to keep us dry. We would huddle together and cram tissues in our ears to keep the roaches from crawling in, one eye open for rats until we finally passed out. Carlos, who was a few years younger than me, had been an addict for many years, too, and shot up so much dope that he sometimes had open sores on his skin. I would find maggots crawling on him and have to wake him up so he could brush them off. I worried about him freezing to death on nights when I didn't show up in the alley because I had passed out in a trap house. But I never worried about Carlos during the day because the whole neighborhood looked out for him, bringing him tamales, coffee, and even a few bucks. The workers at McDonald's knew he loved their chocolate-chip cookies, so he had a standing free order every morning, and they even heated the cookies for him. I knew he would be out in front of the Mexican grocery store up the street or over by the McDonald's panhandling, his main hustle. Everyone knew him and liked him, so they always gave him money, even though most people knew he was going to buy drugs with it.

Whenever I got out of prison, I would get off the bus and go straight to Carlos to cop. Inmates were given ten dollars upon release. I always spent mine on drugs, and Carlos helped me out. He was my family now.

Many years later, after I turned my life around, I would go back to check up on Carlos every couple of months. I knew I would find him in the same alley, and I could give him a hug and buy him a meal. I wanted to make sure that he knew he was still my family and that I loved and cared for him. But, as hard as I tried, I could not get him off the streets. He always told me that he liked living outside. He said that after serving too many years in prison, being outside, looking up at the stars at night, made him feel free.

One day I went out to look for him. I hadn't seen him in a few months, and he wasn't in any of his usual spots, not in the alley, or on any of his favorite corners. Everybody in the neighborhood knew the homeless guy named Carlos, so I asked a woman outside the store where he panhandled if she had seen him. She shook her head as she told me that he had overdosed about a month ago. She said they found him dead in the alley behind a Dumpster. I was devastated. I hadn't been there to protect him, and Carlos had died alone, too high to even realize he was freezing to death.

Before I met Carlos, I sometimes passed out in the fenced-off Dumpster corral in the McDonald's parking lot. I felt safe there because the lot was lit all night, even though I knew rats would be crawling all around me. I made sure I could get really high so I would be oblivious. It was nights like this when I would think about Sean, Grandma, my father, Pat, and all the loving people I had hurt in my life. It was so painful.

When that feeling would hit me, I would do more dope and try to sink deeper and get farther away from what my life had become. When I met Carlos and he was so kind to me, I was grateful and knew that I would share whatever I could with him, and he would do the same for me.

I understood why he had to panhandle; he didn't have a lot of choices. But I never panhandled. In my twisted mind, I actually believed I was above begging. I had pulled off so many hustles over the years that even when I was at my lowest I still had an angle to work, pickpocketing at Union Station, or using my well-honed skills as a department store thief. I did what I could to clean myself up every day before heading to Macy's on Michigan Avenue or another upscale department store to lift jewelry and perfume and pickpocket the rich people shopping on the Gold Coast. I had lost everything, but not my skills as a thief.

I knew how important it was to blend in downtown, so I tried to keep up my appearance, even though I was living on the street. I stole hair dye, soap, and makeup from Walgreen's. Sometimes the guy who worked in the Dollar Store would just give me a box of hair dye. I would wash up and dye my hair in the sink at McDonald's or, if I was kicked out, I'd use the ladies' room in the taco joint up the street, blow-dry it with the hand drier on the wall, then draw perfect eyebrows and add eyeliner, mascara, blush, and lipstick. Whenever I woke up, I first checked for my false teeth. I had always tried to take good care of my teeth no matter where I was, even if I had to use a running fire hydrant, but I would grind my teeth when I was high, and over time the pressure had loosened three of my teeth, right in front. Years before, while I was in the joint, the prison dentist pulled them, and I had a partial made that snapped in. But I broke the partial after a while on the street, and it no longer fit correctly, so it would come loose. I could get a little crazy worrying about what I would do if I ever lost it, having no money or a dentist I could go to. Losing those teeth put a serious dent in my self-esteem, and it affected my confidence and my ability to hustle. There wasn't any makeup I could steal that would cover a gaping hole in my front teeth. For a time, I actually used Krazy Glue to attach what was left of the partial to the roof of my mouth. It would stay put for a few hours, and then I'd have to redo it. But when you go to jail, you're not allowed to have Krazy Glue. On one of my trips back in, I discovered Poligrip at the commissary. From that day on, I kept a tube of Poligrip tucked in my bra, so I could glue my partial back into place if it fell out.

I kept just about everything I owned tucked inside my bra, knowing that, since I had so many felony warrants out on me, I could be picked up and sent to prison at any time. I considered it an occupational hazard. But I wanted to be prepared. I slit open the lining of my bra to hide the bare necessities inside. On one side, I stashed a Xanax and a dime bag of heroin to get me through intake and the dope sickness that would start there. On the other side, I kept a small piece of eyebrow pencil—because I would rather die than be caught without my eyebrows on—and a small wad of cellophane with Poligrip squeezed inside so I could get through the first few days until I could buy a tube at the commissary.

Using my bra as a purse was an old trick I had learned from Grandma years ago. I would laugh and cry whenever I thought about her now. I hadn't seen her in more than ten years and was in prison when she passed away, so I couldn't even go to her funeral. For so many years, I justified staying away from my family because I loved my life and I loved Blue. I knew Sean was in good hands, and my other kids were, too. Now, I had sunk so low that if I didn't stay high enough to be oblivious I couldn't handle the reality of what my life had become. I didn't care if I died, and I came close to OD'ing all the time. I had done so much damage and caused so much heartache; I truly believed there was nothing I could do to change anything.

On this sunny morning, I sat up in the alley, looked around to make sure no one was watching, and snorted the dope I had left from the night before. I got up and started my day, walking past the Dumpsters and open garbage piled behind the buildings. I passed many spots, cubbyholes, back doorways, and covered back entrances where Carlos and I went to get high and spend the night. Sometimes we got lucky and found a way to break into a building at night and get away from the rats and out of the winter cold. I walked out of the alley to the sidewalk, made a stop at Walgreen's to lift some supplies, and was heading for the McDonald's to use the restroom when a cop who knew me pulled his car over.

He rolled down his window and said, "Hey, Bianca, you are lookin' a little shaggy today, girl," he laughed at me and then held up a bag of dope. "But I'm a little horny, so how about you take care of me right now? I think a BJ to start the day is a good idea. Otherwise, I believe this is yours, and I'm gonna have to take you in for another possession charge. Whaddaya say?"

He was holding up what we called a "jab," a ziplock baggie with twelve smaller bags of heroin inside. This was a frequent form of harassment for junkies on the street. Sometimes the cops would dangle a "bundle," about ten jabs in a huge ziplock bag, enough dope to send someone away for years. In those days, the police were known to confiscate drugs and money from dealers without making an arrest and keep whatever they found. They kept the drugs handy, in the trunks of their squad cars. On a whim, they would plant them on known junkies or dealers to put them in jail or to barter for sex. It happened to me regularly, and I knew many others who were subjected to the same threat. A cop put a jab on me once, and I did go to jail because it wasn't sex that he wanted; he thought I should go back to the joint, so I did. I wrote it off as being part of the price I had to pay since I had gotten away with so much in my life. Now I was not only homeless and helpless but a well-known criminal, and that made me an easy target. Sometimes the police would stop me, and I really would have one or two bags of heroin on me. They would make a deal with me to have sex, and they'd look the other way. I always did it, never really knowing if they would keep their word. Oddly enough, they always did.

On this morning, I did what the cop wanted and gave him a blow job in the front seat of his squad car. He put away the jab and moved on when we were done. This had become so normal to me that I was inured to it and never gave it another thought, other than being mad about giving a blow job away for free. At this point in my life, I considered most men incompetent and irrelevant. If another woman was dope sick and asked me for a taste, I would gladly share. But whenever a man asked, I would yell at him and say, "Really? You want my fuck money? I had to fuck somebody for this dope." Of course, I would cave eventually, but I had to give him some shit first.

I walked toward the McDonald's thinking about my time in the joint. I had gone from voluntarily having sex with prison guards because they were cute or for the many favors I got to sinking so far down in the hood that police officers, lieutenants, and even a sergeant could force me to have sex just by dangling a bag of dope in front of me. It was always the same threat: if I refused to give them what they wanted, the drugs would become mine and I would go to prison. I had a good time in jail with the COs because it was always a mutually beneficial arrangement. Now I was threatened and forced into sex just to stay out on the street.

On my way to McDonald's I stopped to say hello to a friend who owned a small beauty salon. I had met her a few months before. I walked the streets near her shop all the time, but didn't look like the typical homeless person. She had been curious to know my story and came out to the sidewalk one day to introduce herself. We chatted, and after that she continued to welcome me whenever I stopped in. She was a warm-hearted, caring person, and when I walked into the shop on this day I could tell by the look on her face that I was not in very good shape.

"Bianca, damn, you lookin' a little rough, girl. Let me give you a nice shampoo and a blow-out. Whaddaya say? Got time in your busy schedule for a little beauty?"

"Oh, Liz, that would be so nice! Thanks!" I could have cried. I was so grateful.

She treated me to a shampoo, trimmed my hair, and styled it. My next stop was a small secondhand shop owned by a very devout Jehovah's Witness, another kind woman who looked out for me. She let me choose some clean clothes, something she did on a regular basis, and I used the mirror in her bathroom to put on some makeup. I walked the block, stopping in to visit my regular customers. I actually did some pre-sales with the shop clerks and waitresses in a few places on Eighteenth Street. The woman who managed the Payless shoe store gave me fifty or sixty dollars and told me to bring back her favorite perfume. Others would give me ten- or twenty-dollar bills and orders for jewelry. This was how I managed to get by, because not only were these women kind and compassionate to me, but I still had a personality that could engage just about anybody. We were like girlfriends, and they liked talking to me. Being an honorable crook, I always came back with the goods, so they trusted me. By midday, I had money, clean clothes, and my hair was perfect. I was ready to head downtown and do some business.

I caught the #60 Blue Island bus, sat in the window, and watched the neighborhood go by. There were many places with my footprints on them along this route; it was a warped trip down memory lane as I gazed out the window. I passed an abandoned building with a crumbling back porch and remembered how I had been trapped there one Fourth of July. I was hanging out with a young guy named Jimmy, probably not much older than Sean. He was from the suburbs, had caught a bad heroin habit, and was now homeless and addicted. I took him under my wing and showed him a few survival tricks. We had a lot of money that day, enough to cop some rocks and blow, and decided to go to a building nearby that was known for the best dope in the area, "rainbow bags." The line to cop was long, and even though the operation was well coordinated, with one guy taking the money and calling out to the next guy exactly what to hand over, it went slower than usual. This location was no place to be after dark, especially on the Fourth of July, a notoriously violent holiday in the city. Everyone who lived on the street knew they had to find a hole to crawl into before the shooting started. Jimmy and I copped and started walking through the neighborhood, but I was feeling dope sick.

"Jimmy, I don't feel good. I gotta stop and do a bag. Let's go inside this building."

"No way I'm going inside," Jimmy said. "There are too many rats in there."

"I hate rats, too. But we can hang out on the second-floor porch. It's cool. I've been up there before."

Though it was getting late and there wasn't much sunlight left, we climbed the rotting stairs to the second floor, made our way through piles of rubble, and sat out on the porch. We could see the sun getting lower behind the Chicago skyline, always an awe-inspiring sight to me. Soon it was completely dark. Now we were in the worst part of the old projects on the West Side, on the Fourth of July. The colorful bursts of fireworks coming from all over the city mixed with the sound of gunshots ricocheting off the buildings all around us. There was no way we could leave until morning, so we stayed there all night. Thankfully, we had enough dope to keep us happy, and when the sun rose, we made our way back to the street to start the hustle all over again.

I had so many memories of witnessing violence up close, some that stuck in my mind as vividly as the day they happened. Another came to me as I sat on the bus. It was a hot summer night and I was meeting one of my gang connections to cop. We were sitting in his car, and I had just handed him a wad of cash. The car windows were down. I was in the front seat on the passenger side and we were facing one another, talking. In an instant, before either of us could react, two guys masked in black bandannas walked up to his window, aimed a gun right at his head, and shot him at close range. Blood and gray matter splattered on my face and clothes. He was dead. The guy with the gun looked me in the eye and put his finger over his lips, letting me know, "Keep your fucking mouth shut, or you're next." They ran off. In shock, I grabbed the bloody money that was on the seat and stuffed it into my pocket. When the cops came, I claimed that I was a hooker and he was a trick, and I knew nothing. The money was seized as evidence, and they eventually let me go after a few hours of questioning.

The bus moved slowly through traffic, stopping every few minutes. We passed a viaduct I had once run under trying to get away from a trick I had robbed. I had told him to put on a condom. While he was fumbling with that, I grabbed his wallet and ran. It was a scam that I worked all the time. I knew I had stolen a lot of money from him when I pulled out a wad of cash before tossing the wallet into an alley. I kept running but realized when I stopped under the viaduct that there was no way out on the other side, so I decided I had to hide the money someplace where the trick or the cops couldn't find it if they caught me. I did what I had done many times and began shoving the cash into my vagina. I used to think of it as my "safe." Many times I shoved stolen watches and jewelry up there. I started spitting on the money, somehow managing to actually get it all inside me. I calmly walked out from under the viaduct, saw that no one was chasing me, and got to my friend Peaches' apartment in the projects nearby. Peaches had to wear latex gloves smeared with Vaseline to get all the cash out of me. It wasn't easy, but in between fits of laughter, we did it. All told, I had stuffed $5,000 up there. Peaches and I bought a lot of dope and had a really good time.

The bus came to my stop, and I stepped out into the sunshine. I realized I was on the same corner where, as a headstrong teenager, I had hustled for money, standing out on the sidewalk in my bathing suit, begging for bus fare to get home to Oak Park from the lakefront. I remembered that look of surprise and a little bit of pride on my father's face when I produced my half of the money, and he had to cough up his half. My father knew me well because I was so much like him. I know he felt guilty and lost in the end, but I never blamed anyone in my family for anything that happened in my life. I knew deep in my heroin-clouded heart that all the choices were mine. I realized far too late just how much I had thrown away.

I got through that day, just as I did so many others, stealing jewelry from Nordstrom and perfume from Macy's, and catching the same bus back to Pilsen. I had already spent the up-front money from my customers on dope, so when I got back to the hood I made my deliveries and went back to the alley to get high and pass out.

Soon, I would get arrested for shoplifting again and end up back in prison. It was 2010 and I was fifty-two years old. I had been living with a guy and we got high that morning, but I was tired of my life. He offered me a little more dope but I turned away, thinking to myself, *When is this going to end?* In many ways, I had given up. I wanted to die. I really thought that was all that was left for me to do. Back in prison, I saw some old friends, and I managed to work some of the same hustles, like working the sugar daddies on the sex sites. But things were changing in prison. It was getting much more crowded, and the rules were tighter and more strictly enforced. There were cameras everywhere, and I knew I could not scam the system the way I used to. The powers that be had taken their prisons back. And then, on January 11, 2011, I got the worst possible news.

I was in my cell when the CO told me the warden wanted to see me. I got up from my bunk and quickly ran a mental check of all my recent activities. What had I done that would make the warden call me in? I was thinking about this when the CO knocked on her office door and we were told to enter. The CO left, closing the door behind him. I sensed the tension in the warden and I started to get really scared. There was another woman there, a counselor I recognized from psych intake.

"Bianca, take a seat," the warden said kindly, pointing to the chair facing her desk. "We have some bad news."

"Oh, God, what's going on, Warden?" I could not imagine what she meant.

The counselor came over to me and put her hand on my shoulder. "I'm sorry to tell you that your Aunt Louise called today. Your father has passed away."

I felt as though I had been punched in the stomach. I doubled over in the chair and let out a scream, "No, no, no!"

I was in shock and could not stop sobbing. As the grief overcame me, I felt something else washing over me like a suffocating wave. All the guilt I refused to let in over the last thirty years hit me at once. I doubled over from the sheer weight of it. The counselor did what she could to comfort me, but I recognized what I was at that moment, a real piece-of-shit daughter. I hadn't seen my father in sixteen years, and now he was gone. I could never tell him again how much I loved him, nor could I explain how sorry I was. It was the most overwhelming emotion I had ever experienced.

As I started to calm down enough to breathe, the warden let me use the phone to say a few words to Aunt Louise. When I heard her voice, I fell apart all over again. As I wept into the phone, she said she would keep me posted and send me a prayer card from the funeral. When I hung up, I could barely see through my tears. I murmured my thanks to the warden, and the counselor took my hand.

"Bianca," she said quietly, "you can take comfort in knowing that your father died peacefully, with his loved ones around him." This might have been a standard thing to say, but that counselor could not have realized how much that statement would change my life.

I slowly walked back to the cell house. I was still in shock, but something was beginning to change inside me. When I got back and told my cellies that my father had died, they showed their sympathy like sisters. I thanked them and went to my cell. I lay on my bed, getting choked up and crying over and over again. I thought of all the times my father had done whatever he could to help me. I knew he loved me. Now the guilt in realizing what a disappointment I must have been to him was crushing. I was hysterical with grief and had to use every ounce of mental effort to contain myself. Prison is no place to be in that kind of emotional shape; you could end up locked away on the psych ward in a straitjacket.

I kept replaying the counselor's words in my head, *"He died peacefully, with his loved ones around him."* I had a moment of such clarity, as if a door had been opened and so much light was shining in that I could not turn away. I thought, *It's OK. We all have to die. What better way to die than peacefully, with your loved ones around you?* And I realized at that moment that I would not have that kind of a death. I was going to die alone in the streets from a drug overdose or a bullet, with no one to mourn me or even know I was gone. My mind was racing. I pictured myself in a morgue, my body on a slab being fingerprinted so they could find out my name, since I never carried an ID anymore. But even when they got my name from the files, would they know who to call? Even worse, would anybody come? I imagined that anybody they called in my family would say that I was already dead to them; do whatever you want with her. My uncles and aunts would never put my children through the hell of mourning me all over again. They had considered me gone for a long time. I felt a depth of fear that gripped me like nothing else in my life ever had, not even the threat of gunfire or kidnapping or rape or any of the things I had been up against on the street. In the midst of this, I remembered telling my grandma when I was a kid, "Grandma, I'm going to be somebody. I'm going to make a difference in this world. Just watch."

All this was going through my head as my cellie tried to help me through it. A prostitute who was inside for killing one of her tricks, her name was Miss Barbie, and she was a Bible-reading churchwoman.

"Bianca," she said, "just pray to God and ask Him to help you." I answered her with a blank stare. "Have you ever prayed?" she asked.

I wasn't sure how to answer. The only times I'd ever prayed in my life were when I asked God to keep me from getting caught while I was doing a crime or to help me get dope because I was so sick. I considered God my accomplice. Before I'd go into a store to steal, I'd make the sign of the cross. The only prayers I knew were, "Oh, God, please let me get away with this," and "Please, God, I'm so sick, let the dope guy be there," and I'd make the sign of the cross at the dope spot while the other junkies looked at me like I was crazy. And then, I'd be sure to thank him afterward, "Thank you, Jesus. I love you, God."

So, I told Miss Barbie that I loved God, but I didn't think I really knew how to pray. She told me again to ask God to help me, and He would. So I tried it.

I closed my eyes and made the sign of the cross. "God," I prayed silently, "I'll make a deal with you. If you'll take the taste of heroin and the streets from my mouth, I will help people until my last dying breath."

I never got high again.

# 11

# Shine a Light

ON AUGUST 9, 2011, AFTER eighteen months, I walked out of prison for the last time. I got the standard ten dollars and took the Amtrak train back to Chicago with only a small bag of my belongings. But I was prepared. I had kept in touch with a sugar daddy from the sex site who lived in California. He had been wiring me $300 a month in the hope that I would come and see him when I got out of prison. I lied to him and wrote I could not travel out of state for three months after being released, hoping I could figure out some other way to survive in that time. He bought it and had faithfully sent that month's payment, too, so I went to the Western Union near the train station, collected my money, and put it in my bra. I made another stop and bought myself a cell phone, then hopped the #60 Blue Island bus back to the hood. I had arranged to be paroled to a friend's house but didn't want her and her husband to see me looking so bad. Once a new parolee checks in at her designated location, she's required to stay there for the next seventy-two hours. I knew that anything I needed or wanted to do on the street, I had to get done before I checked in. And that included dyeing my hair. Eighteen months inside without being able to scam any kind of hair dye had left me so gray that I could not live with it another minute. When I got off the bus near Eighteenth Street, I stopped at the Dollar Store, and when the guys saw me they were so shocked at my appearance that they handed me a box of dye, no charge. I walked to the McDonald's to use the ladies' room and get the job done, but the moment I walked in the woman behind the counter looked at me and said, "No way, Bianca. You are not dyeing your hair in our bathroom."

I realized that I had no other choice but to go see Liz at the salon. I hated to ask her to do my hair for free. Over the past months, she had written to me in prison and even sent me some cute crayon pictures her kids had drawn for me. She took one look at me and said, "Oh my God, Bianca. Get in the chair." I couldn't spare the cash, but I wanted to give her something in return. I did a lot of drawing and painting whenever I was inside, work that I knew was good and worth keeping, so I took it with me when I left. I told Liz I wanted to give her a painting I did in prison. At first, she didn't even want to take that. But when I took the painting out of my bag and unrolled it for her, she was impressed and really liked it. To this day, my painting of Cleopatra hangs in a frame in her house.

Feeling like myself again, I left the salon and made my way to my friend's house to begin my parole. I was determined to make this time different. Failure was not on my agenda. I was going to stay clean, get a job, and make a legitimate life for myself. I felt a sense of resolve about turning my life around that I had never felt before. I followed the rules and called my parole officer's number as soon as I got there, getting the automated message that meant I was officially signed in. You never talk to a real person. Now, anytime over the next seventy-two hours, my PO could show up unannounced, to check in on me. But the minute I walked into my friend's house, I realized I had made a big mistake. I knew she and her husband were getting high, and as much as I loved them and knew they meant me no harm, I realized that if I stayed, I would end up back on the street, caught up in the same cycle. I had to do whatever I could to get out of there. On top of the stress of trying to stay clean, the house had roaches and, even worse, bedbugs. I was scratching within twenty-four hours, and it was all getting to be too much. I had just come from a clean cell with a clean bed, no bugs, and no temptation toward drugs. Now, I felt overwhelmed and incredibly vulnerable. The itching was so bad by the second day. I felt like I was detoxing all over again. I had to get some help, which meant I had to leave the house, which meant I needed permission from my parole officer. I left a message again, saying I was going to Stroger, which we still called Cook County Hospital, and never got an answer, but I took a risk and went anyway. The nurse at the hospital explained what bedbugs were and gave me lotion for the itching. I had to go back to the house or risk violating my parole and having a warrant out on me again. Finally, at the last possible minute, after the seventy-two hours were just about past, my PO showed up. I was desperate, but I had a plan.

When discharged from prison, you get a release document that includes your "parole stipulations." I took another look at mine. Some of the usual requirements were listed: a drug and alcohol assessment and a mental health assessment. Judges tended to add the mental health checkup for me because they were always trying to figure me out, recognizing that I was intelligent and well spoken, especially when I tried to argue my own cases, and they could not figure out why I kept living the life, not seeming to realize what I was doing to myself. So, they all concluded that I must have been mentally ill. This time, below all the regular assessments, Judge Porter had also recommended that I go into treatment at A Safe Haven (ASH), a homeless shelter in Chicago that offered many services, including treating addiction. I had been there five years earlier to serve a three-month stay imposed by drug court, but I was back on the street as soon as I left. Now, I knew I could work the program if they would just let me back in. The waiting list for ASH was long, but if you were on parole, you got moved to the top. I figured that, along with Judge Porter's recommendation, had to help.

When my PO finally showed up, I asked her if we could step outside to talk. "Listen, I can't stay here," I said, and showed her my discharge papers. "I want to go to A Safe Haven, please. You have to get me out of here."

I was begging and I knew she could see how desperate I was. But, being an overworked, overwhelmed officer of the court, she saw a lot of paperwork and overtime, and she was not willing to take it on, so she told me I'd be OK. Standing in the dark living room, mattresses on the floor, dirty dishes, trash, and clothes strewn all around, she told me this house was just fine. I tried to persuade her without throwing my friend under the bus.

"Please," I was begging her. "This is a bad neighborhood for me since I got high here all the time, plus there are bedbugs in this house, and I'm not used to it. I'm really worried I'll start using again. I want to do better, but this situation is not going to help me."

"Well, we'll see, but just give it some time," was all she said.

I thought, *Really, does it look like I'm going to thrive here?* but I could see that it was futile.

My PO left, and I knew that, as usual, I was on my own. If I wanted to solve this, I would have to do it myself. I called ASH and Ms. Flores answered. I remembered her from five years ago, and was so happy to hear her voice again. But she said my parole officer had to call ASH first. I called my PO twice that day. She kept saying I'd be fine, but I knew she did not want to do the paperwork it would take for me to change addresses. I refused to give up and called Ms. Flores again, this time in tears.

"I can't take it, Ms. Flores! I'll tell you the truth. There's a lot of drugs here, and I don't want to get high. I don't want to get addicted again. Please help me. I have to get out of here."

A compassionate and caring woman, she said the simplest, most wonderful words I could have imagined at that moment: "Do you have bus fare?"

"I have money," I answered, feeling like I could breathe again.

"Do you have a lot of stuff?" She knew I was on the opposite side of the city from where ASH was located, and it would take a few transfers on public transportation.

"No, just one small bag."

"OK, grab your bag and walk out of there. Get on the El and come straight here. I'll call the parole department." She sorted everything out with them and got me transferred to the parole officers and support staff that served ASH. I moved in immediately.

After a month of observation at ASH, I asked Ms. Flores if I could get permission to look for a job. She gave me a pass, and I headed to the Merchandise Mart, a huge center in the Chicago Loop that houses all types of design firms, furniture showrooms, and other businesses. It is also the location of many food service businesses that cater to the thousands of people who work there every day. I figured one of them had to need help, and it had to be something I could do. I got off the train that stops right next to the mart so early that the food court wasn't even open yet. But I was ready. A Safe Haven had sent me to a thrift store for new clothes and helped me create a résumé. I had never even heard of a résumé and had no idea what it should include. I hadn't had a full-time job since I worked at the board of trade more than thirty-five years ago. So for work experience we listed the skills I had acquired inside prison. I could buff floors, wash dishes, polish brass, and I even had a sanitation license from a class I'd taken in the joint. I added my volunteer time with the youth program at ASH, something I now did on a regular basis. I looked and felt so respectable that morning that it seemed impossible for me to fail.

I stayed at the Merchandise Mart all day long, until my folder of twenty résumés was empty. I went up to each food service establishment and asked if I could apply for a job. It went the same every single time:

"Excuse me, are you hiring?" I asked in my most patient and respectful tone.

"Yes, we are. Here's an application. Fill it out."

"OK, sure, thank you. Um, can I talk to the manager?"

"You can just fill it out, and I'll make sure he gets it."

"Thanks, but I have a question, and I want to be up front."

The manager would come over to me and ask, "Can I help you?"

"Yes, thanks. I need a job, and I do hope you can give me a chance, but I want to be up front and transparent with you. I'm honest and law abiding, but I have a really bad record. I'm on parole—no violence—and I just need a chance so I can become a productive citizen."

I would watch the awkwardness creep over their faces; the answer was always the same, "Oh, I'm sorry, honey. We don't hire ex-felons."

I sympathized with their obvious embarrassment and couldn't help but let them off the hook. "OK, thank you, I appreciate that. I don't want to waste your time."

They would say OK, and as I was getting ready to walk away add, "Oh, but what a great story! Good luck. I hope you make it."

I did this for two days. On the third day, after trying a few other places cold, I went to a gourmet salad bar that was recommended by one of the counselors at A Safe Haven. The owner, Cynthia, was a recovering alcoholic, in AA, and the counselor thought maybe she would be sympathetic.

I started with the same conversation, asking if they were hiring and could I please see the manager. When the manager came out, I asked if she was Cynthia and she said she was.

"I'm Bianca and I live at Safe Haven. I'm on parole. I really need a chance."

"Hmm," she looked me over and then said, "Let's sit down. Do you want some coffee?"

We sat and talked, and I could see that she was sizing me up, trying to make a judgment.

"I have a sanitation license," I told her.

"Oh that's great! You got that in prison?"

"Yes, I did. I took a lot of classes in prison. I really like to learn."

"Well, that's definitely a plus." She smiled when she said it.

"Listen, I haven't had a job since I was a teenager, but I'm willing to learn anything. I just need a chance."

"Hmm," she said again, taking her time. Then, after an excruciating silence, she said, "You know what, I'm gonna give you a chance. Can you be here tomorrow morning?"

"Oh my God, yes!" I was almost in tears.

"OK, we'll train you for the rest of this week and then give you some hours."

I had no idea what they actually did at this place or what a gourmet salad even was, but I was so happy that it didn't matter. Cynthia took me to the back of the store and gave me a shirt, an apron, and a hat to wear. "Do you have black pants?" she asked. "Sure," I answered, figuring I could get a pair at the thrift store.

The next morning I showed up and was hopelessly confused from the get-go. I looked the part in my shirt and apron and hat, and as I walked through the food court at the Merchandise Mart that morning, I was feeling so cool. Cynthia wasn't there yet, but the other workers knew I was the new hire and started to show me the ropes. They all spoke so fast and assumed that I knew the basics. I had no idea how to punch in or enter orders on the computer. I had never seen a touch screen before. I desperately tried to take mental notes, but I couldn't grasp everything. I figured I'd find someone to help me again later. I took my place on the order line, behind the open salad bar where all the choices were laid out, thinking, *How hard could it be to make a salad?* But I had no idea what I was looking at. I thought a salad was lettuce, tomatoes, and maybe a cucumber. Here, there were two kinds of lettuce, one labeled "mixed greens," plus spinach, multiple containers of chopped veggies, and fixings I had never heard of before, like garbanzo beans and kalamata olives. We never had those things in prison. I thought I knew what choices existed for salad dressings, but there was something called balsamic vinegar that terrified me because I had never heard of it, and there were many kinds of balsamic dressings, like raspberry balsamic, ginger balsamic, and balsamic mustard. Even the bowls were different sizes. *What the FUCK!*

Once we opened, the day started slowly, with a few orders trickling in, and I thought, *OK, I can handle this.* When my first customer asked for the mixed greens, I thought, *They're all fuckin' green.* But the pace was manageable, and I figured I would learn as I went along. Then lunchtime hit. I was like Lucille Ball working on the candy factory assembly line in the famous *I Love Lucy* episode. She gets so behind that she ends up frantically stuffing the candies into her mouth. Each customer had a different order. I tried to chop and mix and dress as fast as I could, but it was hopeless. I was holding up the line, people were getting impatient, and I was traumatized. I looked up and saw an endless sea of hungry white people in suits, all rabid for a salad.

Cynthia finally came along and rescued me. She was so kind and patient.

"Bianca, this is too crazy right now. Come out back and you can wash the salad bowls."

I was so relieved, but I didn't know how to use the sink and the hose; it was different from the one I used in prison. I was doing fine, but I got soaking wet and the floor was flooded all around me. Cynthia came by to check on me and was horrified. "Bianca, you're supposed to put this big apron on," and pointed to something that looked like a giant X-ray shield hanging on a hook nearby. She got the guys to mop up the floor and said, "OK, I'm going to have you restock the walk-in freezer." That also ended badly. The oily olive jars had to be refilled, but as I poured olives from the giant slippery plastic container into the half-empty jars, I dropped it and expensive kalamata olives were sent rolling all over the walk-in floor. I did my best to help pick them up, apologizing to Cynthia, but I only made things worse. I was sure she would fire me now. I had hit the place like a tsunami. Instead, she told me to take the rest of the day off, and we would start fresh in the morning. The same craziness happened all over again the next day. Somehow, Cynthia had the patience to keep me on and tried to help me fit in.

I got my first paycheck at the end of two weeks. After years of hustling on the streets, sometimes taking in thousands of dollars a day, I was so excited to see a legitimate check. It was eighty-seven dollars. At first, I thought Cynthia had taken money out to cover all the things I had broken during my first week. But she told me she had not, that she would never do anything like that. That was my minimum wage part-time pay. Riding the El back to A Save Haven with that check in my hand, I gave myself a pep talk. I told myself that it was not about the check; this job was teaching me how to be responsible, how to get up early and actually show up at the same time every day, staying all day and doing what I had to do. And, to be honest, I still had the sugar daddy I had been milking from prison. He thought I still had a few months before I could leave the state, so I strung him along for a few more checks, eventually cutting him loose. I realized I could not have a foot in my past if I truly wanted to move forward. If I were really going to change my life, it had to be all or nothing.

I continued to work part-time at the salad place, but I wanted to keep busy while I was living at A Safe Haven. And, more important, I was determined to keep my promise to God about helping people every day for the rest of my life. The counselors at ASH started sending me out into the hood to visit the community centers and other youth programs nearby and even to apply for jobs at some of them. On my way there, I walked past young guys hanging out on the corner. I didn't know any of them by name yet, but I knew exactly what they were doing, and I would stop and just start talking to them. These guys were fifteen, sixteen, and seventeen years old, probably with guns under their jackets, and some of them did look at me a little sideways, but a few of them would say, "What's up, what do you need?" assuming that I wanted to cop some dope. I would just start talking to them, and, being the good talker that I am, they would listen.

"No, no, no, I don't want anything," I would quickly clarify. "But listen, my name's Bianca, and let me tell you somethin'. I just got out of the joint and I used to be you. I want to tell you the ugly side right up front so that way when you go to jail—and trust me, you will—you won't be shocked like I was when they slam that cell door and you know you're not gettin' out for some years. Let me lighten that load for you a little bit."

Their first reaction was to laugh a little, but I could see that they were impressed and engaged. So, even though this wasn't my old neighborhood, street is street, and I was starting to gain their trust. Talking to them out on the corners became a regular thing for me.

At the same time, ASH sent me to help Kelly Cassidy, the state representative in their district, who was running for reelection and needed to collect signatures. The alderman's office was organizing her volunteers and would pay fifty cents a sheet for valid signatures, and, ever the hustler, I collected the most of anyone working for her. I would come back to the office at the end of the day with my pile, they would review the signatures to make sure they were all good, and I would collect my money. I followed every rule and made sure each of those hundreds of signatures met the requirements. When I had first arrived at ASH, Ms. Flores told me, "If you don't break a small rule, you won't break a big rule," and I really took that to heart. So, once again, my ability to talk to anyone was paying off, and I was becoming known in the neighborhood, but for legal activities this time. I started to bond with Kelly, who would eventually end up getting reelected and is still a good friend today. I became an activist, showing up at candlelight vigils when someone was shot, helping to comfort the families, and generally being there for the people in the hood who needed some support. Candy, a case manager at ASH, would take me out to work with her youth group. I loved being with the young people, and they responded to me. Candy brought me to every violence prevention meeting, every rally, and every peace walk. People began to see my passion and appreciate my involvement. After less than a month of working at the salad place, I even got Cynthia to change my schedule so I could keep up all my volunteer activities.

My time hanging out on the corners was not going unnoticed. One day, I caught the attention of J. W. Hughes, the program manager of the Rogers Park site for Cure Violence, which at the time was still known as CeaseFire. JW was driving around with one of his workers when he noticed me talking to a group of guys. He saw me and remarked on what an odd sight it was to see an older white woman talking to a group of young guys and, even stranger, the guys seemed to be engaged with her. He assumed that I knew them and was probably friends with one of their mothers. Finally, after seeing me on the street, doing the same thing a few more times, JW had to know what was going on. He pulled the car over, got out, and walked over to me in his orange CeaseFire jacket.

"Excuse me, sister. Can I talk to you?" he said.

"Um, yeah, sure." I was very impressed by the jacket. The young guys knew him; CeaseFire workers are well known in the hood. They were all saying, "Hey, J-Dub," and seemed happy to see him.

We walked a few feet away from the group, and JW said, "I don't mean to sound strange at all, but do you know those guys?"

"Well"—I hesitated for just a second, not sure what he was getting at—"I do now."

"What do you mean?" He was truly baffled.

"I didn't know them an hour ago."

"Really? Listen, I'm so sorry. I don't mean any harm, but I am so confused right now. I have never seen—and I don't mean this in a bad way—an older white woman in the hood. . . . You do know that's a dangerous corner, right?"

"Yeah, of course I know." I tried not to laugh. "I used to be those guys."

"Really? What are you sayin' to them?"

"Well, I'm laughing with them, but I'm keepin' it real. I'm letting them know what that looks like when you pull the trigger. I'm trying to help them with the ugly side up front in a lighter way, so that when they're done laughing, they might think about it."

I could see that he was impressed and a little surprised. "Man, they're really engaging with you. Have you ever heard of CeaseFire?"

"Oh, yeah, of course I have. I'm from the West Side."

"So, what do you know about CeaseFire?"

"Well, I see the posters on the bus with the little kid who says, 'Don't shoot, I want to grow up,'" I answered. "And you march in the neighborhoods, right?" I didn't know much about what the organization actually did.

"Well, we do all that, but we also train and support violence interrupters who work in the street and try to stop kids before they even pull the trigger. I need to hire another violence interrupter for this site. Would you be interested? Full time. You're doing the job right now. I don't know if you realize it. That's what we do."

"Wow, I am definitely interested." I was flabbergasted.

He told me where to go for an interview. I could not believe it. I didn't tell Cynthia at the salad shop right away, in case it didn't work out, but I did tell the counselors at A Safe Haven because I needed a suit. They helped me get one and Candy even drove me to the interview. I felt so good that day. The suit was really nice, my hair looked perfect, and I even had my nails done. I had my résumé copies in a folder, and I felt organized and professional. I was a little nervous because I had to go in front of a panel of five people, community activists and representatives, including JW, but I felt confident and sure that they would see how eager I was to make a difference. They grilled me.

One man asked, "What does Bianca do alone in the dark when nobody is looking?"

"Excuse me?" was all I could say.

"This job pays fifteen dollars an hour. How do we know you don't get your first check and go back on the heroin? After all, you're living in a homeless shelter. You're just out of jail and still in a program. How do we know you're not going to get high?"

"I can tell you exactly what will happen when I get my first check," I answered, staying calm and trying my best to sound reasonable, "because I have a job now. That first paycheck will go right into my bank account like all my others have for the last month."

"Well that sounds good," he said, "but I think you'd be better fit for a desk job somewhere, maybe an admin position. This is really dangerous work."

"With all due respect, I come from that life. I think I have enough passion to be effective and, believe me, I know what goes on in the streets."

Every single person on the panel voted no. They thought I was too old, too white, and still too close to my past. I was devastated, but my disappointment was short lived. I didn't realize it until he spoke, but the final decision was up to JW.

He politely thanked the panel and said, "I don't know what it is about Bianca, but I'm going to hire her. If she doesn't work out, it's on me and I will take responsibility."

I could not believe my ears. That decision would change my life in immeasurable ways. To this day, after years of being a supervisor, JW still claims I was his best hire. I started my training three days later, a full-time employee earning fifteen dollars an hour. I had to tell Cynthia and worried that she would take it badly since I wasn't giving her two weeks' notice. I even offered to work both jobs at the same time if we could figure it out. She had given me a chance, and I was so grateful to her. I wanted to make it right. But she was genuinely thrilled for me, and certainly also secretly relieved. "I'm so proud of you," she said as she hugged me and we said good-bye. It had only been a month since we first met, and I had practically destroyed her shop. Now I was about to start doing work that was challenging and important. I was given a unique opportunity to take all the mistakes I'd made, everything I had endured, and all that I'd learned and turn them into a force for good. I could not believe my blessings.

After a few months with Cure Violence, I knew it was time for me to move out of A Safe Haven. Every counselor supported my decision, agreeing that I was doing so well, I was more than ready to be on my own. I got an early release on my parole, six months before the designated completion, something that rarely happened. I started looking for apartments in Rogers Park near my Cure Violence site. I had so much support; JW even advised me about which buildings would be good for me. When I found the building that seemed to meet all my requirements and I went to apply for a studio apartment, however, I found myself facing the same situation I had gone through when I was looking for a job.

"I have a record and just recently got off parole, and I don't have any credit," I admitted right up front, as I handed over the thirty-five-dollar application fee.

"Well, let's run it anyway," the building supervisor said.

The next day, he called and agreed that I didn't have much to go on, but he thought I was a nice person and asked if I had anybody who would cosign for me. I was at a loss at first. No one in my family had agreed to even see me since I'd gotten out of jail, so of course I didn't dare ask any of them. I decided to call Alderman Joe Moore, the representative from my ward, who had gotten to know me through my activism and Cure Violence. Though he knew a lot about me and I reminded him that I had a horrific record, once again someone took a chance on me.

"I'll write you a reference letter," he said without hesitation, and faxed the letter the next day.

The building supervisor called and said, "If Alderman Moore believes in you, we believe in you. When do you want to move in?"

I had the deposit ready, signed the lease, and found myself with the keys to my own studio apartment. I was thrilled but also more than a little hesitant. I actually ended up staying at A Safe Haven for a few more weeks. I was surprised to realize that I was feeling shaky about this move, wondering if I really was ready. I had never lived alone before. I had lived in prison, shelters, trap houses, and even with other homeless people like Carlos on the street. I was happy I had the apartment and could pay the rent, but I was afraid to move in.

While still living at ASH, I happened to run into Neli Vazquez Rowland, the cofounder and president of ASH, someone I had heard so much about and had been wanting to meet in person. I walked right up to her and said, "Are you Neli?"

"Yes, I am," she said in a very sweet voice, her arms overflowing with files of paperwork. But she stopped and asked me who I was.

"My name is Bianca, I came here on parole from prison almost eight months ago, and I want to thank you for saving my life. I've been to rehabs before and they never worked, but this program has truly changed everything for me."

"Oh my God, I live for moments like this," she said. "I'm on my way up to a board meeting right now to talk about funding for the ASH Re-entry Program, you know, the one that funds Illinois inmates to be paroled to places like this. Would you mind coming up and talking to the board members and telling them exactly what you just said to me?"

"Um, OK, but do I have time to run to my room and fix my eyebrows?"

"They look OK to me," she laughed, "but sure, go ahead. And would you be OK with us filming what you say to them?"

"Yes, of course! But now I need some mascara, too."

She smiled and said, "OK, meet me upstairs when you're ready."

After getting myself together, I went up to the third floor where all the executive offices were and walked into a large boardroom filled with people waiting to hear from me. Neli gave me a hug and thanked me for being willing to share my story. "This is exactly what we need to help so many others," she said.

I told my story as honestly as I could, keeping my language clean. I told that roomful of strangers how grateful I was for A Safe Haven because no other program, no person, judge, counselor, family member, parole officer, no matter how much they tried, could help me change. I told the board that I had a job and I was about to move into my own apartment. Even though I got choked up, I knew they heard every word.

About a week later I was still hesitating about moving out and Ms. Flores finally said, "Bianca, why are you still living here?"

"Well, I need a few more things, like a coffeemaker." I tried not to let her see how hesitant I was.

When she heard my excuses, she just said, "No, it's time now. You have to fly out of the nest." I knew she was right. She could see that I was scared, so she helped me. She bought me a care package, including a coffeemaker, and arranged for a van to help me move my things. After the moving guys left, I closed the door, leaned against the wall, slid to the floor, and started to sob. I could not believe I was there. I had an apartment. It was empty, the walls were bare, but it was mine. There were no bugs, it was clean, and I could even see Lake Michigan from my window. To say it was an amazing feeling doesn't begin to describe the joy I felt that day.

The next few months were filled with long hours working with Cure Violence and settling into the apartment as best I could. I was so happy to be alive. I slept the bare minimum I needed because I couldn't wait to get up every day and get back to work. My dedication grew, and I worked nonstop. I was honored to be working alongside ex–gang leaders whose names I recognized as legends from the streets and who had turned their influence and street cred into a force for good. While I knew all about what happens on the streets, I felt empowered by the training I received and by the team that I worked with. When we went out at night to answer a call or respond to an escalating conflict, armed only with our orange jackets and our determination to save young lives, I felt like I was with family. After so many years on the street, learning the hard lessons that come from hustles and drug deals, living the same life as my colleagues and those we were trying to save, I knew that I was doing important, effective work. Cure Violence was more than a job to me; it became my life, and working with at-risk youth remains my passion and my calling. I knew from the minute I started that it was exactly what I was put on this earth to do. Every day I saw the need for violence interruption grow, and my desire to help grew along with it. I was grateful beyond words.

I even mediated conflicts on my off-hours. Riding the bus to the Cure Violence offices one day, I saw a conflict brewing on the street. There wasn't any shooting yet, but the shouting and shoving was escalating. I knew what would come next.

"Stop the bus!" I shouted.

"You have to wait for the next stop, lady," the driver shouted back, and I could see that he was trying to just get past the trouble.

"No, I mean it, stop this bus right now. I'm a violence interrupter. Let me out right now."

He stopped the bus, opened the door, and I ran to the scene of the conflict without hesitation. It was escalating from two guys to four guys. I knew all of them. I stood in between the opposing young men and started talking.

"What the hell is going on? No, no, no!" I yelled as I tried to get one of them to look at me. They kept arguing as if I weren't there, and I knew they were about to start fighting. I could hear sirens in the background. "Listen, you have to leave now before the cops get here," I screamed.

I knew from my training to always focus on the most aggressive person, whom I happened to know really well, a guy named Mikey. I pulled him by his arm and tried to lead him into the train station. The ticket taker said, "Oh, hell no! Don't bring that shit in here."

"I'm a violence interrupter. I got this," I said, which made Mikey shake his head. The tension was broken, and he started laughing. "You crazy as hell, Bianca."

The CTA worker was still yelling for us to leave, so I locked arms with Mikey and would not let go. I steered him toward the ticket machine and bought two tickets, one for him and one for me. Once on the platform, out of harm's way, I called one of my team members, Felix, and told him where I was headed and asked him to go talk to the guys still on the street. The whole team went there and started to figure out what the beef was about and to keep it from escalating again. Mikey and I got on the train and he wanted to get off two stops later in his own hood. I made him stay on the train and ride it to the end of the line with me, which gave him plenty of time to cool down. We turned around, got on the next train back, and I let him get off at his stop this time. We had been riding for over an hour each way, with Mikey still shaking his head, laughing in disbelief. By the time he got off the train he had calmed down, and my coworkers were with the other guys. Our team was working in the coordinated way we were trained to, and it was a great feeling to divert a situation that could have ended in another tragedy.

Every day ended on a high note for me. When I wasn't part of conflict mediation, I worked at the Cure Violence offices and learned more about how the organization functioned, learning how to use a computer and track the data from each site. I became a valued member beyond what I did in the street. At the end of a long day or night, I went back to my empty apartment. I barely had any furniture. I used some blankets and pillows on the floor for a bed, and the walls were still bare. After leaving the warm acceptance of my coworkers, people I really did think of as family, I started to miss my real family and began to think that maybe, just maybe, I could reconnect with them. This was a small ray of hope that, once it had been let in, started to spread in my heart and mind until I felt myself longing to see my mother, my sisters and brothers, and, by some miracle, my children and grandchildren. Coming home to an empty apartment got harder. As she had done throughout my life, Aunt Louise kept in touch. During my parole, I would get weekend passes from ASH to stay with her. I kept visiting her, and now that I had my own apartment, Aunt Louise started pulling out boxes of my things that she had saved over all the years I was gone. She had so many pictures, and we would sit and reminisce together, laughing and remembering all the better times when I was young.

There was one picture of Sean that I had taken when he was about eight months old, a Polaroid that I had stuck into a metal frame. The frame was rusty now, but seeing the picture broke my heart. He was wearing a pair of little white socks, and you could see the dirty bottoms. Grandma used to give me such a hard time about how filthy those little socks were. She couldn't believe that was the picture I had chosen to frame, and I would just laugh. Now, I looked at that fading image and the enormity of my loss crashed down on me. I took the picture back to my apartment. It became the first thing I hung on the wall. I would look at it at night and cry myself to sleep. I had no idea if I would ever see my son again. The gulf between us felt enormous.

Along with Aunt Louise, I reached out to my mother and her sister, Aunt Trisha, while I was still at ASH. My mother was not ready to see me and didn't answer my calls at first, but we eventually started talking regularly. Aunt Trisha came to visit me and took me on weekend passes to her house. It meant the world to me. I had done so much damage. Most of my family would have to take the risk of getting close to me again on their own time, and I completely respected that.

My first six months out of prison went by quickly, and soon Aunt Trisha was visiting me at my apartment. When she saw how empty and bare it was, she took me to thrift stores to buy things and finally persuaded me to get a bed. It was the oddest feeling in the world. When I wasn't in prison, I lived such a transient life. It felt like having my own bed was some kind of huge commitment. It was more normal to sleep on the floor, but I gave in. With the help of one of my coworkers, I bought a futon with a frame that I had to assemble myself. I didn't get it quite right, but I slapped the futon on top, worked around the metal bar that had somehow ended up in the middle, and got used to sleeping in my own bed. I had a tiny seven-inch television, a few chairs, and my futon. When the sunlight came in through my window, I realized I had never been happier in my life. I felt like I had made it.

By the spring of 2012, about seven months after I walked out of prison, a few more of my family members had decided to call me. I had been talking to my mother from A Safe Haven but had still not seen her in almost sixteen years, since Alia was a baby. When we talked, she would tell me about Sean and the other kids, trying to catch me up and make me feel connected to them. Finally, she told me that she had spoken to Sean about me.

"Ang," she was trying so hard to be kind about it, "I talked to Sean and he told me not to say your name anymore. 'Grandma, don't say her name again.' That's all he says, Ang."

"I understand, Ma." I tried not to cry over the phone. I knew I had fucked up so badly. "How could I have ever left that sweet little baby?"

I wondered over and over again. And I thought it was too late for us; I could never get him back.

"I'm tryin', Ang. I'm really tryin'," my mother would say over and over, but Sean was the one child who was with me enough to remember all the worst times, and I realized how deeply I had hurt him. I asked another favor of God, praying for him to soften my son's heart, promising to give up anything that I had, anything that mattered to me now, if he would just let me be Sean's mother again. I was grateful for so many things in my life by then. I would come home from work feeling so good about making a difference, maybe saving a life, stopping a shooting, connecting and laughing with my coworkers, but walking into that empty apartment and looking at that baby picture of Sean just made me want to cry myself to sleep again.

One day I was running to catch the train downtown when my cell phone buzzed. I said hello, and a voice I hadn't heard in almost twenty years said, "Ang?"

"Uncle Joey? Oh my God, Uncle Joey!" I started crying right there on the street. Uncle Joey had given up on me a long time ago, banning me from his house, the place where I had hidden almost $50,000 in the wall, and even telling his neighbors to call the police if they ever saw me coming around. I knew that it took a huge leap of faith for him to reach out. We both cried and talked for almost an hour. When I told Uncle Joey about Sean and how much I wanted to see him, he just said, "Keep doing what you're doing, Ang, and he'll come around."

In July of 2012, I was given one of the greatest gifts of my life. Uncle Joey decided it was time for a reunion. He invited everyone in the family who was talking to me at that point to come to his house so we could finally be together again. I was thrilled. My mother was coming, my aunt, my dear old friend Mark, who had also gotten clean, and Uncle Joey's husband, Uncle Michael. My mother had stayed close to Alia and Anthony's adoptive parents, Mira and Jack, over the years, and now she had been telling them all about my recovery. While Mira was leery about how far I had really come, she genuinely wanted to keep her promise to me. It had been almost fifteen years since she had taken

Alia from my arms in that courtroom and given me her word that if I ever got my life back together, she would let me see my kids. After so many years of wondering if I was still alive and if the kids would ever meet their birth mother, that day had come. Mira told my mother that even if I wasn't completely recovered, even if I relapsed, she could not live with herself if she didn't at least let me see them. I could not fathom the generosity of her heart, and I am still humbled by it.

The big day came. I was so excited that I could barely get myself ready. I was going to see my mother, my uncle, and two of my children for the first time in fifteen years. I tried not to dwell on the fact that Sean wouldn't be there and just focused on how grateful I was for that day. When I got to Uncle Joey's house and walked up the steps to the front porch, my mind was flooded with memories. So many bad times had taken place in this house. I remembered standing in the same spot fifteen years ago, on a freezing winter day when I still had Alia, a tiny baby wrapped tight in my arms. I was so desperate and dope sick that I went to the one person in the world who I knew would still help me, my grandma. When she came to the door, she was shocked to see me with a baby.

"Oh my God, Ang, is that a real baby? Is it your baby?" she said, her voice trembling with age and the sorrow I knew she felt.

"Yeah, it's a real baby, Grandma, but it's not mine. I'm babysitting," I answered, knowing that if I told her Alia was my daughter, her great-granddaughter, she would not let us leave, and she would be even more worried than she already was. It would set off a storm in my family that would only make things worse.

"Come in, honey, get out of the cold."

"No, no, Grandma, I can't. If Uncle Joey catches me, he'll kill me. I just need twenty dollars. I have to buy some stuff for the baby. Can you give me twenty dollars, please?" I was genuinely scared that my uncle would make good on his promise to call the police if he ever caught me near his house again. I desperately needed the money to cop, and the sickness was talking for me.

"Sure, sure," Grandma said as she turned into the house, returning a few minutes later with two twenty-dollar bills. She shoved them into my hand, held it for a minute and said, "Please buy what you need for the baby. She's so beautiful!"

I pulled my hand away and hurried back down the porch steps. It was the last time I would see my grandmother alive. She was the love of my life. She never really gave up on me and tried relentlessly to save me. She did not get to see me change. The day she died and I was in prison was one of the worst days of my life.

I shook off the sadness of that memory. I steadied my nerves and knocked on the door. I saw Uncle Joey and Michael first, and then my mother walked into the room. We hugged and cried. The kids weren't there yet, so we all sat and had coffee and talked. Uncle Joey was beaming with pride. I had been out of prison for almost a year. I had a job. I was helping kids. I was even friends with the state representative, and a reporter for the *Chicago Tribune* had written an article about Cure Violence that focused on me. There I sat, alive and well. It was truly hard for them to believe.

I was so anxious when the doorbell rang. I opened it, and there stood Anthony and Alia. Even though Aunt Louise had sent me pictures of them over the years when I was in prison, how beautiful they looked at that moment honestly took my breath away. They were babies when I gave them up, and I never thought I would see them again.

I hugged Mira and Jack, and she said to the kids in such a completely joyous and sincere way, "This is your mother!" I lost it and could barely talk. They were a little awkward and shy, but they wanted to meet me, so there was a lot of hugging and crying all around.

"We thought you died, Ang. We thought it was too late, and it broke our hearts to think that these kids would never get to see their birth mother." Then she said to the kids, "What did we do every night when we said our prayers?"

And the kids answered almost in unison, "We prayed for our mother and hoped that she was still alive."

"Thank you, Mira, for keeping your promise and being there when I couldn't," I said, and then I turned to the kids. "I want you to know I loved you with all my heart. I was really lost and on drugs, and I'm so sorry. But you have the best parents in the world!"

Alia just smiled, and Anthony said, "We know, we know. It's OK."

Mira told the three of us to go out to the backyard and talk. We got to know one another, laughed together, and it was one of the best days of my life.

My family continued to take their time, each one cautious for their own reasons and hesitant to get taken or heartbroken by me yet again. The next one to come around was my sister Dina. She and I had been so close, but she became one of my harshest critics when things started getting bad and washed her hands of me. She adopted my daughter Christina and was adamant that she would never let me near her again. But my mom had been working on her, too, and one day, a few weeks before Christmas of 2012, she called me.

"Ang? It's me," she said and then would not let me get a word in. "Look, I'm not saying that I hate you. I'm not forgetting yet, but I'm willing to give you a chance. But first, let me just get this out of my system and that will be the end of it."

"Dina, I can't believe you called! I missed you so much. I love you!"

"Yeah, I don't want to hear that," she said.

"I'm just happy to hear your voice!"

"Listen," she jumped right in, "You fuckin', son of a bitch, you left your family. Where the hell were you all these years? What the fuck was wrong with you?" She went on like that for a few minutes, really letting me have it. I listened and just took it, like being initiated on the wall by my gang sisters. If this was what I had to do to get my sister back, I was fine with it. When she was done, she said, "So, what's goin' on? Do you wanna come and see Christina?"

"Oh my God, yes!"

We talked as if no time had passed since we were young and were the best of friends. She gave me her address and told me what Amtrak to take. Her husband, Ron, picked me up at the train. Christina was with him. She got out of the car, and we both started crying. Christina was shaking, looked at me in disbelief, and said, "Are you Ang? I came from you." Then she looked me up and down and said, "Oh, now I see where I get my butt from!"

We spent the weekend getting close, and I felt the same way I did about Alia and Anthony. I was so grateful to be reunited with another one of my children and my sister. Dina wanted me to come again for Christmas, but Sean and my other daughter, Rachel, would be there, and even though Dina didn't want it to be that way, she knew it would be better for them if I stayed away. "I could tell them that you are my sister and I want you there, but these Christmases at my house have been the only holidays those kids have had together."

"No, no, no," I said. "I've already taken enough away from them. I would never force it."

My sister Crickie called me from Florida, and the same emotional reunion replayed. She flew to Chicago from Florida in the spring of 2013 to see me and stayed at my apartment. We both cried when I picked her up at the airport. The day she arrived happened to coincide with a fundraiser at A Safe Haven that I had helped organize, so I took her there and was so happy to show her off and for her to meet my colleagues, professional women whom I had come to admire, especially Neli. Neli had been in my corner from the start, as she was for so many who made their way to ASH. Crickie could see just how much my life had changed and was truly impressed. It was a proud day for me.

I was grateful for all of it, but I still held out hope for my oldest son. It would take until 2015, three years since I was released from prison, before Sean would see me. Like the others, he called me one day out of the blue.

"It's time," he said. "It's time for us to have a conversation. Let's have lunch."

We met at an Italian restaurant in Elmwood Park. I got there first and sat in my car texting with the Rolling Stones blasting on my CD player. He knocked on the window.

"Oh my God, Sean!" I hollered.

"So you still like the Rolling Stones," he smiled.

I got out of the car and hugged him and started crying. "Look," he said. "I don't want to get emotional. I promised myself I wouldn't."

We went inside, got a table, and sat across from one another.

"First, I want to say thank you," he said.

"Thank me for what?"

"That I didn't have to see my mom the next time in a casket. I honestly thought that's what would happen. So I appreciate that."

My words were slow in coming, but we managed to talk, and I even made him laugh.

"You are still the same," he said. "And you look really great. I'm really proud of you, but it will take some time. I'm willing to work on it, though."

"You take your time." I tried not to cry. "Sean, if it takes to my last dying breath, I will be here. I understand." We parted on good terms, but he still would not give me his phone number.

I spent Christmas 2013 at Dina's. Rachel and Sean were there with their kids. The kids were all little, under seven, but Sean was still not ready to let my grandchildren know me, and Rachel followed his lead and said the same about her daughter. So I was there, but I did not get to be their grandmother yet. I understood and did not want to push it. There was no way I would tell their kids who I was until I got permission. The following July, Uncle Joey invited me to his annual family picnic. Everyone was there, and I assumed I was still just "the nice lady from Aunt Dina's house" to my grandchildren. But Sean really was coming around, just as Uncle Joey had predicted. I didn't know it, but he had told them that the lady they saw at Christmas was his mommy.

At the picnic, his four-year-old daughter, Gemma, came up to me, put her little hands on my face, and pulled me toward her so she could whisper in my ear. "Are you my daddy's mommy?"

"Who told you that?" I asked.

"My daddy said that you are his mommy. So are you my grandma?"

"Yes, I'm your grandma," I said, and laughed so I would not cry.

I looked around at the beautiful force of nature that was my family, talking loud and laughing in the sunshine. I could see how blessed I was. I was finally home.

# Epilogue

## A Life Worth Living

I WALK OUT OF STARBUCKS, latte in hand, into the heat of a humid July day. Downtown Chicago swarms to life in the summer, transforming into a different city, with crowded outdoor cafés, curious tourists streaming in and out of museums, and parks littered with families spreading blankets in the grass and sending barbeque smoke wafting into the blue sky over Lake Michigan. The suit I'm wearing is a little warm for the day, but I have just come from giving a presentation to a roomful of executives concerned about the rising violence in the city, another hallmark of Chicago summers. I speak often to all kinds of groups, hoping to help them see the value of violence interruption and how it works to save lives. I feel great in this suit. In my lowest days, homeless and walking down Michigan Avenue, getting ready to steal and get money for dope, I would watch the businesswomen clipping along, so crisp in their heels and perfectly tailored suits, carrying their briefcases and themselves with such confidence and I would think, *That should have been me.* Now, I walk past a department store window and catch a glimpse of my reflection and realize it *is* me. *So that's why they call it a power suit,* I think.

I walk to my car, throw my suit jacket onto the backseat, pull out of the parking garage, and head back to my office at the University of Illinois. Instead of taking the highway, I do what I always do and drive through the West Side neighborhoods, taking a detour down some of the alleys and side streets that I used to call home. I spot a homeless man panhandling on a corner, recognize him, and pull over to say hello.

"Hey, baby, how you doin'," I say as he walks over to my car.

"Girl, look atchu! You are lookin' so fine. You're doing really good, huh?"

"Oh yeah, you know," I answer, feeling myself blush a little. "I'm just tryin' to keep it real."

We hug and I ask him about Larry, another guy we both know. We're not far from a highway overpass, and I know many of my old friends are living and getting high under there, as I had not that long ago. I figure Larry might be hanging out there, taking a break from the hot sun. I want to see how he's doing.

"Where's Larry at now?" I ask my friend. "Have you seen him today?"

"Oh yeah, last time I seen him he was passed out."

"Whaddya mean he was passed out?"

"Yeah, he was shooting some dope, and he passed out."

"And you just left him there?" I'm alarmed.

"Ah, he'll be fine. You know, baby, it happens all the time."

"No, no." I'm worried. "Where? Show me where you saw him."

He points under the bridge. There is a fence blocking the area, but we used to climb over it all the time, so I don't let it stop me now. I have a bad feeling. Larry was left passed out with a needle in his arm. I have to see if he needs help. I put the hazard blinkers on in my car, and walk over to the fence. Kicking off my high heels, I hike up my pencil skirt and climb the fence. I walk down the slight embankment, and there he is, lying motionless on the ground. I run to him and can see that he has OD'd and is turning blue, the needle still in his arm. I start giving him mouth-to-mouth, beating on his heart, stopping only long enough to use my phone and call 911. Soon I hear the siren, and the ambulance pulls up near the fence. The paramedics are able to stabilize him and get him to the hospital, where he recovers. Once again, I am reminded that no matter how much my life has changed I can never forget where I have been, and I silently renew my vow to help someone every day.

Gang violence and all its root causes—poverty, homelessness, lack of jobs, lack of support for youth—fuse together to create a parallel reality in Chicago, so different from the shiny city that tourists roam. I lived for many years in that other universe. I know and love the families and young people who try every day to survive there. I never think in terms of escaping any part of my past because it is always with me, reflected in the faces of people I have met—real people—who need and deserve so much more from all of us.

In the years since changing my life around, I have learned a great deal. My role as a violence interrupter has grown, bringing me both satisfaction and heartache. The social conditions that lead young men and women to violent behavior and drug abuse sadly remain the same. The streets continue to steal young lives and are unforgiving for those who lack support and guidance. After incarceration, reentry and recovery is still an enormously difficult process. Recidivism rates remain high, and the cycle of failure continues to trap young people and rob them of their potential.

My passion runs deep, but I have to accept the sadness and tragedy I must also endure. The young man whose life I saved and wrote about in chapter 1 of this book was gunned down again and killed on May 27, 2017. He was only sixteen, and I thought of him as my own child. I held his mother in my arms as she wept for yet another lost son. My passion and sense of purpose is both a blessing and a burden. I feel a deep sense of responsibility as I work to keep the promise I made to God when my father passed, especially when I lose someone to the streets. For every victory I experience, there are many losses. They are all unacceptable. While I grieve, I also recommit myself and continue to help as many young people as I can, every day.

My work as a violence interrupter has led me to become an expert in the field. I am invited to speak at professional summits and conferences, adding my unique perspective to the work that so many others are also engaged in. I travel around the world to sit on panels with leaders in related fields: antiterrorism, countering violent extremists, social work, community outreach, trauma treatment, and addiction recovery. And, closest to my heart, I regularly speak at high schools in Chicago and around the country, going directly to those who need me the most.

I am constantly humbled and honored by all the people who understand and share the work I do, and for that I am endlessly astonished and grateful. I received a Humanitarian Award presented by Illinois state representative Kelly Cassidy for my "invaluable contributions to the community and the fight against violence." I was honored with the IChange Nations Global Leadership Award for "your exemplary leadership to empower all of mankind," and appointed as a goodwill ambassador for the Golden Rule International by Dr. Clyde Rivers, honorary ambassador of Burundi and representative to the United Nations. I received an honorary doctorate of philosophy in humanities, also presented by Dr. Rivers. I received the Community Leadership Award from the Jane Addams College of Social Work & Policy Change, for "her transition from prisoner to world crusader for youth." I was named in a resolution by the City of Chicago, Mayor Rahm Emanuel honoring me because I "ran to a fifteen-year-old boy who had been shot and applied enough pressure to the bullet wound in his artery to save his life . . . for her steadfast commitment to preventing violence and saving lives in the City of Chicago and throughout the world." I was awarded NASW Public Citizen of the Year, 2017, by the National Association of Social Workers Illinois chapter.

Throughout every twist and turn in my life, the people I have met along this journey mean the most to me. I am in awe at their dedication and have endless respect for their determination; they make a difference every single day. To name every person who kept me from stumbling and who gave me a chance would take a very long time.

If, as quoted by Gil Scott-Heron at the start of this book, "the first revolution is when you change your mind," then the next revolution is when you free your heart. For me, the dismantling of that wall I built around my heart, brick by brick, has allowed a blessed light to shine in, illuminating my purpose. I have been given a precious gift, the gift of a life worth living.

# Acknowledgments

**Angalia Bianca** would like to thank: my friend and coauthor Linda Beckstrom for making the words in this book come to life and for keeping my voice throughout; my uncles Joseph Bianco and Michael Thorp for their endless love; my sister Crickie for the laughter and love we share; my brother Rich "Big Daddy Woo Woo," who I love to argue with; my family for their love; my friend Mark Terran, who fondly refers to us as Will and Grace; my Uptown Girl Lynn Orman-Weiss for NYC, sunsets, and the oceans; my pal Rose Elenz for the Hollywood Hills and for always caring; my close friend Carmine Appice for all of his support and advice; my Julie for keeping me smiling in spite of the darkness; Kevin Gates and Dreka Gates for becoming family; Belo Zero of Do or Die for always having my back; Niko "Trap" Williams for the utmost respect and love he always shows me; Mary Jean and Joanne Galivan for their lifelong friendship; Tio Hardiman for his guidance; Judy Roth for Apache Junction; the Captain and the boy for putting up with me; Dr. Gary Slutkin, founder of Cure Violence; my mentor Timothy White; Andre Thomas for his love of community; Cheyenne Hardy, a passionate teenage humanitarian in Nova Scotia; my good friend Christian Picciolini for always being there; my boss Jalon Arthur for pushing me to be the best I can be; my colleague Felix Jusino for helping me help others; my sister Angela King for turning hate into love; LeVon Stone Sr. for encouraging me to go back to college; Stevie for his advice; the Francis family; Chicago alderman James

Cappleman for always believing in me; and Illinois state representative Kelly Cassidy for inspiring me to be the voice for the voiceless. To those I have lost—Daddy, Mom, Pat, and Aunt Kathy—and to all those who have lost their lives to addiction and gun violence, may they eternally rest in peace.

**Linda Beckstrom** would like to thank Angalia Bianca for her courage, honesty, and determination; our dreams are forever connected, and for that I am eternally grateful. I would like to thank: my family, especially my husband, Blake Beckstrom, for his unwavering support, superb editing advice, and clear vision; my son, Lane, for his loving attitude; my mother, Norma DeLuccia, and my late father, Bill DeLuccia Sr., for knowing I could do this, and my brother Bill DeLuccia Jr. for always being there; Fran and Elena DeLuccia, Laura Beckstrom, and Page Walter for their early reading, honest comments, and gratifying encouragement. I cannot thank my loyal friends enough for believing in this project, reading early drafts, and supporting my work, especially Kari McGlinnen, Laura Pusateri, Stacey Platt, Susan Schmeer, Karyn Kerner, Kristen Green, Linda Licocci, Vicki Capalbo, Annalise Raziq, Cindy Coakes, and Carla Sloan. And much gratitude goes to Larry Kay for being a good friend and a trusted adviser from the beginning of this endeavor.

**The authors would both** like to thank: Linda Mensch for her generosity and good counsel; Paul Scheuerlein for his sage advice; Pamela Des Barres for bringing us together; all the Chicago Dolls; our editor, Yuval Taylor, for his patience; Chicago Review Press for taking a chance on us; and our many early readers for their honesty and encouragement, including Carmine Appice, Kelly Cassidy, Neli Vazquez-Rowland, George Blaise, Christian Picciolini, Vera Ramone King, Vic Mensa, Saverio Cali, Lynda Franco, Carie Antepenko, Carla Rodriguez, Bonita Falco, Greg Guy, Vicky Guy, J. W. Hughes, and Sheila Regan.

And finally, to all those struggling with addiction, homelessness, and incarceration, this book is given as an offer of hope in your darkest times.